MANAGEMENT OF KNOWLEDGE & INFORMATION SERVICES:
A CONCEPTUAL APPROACH

Editors

Dr Bal Ram

Dr. Shalini Singh

EDSOL

Published by **EDSOL INFORMATICS**
Plot No 9, Add India Center Building,
7th floor, Supreme work, Sector 125,
Noida, Uttar Pradesh 201303

ISBN: 978-81-984808-0-4
First Edition: 2025

Management of Knowledge & Information Services: A Conceptual Approach

Dr Bal Ram | Dr. Shalini Singh

For more information regarding **EDSOL INFORMATICS** and its products, please visit the publisher's website
www.edsolinformatics.com

Acknowledgement

The publication of this edited book has been a journey enriched by the contributions and support of many individuals and organisations to whom we are most deeply indebted.

First, we would like to extend our sincerest thanks to all the authors of these chapters. Their expertise, dedication, and insight have formed the foundation of this book. Collaborating with such a diverse and knowledgeable group has been an honor and a joy.

We would also like to thank our current organisation for their support, resources, and encouragement, making this book possible. We want to sincerely thank our Registrar, senior officials and colleagues for their constructive advice and insights that have greatly improved the quality of this work. We are also extremely grateful to the publisher for their unwavering support and belief in this project.

Finally, we sincerely thank our family and friends for their unfailing support and understanding. Their patience and encouragement have been a constant source of strength and inspiration throughout the many hours spent on this endeavor. This book results from a collective effort, and we are sincerely grateful to all who have contributed to its creation.

Editors

Table of Contents

Dr. Devendra Kumar Sharma
Deputy Librarian Central University of Himachal Pradesh, Dharamshala, Dist-Kangra (HP), (India) Email: sharmadk73@gmail.com

Prasanna Kumar Konch
Assistant Librarian, The Assam Royal Global University, Guwahati
Email: prasannakonch@gmail.com

Dr Sailendra Das
Assistant Professor, Mass Communication The Assam Royal Global Uni-versity, Guwahati
Email: sailendas.das@gmail.com

Rajshree Dutta
LIS Intern, Central Reference Library, Kolkata MLIS, PGDCA
rajsheedutta35@gmail.com

Dr. HARIKRISHNAN CA
Librarian, ISRO/VSSC/SCS, Trivandrum, Kerala, India.
harikrishnan.harikrishnan@gmail.com

Sonal Singh
Professor & Dean- Faculty of Arts
School of Studies in Library and Information Science
Vikram university, Ujjain, M.P.
E mail drssonal@rediffmail.com

Richa Sharma
JRF
School of Studies in Library and Information Science
Vikram University Ujjain, M.P.
E mail s.richa1512@gmail.com

Ansh Sehgal
MBA 1st year student, IITM
E-mail: anshsehgaldelhi@gmail.com

Sarthak Tyagi
MBA 1st year student, IITM
Priya Gupta
MBA 1st year student, IITM

Mohd Noman Mansoori
Network Administrator; Integral University,
noman.integral@gmail.com

Priyanka Tripathi
Assistant Librarian, Integral University,
Email: priyanka111444@gmail.com

Ajay Saini
Librarian, Directorate of Education Delhi
ajjaysaini@gmail.com

Vikas Saini
Librarian, Directorate of Training and Technical Education, Delhi
vikashsaini2011@gmail.com

Dr.Anjali Srivastava
Assistant Professor, Sarala Birla University
Email:anjali.srivastava@sbu.ac.in

Dr.Afshan Anees
(Assistant Professor)
Al-Barkaat Institute of Education, Aligarh
E-mail: afshan.anees1@gmail.com

Vikash Kumar Singh
Librarian
Sainik School Tilaiya
(Under Sainik School Society, Ministry of Defence)
Koderma Jharkhand
Email: vksingh1718@gmail.com

S. Weerasinghe
Senior Assistant Librarian,
Science Library, University of Peradeniya, Sri Lanka
E-mail:-sureniw1@yahoo.com

Ms. Padma Harsora
Research Scholar (Ph.D.)
Veer Narmad South Gujarat University Surat
E-mail: padma.harsora@gmail.com

Dr. Ajit Prajapati
Librarian
Government Arts and Commerce College,
Netrang, Bharuch, Gujarat
Email: ajit.prajapati2010@gmail

Nattha Ram
Assistant Librarian
Army Public School Jodhpur
E-mail: nattharam1894@gmail.com

Dr. Pushpendra Singh
Librarian & Head Central Library G.L. Bajaj Group of Institutions, Mathura
om.mahaur@gmail.com

Vishal Saxena
Chief Librarian Central Library Babu Banarasi Das University, Lucknow
vishalsaxena7786@gmail.com

CHAPTER 1

Innovative Library Services: Challenges and Strategies for Effective Management

Dr. Devendra Kumar Sharma
Deputy Librarian Central University of Himachal Pradesh, Dharamshala, Dist-Kangra (HP), (India) *Email: sharmadk73@gmail.com*

Abstract

In today's digital age, libraries are undergoing significant transformations to remain relevant and meet the evolving needs of their users. The effective management of innovative library services is a cornerstone in this process, ensuring libraries adapt and thrive in serving their communities. This paper delves into the multifaceted realm of managing innovative library services, shedding light on libraries' diverse strategies while addressing the inherent management challenges. Drawing from a comprehensive literature review and insightful case studies, this paper offers a nuanced exploration of the landscape of library innovation, providing valuable insights and recommendations for library managers navigating this complex terrain. Libraries are no longer confined to traditional roles as repositories of books and information; they have evolved into dynamic knowledge and community engagement hubs. Embracing this evolution, libraries are increasingly exploring innovative strategies to enhance user experiences, expand access to information, and foster meaningful connections with their communities.

Keywords: Innovative Library Services, Management, Strategic Planning, Stakeholder Engagement, Evaluation, Challenges, Best Practices

1. Introduction

Libraries have long been recognised as pillars of knowledge and enlightenment, as bastions of information accessibility and community engagement.

In an era marked by rapid technological advancements and shifting user expectations, libraries' role has profoundly evolved. No longer confined to the traditional paradigms of book repositories, libraries are now dynamic entities at the forefront of innovation, continuously adapting to meet their patrons' diverse and evolving needs. Digital technologies have heralded a new era of possibilities and challenges for libraries. On one hand, it has democratised access to information, enabling users to retrieve vast knowledge. On the other hand, it has ushered in an unprecedented change, necessitating libraries to rethink their service models and embrace innovation to remain relevant in the digital landscape. The traditional notion of libraries as static repositories of books has given way to a more dynamic conception, wherein libraries serve as hubs of learning, collaboration, and exploration. In this context, effectively managing innovative library services is a paramount concern. The ability of libraries to innovate and adapt to changing user needs is contingent upon strategically managing resources, expertise, and partnerships. Indeed, effective management practices are essential for the successful implementation of innovative initiatives and for maximising the impact of library resources and services on their communities. This paper explores the multifaceted landscape of managing innovative library services, shedding light on the diverse strategies, challenges, and best practices characterising this endeavour. A comprehensive review of existing literature and illustrative case studies aims to provide library managers with valuable insights and recommendations for navigating the complexities of innovation in library services. Central to this exploration is recognising libraries as dynamic and adaptive institutions capable of leveraging innovation to serve their communities better. By embracing innovation, libraries have the opportunity to transcend traditional boundaries and foster deeper connections with users, thereby reaffirming their relevance and indispensability in the digital age. In the subsequent sections of this paper, we will delve into various aspects of managing innovative library services, ranging from needs assessment and strategic planning to stakeholder engagement and evaluation. Through a nuanced examination of these dimensions, we aim to equip library managers with the tools and strategies necessary to navigate the challenges and opportunities presented by innovation in library services.

2. Understanding Innovative Library Services

Innovative library services represent a paradigm shift in the traditional role of libraries, moving beyond mere repositories of books to dynamic hubs of knowledge and community interaction. These services encompass diverse initiatives aimed at meeting the evolving needs of users, enhancing their experience, and fostering deeper engagement with the library and its resources. At the heart of innovative library services lies a commitment to embracing emerging technologies and novel approaches to information dissemination. Digitization efforts, for instance, are pivotal in making library resources more accessible and convenient to users. By digitizing collections, libraries can transcend physical limitations, allowing users to access materials remotely and conveniently. This enhances access to information and opens up new avenues for scholarly research, education, and lifelong learning. In addition to digitization, implementing new technologies forms a cornerstone of innovative library services. From state-of-the-art search algorithms to immersive virtual reality experiences, libraries leverage cutting-edge technologies to revolutionize how users interact with information. For example, integrating artificial intelligence and machine learning algorithms can enhance the discoverability of library resources, providing personalized recommendations and tailored assistance to users based on their preferences and past interactions. Furthermore, innovative library services extend beyond technology, encompassing the development of specialized programs and services tailored to diverse user groups' unique needs and interests. These programs may include workshops, seminars, and training sessions to enhance users' digital literacy skills, research methodologies, and information literacy competencies. By empowering users with the knowledge and skills they need to navigate the complexities of the digital age, libraries promote lifelong learning and foster a culture of intellectual curiosity. Collaboration with external partners also plays a crucial role in driving innovation in library services. By forging strategic partnerships with academic institutions, community organizations, and industry stakeholders, libraries can tap into a wealth of expertise, resources, and perspectives to enrich their offerings and expand their reach. Collaborative initiatives such as joint research projects, co-sponsored events, and shared collections enable libraries to leverage complementary strengths and maximize their impact on their communities. In summary, innovative library services represent a dynamic and multifaceted approach to meeting the diverse needs of users in the digital age. By embracing digitization, leveraging new technologies, developing specialized programs and services, and fostering collaboration with external partners, libraries can position themselves as vibrant centers of knowledge, learning, and community engagement. Through a commitment to innovation, libraries have the opportunity to transcend traditional boundaries and remain relevant and indispensable in an ever-changing world.

3. Strategies for Managing Innovative Library Services

Innovative library services require careful planning, coordination, and management to ensure successful implementation and long-term sustainability. The following strategies outline key approaches for effectively managing innovative initiatives within libraries:

a. Needs Assessment

Conducting thorough needs assessments is the foundation for identifying areas ripe for innovation within the library. By soliciting feedback from users, staff, and other stakeholders, libraries can gain valuable insights into emerging needs, preferences, and challenges. Needs assessments help prioritise initiatives most aligned with user expectations and strategic priorities, ensuring that resources are allocated effectively to address areas of greatest impact.

b. Strategic Planning

Developing comprehensive strategic plans is essential for guiding the implementation of innovative initiatives within the library. Strategic plans provide a roadmap for aligning innovative projects with the library's mission, goals, and available resources. By articulating clear objectives, timelines, and performance indicators, strategic plans enable libraries to focus their efforts and resources on initiatives that have the greatest potential to advance their mission and meet the needs of their users.

c. *Stakeholder Engagement*

Engaging stakeholders is critical for garnering support and buy-in for innovative projects within the library. Stakeholders may include library staff, users, community partners, funding agencies, and other relevant parties. By involving stakeholders in the planning, implementing, and evaluating innovative initiatives, libraries can foster collaboration, build relationships, and leverage diverse perspectives and expertise. This collaborative approach increases the likelihood of success and sustainability for innovative projects, while also enhancing the library's relevance and impact within the community.

d. *Resource Allocation*

Effective resource allocation is essential for implementing and sustaining innovative services within the library. This includes allocating budgetary resources, staff time, and technology infrastructure to support innovative initiatives. Libraries must carefully prioritize and allocate resources based on each initiative's potential impact and strategic importance. By investing resources strategically, libraries can maximize the value generated by innovative projects and ensure their long-term viability.

e. *Training and Professional Development*

Providing library staff training and professional development opportunities is crucial for building the capacity to support innovative initiatives. Training programs may focus on developing skills in technology, project management, communication, and user engagement. By investing in staff development, libraries can cultivate a culture of innovation, empower staff to embrace new ideas and approaches, and ensure the successful implementation of innovative projects.

f. Evaluation and Assessment

Continuous evaluation and assessment are essential for measuring the impact and effectiveness of innovative services within the library. By collecting and analyzing data on key performance indicators, libraries can assess innovative initiatives' success, identify improvement areas, and make data-driven decisions to optimize their services. Evaluation and assessment also provide valuable feedback for stakeholders, enabling them to understand the value generated by innovative projects and make informed decisions about future investments and priorities.

4. Challenges in Managing Innovative Library Services

Despite innovative library services' numerous benefits and opportunities, their successful management is often challenging. Understanding and addressing these challenges are essential for ensuring the effective implementation and long-term sustainability of innovative initiatives within libraries. The following highlights key challenges faced by libraries in managing innovative services:

a. Financial Constraints

One of the primary challenges in managing innovative library services is the presence of financial constraints. Libraries often operate within tight budgets, limiting their ability to invest in new technologies, staff training, and other resources necessary for innovation. Limited funding may constrain the scope and scale of innovative projects, forcing libraries to seek alternative funding sources, such as grants, donations, or partnerships, to support their initiatives. Prioritizing projects based on their potential impact and aligning them with available resources is essential for navigating financial constraints and maximizing the effectiveness of innovative services.

b. Technological Barriers

Technological barriers pose significant challenges to adopting and implementing innovative services within libraries. Outdated infrastructure, legacy systems, and limited IT expertise can hinder libraries' ability to leverage new technologies effectively. Inadequate technological infrastructure may impede the delivery of digital services, such as online databases, virtual reference services, and digital collections, limiting access to information and hindering user engagement. Overcoming technological barriers requires libraries to upgrade their infrastructure, provide staff with training and support, and foster a technological innovation and experimentation culture.

c. Resistance to Change

Resistance to change among library staff and users presents another significant challenge in managing innovative services. Staff members may be hesitant to embrace new technologies, workflows, or service models due to fear of job displacement, lack of familiarity, or concerns about the impact on traditional library services. Similarly, users may resist changes in service delivery methods or user interfaces, preferring familiar or traditional approaches. Addressing resistance to change requires proactive communication, stakeholder engagement, and change management strategies to foster acceptance, build buy-in, and facilitate the smooth transition to innovative services.

d. Sustainability

Ensuring the long-term sustainability of innovative services is a critical challenge for libraries. While initial implementation may be successful, maintaining and scaling innovative initiatives over time require careful planning, resource allocation, and ongoing support from library leadership and stakeholders. Sustainability considerations encompass financial viability, staff capacity, technological infrastructure, user demand, and alignment with the library's strategic goals and priorities. Libraries must proactively assess the sustainability of innovative services, identify potential risks and barriers, and develop strategies to address them to ensure their continued success and relevance in the long run.

In summary, managing innovative library services presents various challenges, including financial constraints, technological barriers, resistance to change, and sustainability concerns. Addressing these challenges requires strategic planning, resource allocation, stakeholder engagement, and effective change management strategies to overcome barriers and maximize the impact of innovative initiatives within libraries. By navigating these challenges thoughtfully and proactively, libraries can position themselves as dynamic and responsive institutions that meet the evolving needs of their users and communities.

5. Case Studies

a. Digital Humanities Lab

In response to the growing demand for digital scholarship support, a university library establishes a Digital Humanities Lab to facilitate interdisciplinary research and teaching. The lab provides access to advanced digital tools, software, and resources tailored to the needs of humanities scholars and students. Equipped with high-performance computers, scanners, digitization equipment, and specialized software, the lab offers researchers the technical infrastructure needed to engage in innovative digital projects, such as text mining, data visualization, and digital mapping.

Moreover, the Digital Humanities Lab is a collaborative workspace where scholars from diverse disciplines can collaborate to share ideas, collaborate on projects, and explore new methodologies and approaches. Workshops, training sessions, and seminars are organized regularly to provide instruction on digital tools and methodologies, fostering a culture of digital literacy and innovation within the university community.

b. *Maker Space*

A public library responds to the growing interest in hands-on learning and DIY culture by creating a Maker Space—a dedicated area equipped with 3D printers, laser cutters, CNC machines, and other fabrication tools. The Maker Space allows patrons of all ages to explore technology, unleash their creativity, and learn new skills through experiential learning experiences.

Patrons can attend workshops, classes, and open lab sessions to learn how to use the equipment safely and effectively and engage in guided projects and activities. From prototyping and design to crafting and fabrication, the Maker Space empowers patrons to bring their ideas to life, whether creating custom jewelry, designing prototypes for inventions, or experimenting with robotics and electronics.

Furthermore, the Maker Space is a hub for community engagement and collaboration, hosting events, meetups, and maker fairs that bring together makers, artists, entrepreneurs, and educators. By providing access to cutting-edge technology and fostering a supportive and inclusive learning environment, the Maker Space inspires creativity, innovation, and lifelong learning among library patrons.

c. *Virtual Reference Services*

A library embraces digital transformation by implementing virtual reference services to enhance access to reference assistance and research support. Through chat, email, or video conferencing platforms, users can connect with professional librarians remotely to receive personalized assistance with research inquiries, database searches, citation management, etc.

Virtual reference services offer users the flexibility to seek assistance anytime, anywhere, without the need to visit the library in person. Whether it's a student working on a research paper late at night or a faculty member conducting fieldwork abroad, virtual reference services ensure that users can access expert support whenever needed.

Moreover, virtual reference services enable libraries to reach new audiences, expand their service offerings, and demonstrate their commitment to meeting the evolving needs of users in the digital age. By leveraging technology to deliver high-quality reference services remotely, libraries can enhance user satisfaction, improve access to information, and foster deeper engagement with their collections and resources.

6. Best Practices and Recommendations

Innovating library services requires a strategic and proactive approach encompassing internal processes and external partnerships. The following best practices and recommendations offer guidance for libraries seeking to manage and sustain innovative initiatives effectively:

a. Foster a culture of innovation and collaboration within the library

Encouraging a culture of innovation starts from the top-down, with library leadership setting the tone and expectations for experimentation, creativity, and risk-taking. Creating spaces and platforms for staff to share ideas collaborate on projects, and experiment with new approaches fosters a sense of ownership and empowerment. Emphasizing a user-centered approach ensures that innovation efforts are aligned with user needs and priorities.

b. Build partnerships with external organizations and stakeholders

Collaborating with external organizations, such as academic institutions, community groups, technology companies, and funding agencies, can amplify the impact of library innovation efforts. By leveraging external expertise, resources, and networks, libraries can access new perspectives, technologies, and funding opportunities. Building strategic partnerships fosters innovation, expands the reach of library services, and strengthens the library's role as a community anchor and knowledge hub.

c. Invest in staff training and professional development

Equipping library staff with the skills, knowledge, and support needed to embrace innovation is essential for success. Investing in ongoing training and professional development programs ensures staff are prepared to adopt new technologies, methodologies, and service models. Providing opportunities for staff to learn from experts, attend conferences, and participate in hands-on workshops empowers them to contribute to and drive innovation within the library.

d. Solicit feedback from users and stakeholders

Engaging users and stakeholders in designing, implementing, and evaluating innovative services is crucial for ensuring relevance and effectiveness. Regularly soliciting feedback through surveys, focus groups, user testing, and other methods allows libraries to gain insights into user preferences, pain points, and needs. Actively listening to feedback and incorporating it into decision-making processes enables libraries to improve and refine their services over time iteratively.

e. *Monitor trends in technology, user behavior, and information needs*

Staying abreast of emerging trends in technology, user behavior, and information needs is essential for anticipating future challenges and opportunities. Proactively monitoring trends allows libraries to identify emerging technologies, user preferences, and societal shifts that may impact library services. By staying ahead of the curve, libraries can position themselves as innovators and thought leaders, ensuring their continued relevance and impact in an ever-changing landscape.

In summary, fostering a culture of innovation, building strategic partnerships, investing in staff development, soliciting user feedback, and monitoring trends are key best practices for effectively managing and sustaining innovative library services. By adopting these practices and recommendations, libraries can navigate the complexities of innovation, maximize the impact of their initiatives, and continue to evolve and thrive in serving their communities.

7. Conclusion

In conclusion, the effective management of innovative library services is indispensable for libraries to remain agile, responsive, and impactful in meeting the diverse needs of their users and communities. In an era characterized by rapid technological advancements, shifting user preferences, and evolving societal trends, libraries must embrace innovation to stay relevant and effective in fulfilling their mission. By employing strategic planning, libraries can align their innovative initiatives with their mission, goals, and available resources, ensuring that they are well-positioned to address the evolving needs of their users. Stakeholder engagement is critical in garnering support and collaboration for innovative projects, fostering a sense of ownership and investment among staff, users, and external partners. Continuous evaluation and assessment enable libraries to measure their innovative services' impact and effectiveness, identify improvement areas, and make data-driven decisions to optimize their offerings. By soliciting feedback from users and stakeholders, libraries can ensure that their innovative initiatives are responsive to user needs and preferences, enhancing user satisfaction and engagement. Moreover, libraries must stay attuned to emerging trends in technology, user behavior, and information needs, proactively adapting and innovating to meet new challenges and opportunities. By monitoring trends and anticipating future developments, libraries can position themselves as leaders in the field, driving innovation and shaping the future of library services. In essence, effective management of innovative library services is essential for libraries to thrive and ensure their continued relevance and impact in a rapidly changing world. By embracing innovation, libraries can empower themselves to evolve and adapt to meet the evolving needs of their users, thereby reaffirming their role as indispensable institutions in the fabric of society. Through strategic planning, stakeholder engagement, continuous evaluation, and proactive adaptation, libraries can navigate the complexities of innovation and chart a course toward a future of enhanced service delivery, community engagement, and knowledge dissemination.

References:

1. Alabi, J. (2019). Innovation and change in academic libraries: A case study of using a library innovation framework to explore and support organizational change in libraries. College & Research Libraries, 80(4), 560-576.
2. Bertot, J. C., Jaeger, P. T., & Grimes, J. M. (2010). Using ICTs to create a culture of transparency: E-government and social media as openness and anti-corruption tools for societies. Government Information Quarterly, 27(3), 264-271.
3. Chow, A. S. (2016). Managing the innovation process in academic libraries: A case study. New Review of Academic Librarianship, 22(1-2), 20-39.

4. Cohen, L. (2019). Making in the library: Case studies in digital humanities, publishing, and special collections. Library Juice Press.
5. Popp, J. A., & LeClair, C. (2018). Innovation in academic libraries: A model for advancing strategic initiatives. Journal of Library Administration, 58(3), 290-305.

CHAPTER 2

Role of Libraries for Community Development in Assam: A Study

Prasanna Kumar Konch
Assistant Librarian, The Assam Royal Global University, Guwahati
Email: prasannakonch@gmail.com

Dr Sailendra Das
Assistant Professor, Mass Communication The Assam Royal Global University, Guwahati
Email: sailendas.das@gmail.com

Abstract

Libraries in Assam play a crucial role in providing access to information, pro-moting literacy, and preserving local heritage. They serve as community hubs facilitating learning, collaboration, and empowerment among individuals of all ages and backgrounds. This study delves into the specific context of As-sam, aiming to comprehensively examine the multifaceted role of libraries in contributing to community development. By addressing the unique needs and preferences of diverse communities across the region, this research identifies how libraries serve as integral components of local development initiatives by the people for the people. The study assesses the range of library services and programs offered in Assam, evaluating their impact on education, literacy, and cultural preservation. Through a qualitative exploration of community engage-ment strategies, the research investigates how libraries facilitate social cohesion and inclusivity, transcending boundaries and promoting interconnectedness among varying demographic groups. By collaborating with local organisations and implementing innovative programming, libraries can further enhance their impact on community development. Additionally, fostering partnerships with schools and universities can help libraries expand their reach and provide valu-able resources to a broader audience.

Keywords: Community Development, Library & Communication.

1. Introduction

Assam is a place where the environment in which people live has led to its unique socio-cultural setting characterized by its extensive folklore and wide spectrum of people. As such, it would be good to look at libraries' role in societal growth. Consequently, this research investigates how these institutions have enhanced Assam's overall betterment and forward movement by assessing their specific programmes or strategies. Moreover, libraries are places open for all individuals to exchange ideas, work on joint projects, and establish social ties among themselves. Libraries in Assam can partner with local organisations and government agencies, addressing community concerns and creating a sense of belonging among residents. In rural or urban areas, libraries in Assam have, over time, outgrown being just repositories for books but are now transformed into vibrant learning centres facilitating interaction and growing communities. They have become inclusive, dynamic and relevant to diverse users as they have moved beyond traditional roles, embracing technology, responding to new information needs and reaching different clientele groups.

Assam's traditional education system was based on monasteries and other educational institutions during the ancient period. As a result, religious, philosophical, literary, and scientific manuscripts were kept in their respective places. These ancient manuscripts survived on palm leaves for the most part. The Ahom rulers who ruled Assam from the 13th to the 19th century were instrumental in promoting education and knowledge preservation. A wide range of subjects, such as religion, law, literature, and history, were covered in this collection of royal libraries, which contained diverse manuscripts. These libraries formed part of the royal court complexes.

Assam also experienced a change in the library landscape during British colonial rule. Therefore, The aim was to provide education books for native people, colonial officers who lived there, and missionaries and colonial administrators who established them.

2. Review of literature

Libraries play a pivotal role in providing access to information and knowledge, particularly in regions with limited access to formal education and resources. With Assam's diverse linguistic and cultural groups, libraries act as repositories of indigenous knowledge and local history. Studies by Borah et al. (2017) and Saikia (2019) emphasise how libraries support literacy initiatives, especially in rural areas, and enhance educational opportunities for marginalised communities. Assam's cultural landscape is a mosaic of ethnicities, languages, and traditions. Libraries aid in preserving and promoting this rich cultural heritage. Research by Baruah (2018) highlights the role of libraries in safeguarding endangered languages and promoting traditional art forms through workshops and exhibitions. By serving as cultural hubs, libraries foster a sense of belonging and pride among the local population. In today's digital age, libraries are evolving to provide physical and digital resources. Studies by Rahman (2020) underline how libraries in Assam adapt by offering internet facilities, e-books, and online learning platforms. This shift enhances digital literacy and empowers communities to participate in the global knowledge economy. Libraries can be catalysts for socio-economic development. They serve as platforms for skill development, entrepreneurship, and vocational training. Research by Gogoi and Borkotoky (2018) indicates that libraries have enabled small business initiatives by providing market information and mentorship, thus contributing to local economic growth and poverty reduction. Libraries foster community engagement by hosting events, discussions, and workshops. Such activities facilitate dialogue on important social issues, promoting awareness and activism. Research by Das and Dutta (2019) demonstrates how libraries serve as safe spaces for open discussions on topics ranging from healthcare to gender equality, thereby contributing to social cohesion and progressive change.

3. Challenges and future directions:

While the role of libraries in community development is evident, challenges persist. Infrastructure limitations, funding constraints, and the need for trained librarians are issues highlighted by Bora and Hazarika (2017). There is a need for strategic partnerships between libraries, governments, NGOs, and private organisations to address these challenges and further amplify the impact of libraries on community development.

4. Objectives

i. To Examine Library Services and Programs for community development
ii. To highlight the library as a tool of information.

5. Methodology

Research is an organised investigation using a variety of techniques to find information. Thus, gathering the required data and information is essential to a research project's success. The study is qualitative. For analysis, two primary and secondary categories of data, primary and secondary, have been gathered. Primary and secondary data served as the foundation for the creation of this study. Primary data came from document analysis, surveys, and various interviews.

6. Data presentation & analysis

Here, we can examine the concept of the "community." The community is any size social entity with shared ideals, generally small in size. According to the Oxford Advanced Learner's Dictionary, a "community"[1] is any group of people who live together in a specific geographic region and are discussed as such. A community has traditionally been described in sociology as a collection of socially engaged individuals residing in a shared area. In the context of this definition, community, the term "media" describes the media formats that are mainly created. Thus, considering the foregoing debate, we may state that a library can contribute to the growth of a specific

1 https://www.oxfordlearnersdictionaries.com/definition/english/community#:~:text=%2Fk%C9%99%CB%88mju%CB%90n%C9%99ti%2F,particular%20area%2C%20country%2C%20etc.

community in addition to its regular programming. It might serve as both a platform and an independent tool for community communication.

The role of libraries in community development is multifaceted and significant. Libraries are vital hubs for learning, information access, cultural enrichment, and community social interaction. Here are some key aspects that highlight the role of libraries in community development:

- **Education and literacy**

  Libraries play a pivotal role in promoting education and literacy within communities. They provide access to books, digital resources, and educational programs that contribute to lifelong learning for people of all ages. Libraries often offer reading programs, workshops, and tutoring services to enhance literacy skills among children and adults.

- **Information Access**

  Libraries are reliable sources of information, enabling community members to access a wide range of resources, from books and magazines to online databases and research materials. This access empowers individuals with the knowledge needed for personal growth, informed decision-making, and academic pursuits.

- **Digital Inclusion**

  In the digital age, libraries bridge the digital divide by offering public access to computers, the internet, and digital skills training. This is crucial for individuals who cannot access digital technologies independently. Libraries facilitate online job searches, e-government services, and digital literacy education.

- **Cultural Enrichment**

  Libraries often organise cultural events, exhibitions, and workshops celebrating local heritage and diverse cultures. These activities foster a sense of community identity and pride while promoting understanding and tolerance among different groups.

- **Community Engagement**

  Libraries serve as community gathering spaces where residents can meet, collaborate, and share ideas. They host events like book clubs, lectures, workshops, and performances, encouraging social interaction and strengthening community bonds.

- **Support for Entrepreneurs and Small Businesses**

  Many libraries offer resources and programs to support entrepreneurship and small business development. This includes access to business databases, workshops on business planning, and networking opportunities for local entrepreneurs.

- **Health and Well-being**

  Libraries provide health, wellness, and mental health resources, supporting community members in making informed decisions about their well-being. They may host wellness workshops and health-related talks and provide access to health information databases.

- **Children and Youth Development**

  Libraries offer child-friendly spaces, story times, and educational programs contributing to early childhood development. They provide a safe and enriching environment for children to explore literature, arts, and sciences.

- **Social Services Information**

  Libraries often serve as hubs for information on social services, connecting community members to resources such as housing assistance, employment support, and legal services.

- **Environmental Awareness**

  Some libraries promote environmental awareness and sustainable living through resources, workshops, and initiatives related to ecology, conservation, and environmental advocacy.

- **Civic Engagement**

  Libraries encourage civic participation by providing information on elections, government processes, and community initiatives. They may host forums, debates, and discussions on important local and global issues.

  The **Northeast Educational Trust**, a library in Guwahati, founded a community library in 2009. A community library is where people can access a range of reading materials, including newspapers, books, periodicals, and even digital resources. Such a library seeks to advance literacy, education, and a reading culture in the neighbourhood. It is a priceless resource for those who might not have easy access to books and educational resources. Events, workshops, and reading programs are frequently planned by community libraries to engage people of all ages and backgrounds and promote intellectual curiosity and information exchange.

- **Language Learning Programs**

  The Trust also started language learning initiatives, which aim to assist people in learning new languages or improving their skills in ones they already know. A wide variety of languages, from regional indigenous to widely spoken foreign languages, can be covered in language learning programs. These initiatives can be delivered in many ways, including workshops, classes, online materials, and language-exchange initiatives. These programs are essential for encouraging cultural variety, fostering interlinguistic communication, and giving people more access to career and educational options.

- **Capacity Enhancement Program**

  The Capacity Enhancement Program introduced by the North East Educational Trust focuses on improving the skills, knowledge, and capabilities of individuals in the community. This program could involve training sessions, workshops, and seminars to enhance various skills such as leadership, communication, problem-solving, and technical expertise. Capacity enhancement programs are essential for personal and professional development, empowering individuals to contribute more effectively to their community's growth and development.

- **Early Childhood Care**

  The Trust's dedication to fostering young children's growth throughout their formative years is seen by its participation in early childhood care. Early childhood care programs usually include various services and activities promoting children's physical, mental, emotional, and social development from birth until age eight. Some of these initiatives include preschool education, nutrition and health assistance, parent education, and creating secure and engaging environments for young children. Putting money into early childhood education is essential to laying a solid foundation for a child's well-being and lifetime learning.

  The **North East Educational Trust** in Guwahati has been engaged in a multifaceted education and community development approach. The trust aims to promote education, literacy, skills development, and holistic growth within the local community through initiatives such as the community library, language learning programs, capacity enhancement programs, and early childhood care.

- **Prerana Puthibhoral (Library)** near Nalbari, Assam, is a bright name today. Prerana Library was started in 2000 at Bihampur, Nalbari, under the patronage of teacher Dwijendra Narayan Sharma, and today, it is a remarkable name for Assam and the North East. Members of this library can be from any community. This library has helped promote reading for the students of the society and among the citizens of the society. This is because this library has been doing a lot of work to help poor students and students in need by giving them books. In addition, the library conducts various social activities annually, celebrating language, culture, different significant days, etc., and tries to spread social thought among the people of the society. The library has also helped the people of the society by organising various educational lectures through many university professors. The library has recently organised a book fair and has occupied a special place in the society of Nalbari.

7. Findings and results

Above this discussion, as of our study in September 2021, we can provide some insights into the potential scope of community libraries in Assam, India. However, please note that the information might have changed since then, so verifying the current situation through more recent sources is a good idea. Community libraries are crucial in promoting literacy, education, and community engagement. Here are some aspects of their scope in Assam.

1. Literacy Promotion: Assam, like many other regions in India, faces literacy challenges, particularly in rural areas. Community libraries can improve literacy rates by providing access to books, educational materials, and resources that promote reading and learning.
2. Cultural Preservation: Assam has a rich cultural heritage, including literature, folklore, and history. Community libraries can serve as repositories of local cultural materials, helping preserve and promote the state's unique identity.
3. Language Diversity: Assam is known for its linguistic diversity, with Assamese being the dominant language. Community libraries can support linguistic diversity by offering books and materials in various languages spoken in the region.
4. Education Support: Many students, especially those from poor backgrounds, can benefit from access to educational resources beyond what is available in schools. Community libraries can of-

fer supplementary materials, study resources, and a quiet place to study.

5. Digital Literacy: With the increasing importance of digital skills, community libraries could provide access to computers and the internet, helping people acquire essential digital literacy skills.
6. Promoting Reading Culture: Community libraries can foster a culture of reading from a young age, leading to better cognitive development, improved language skills, and enhanced critical thinking abilities.
7. Community Engagement: These libraries can serve as hubs for community members to come together, share ideas, hold discussions, and organise events, strengthening social bonds and fostering a sense of unity.
8. Health and Well-being: Community libraries can also provide resources on health, hygiene, and general well-being, serving as educational platforms for health-related issues.
9. Skill Development: Libraries can organise workshops, training sessions, and skill development programs to enhance employability and vocational skills within the community.
10. Outreach to Marginalized Groups: Community libraries can be especially beneficial for marginalised groups, including women, children, and indigenous communities, offering a safe space for learning and empowerment.
11. Infrastructure: Establishing and maintaining physical spaces conducive to learning and reading is crucial.
12. Resource Acquisition: Acquiring a diverse range of books, periodicals, and educational materials relevant to the community's needs and interests is essential.
13. Collaboration: Collaborating with local educational institutions, government bodies, NGOs, and volunteers can help enhance the impact of community libraries.
14. Awareness and Outreach: Effective promotion and outreach ef-

forts are necessary to ensure the community knows and participates in library activities.

15. Adaptation to Technology: Integrating digital resources and tools can make libraries more relevant in the digital age.

The scope and success of community libraries depend on the active involvement and support of the local community, as well as sustained efforts by stakeholders. For the most current information about the scope of community libraries in Assam, I recommend contacting local educational and cultural organisations or government agencies.

8. Conclusion

In this study explores the integral role that libraries play in community development in Assam. Libraries serve as dynamic hubs for education, cul-tural preservation, and social cohesion. They bridge the past and the digital age, offering resources that promote knowledge, digital literacy, and access to information technology. Libraries unite diverse groups by preserving Assam's cultural heritage and fostering inclusivity. They provide solutions to challenges like limited education access and socio-economic disparities. Collaboration between libraries, communities, and institutions is crucial to maximise their impact. In essence, libraries are essential agents of positive change, contributing significantly to Assam's progress and inclusiveness.

References

1. Baruah, M. K. (2018). Preserving Cultural Heritage through Library Initia-tives: A Study of Indigenous Language and Art Promotion in Assam. Heri-tage & Society, 11(1), 78-92.

2. Bora, R., & Hazarika, M. (2017). Challenges Faced by Libraries in Assam and Their Implications for Community Development. Library Management, 38(8/9), 507-518.

3. Borah, A., Das, S., & Gogoi, R. (2017). Empowering Rural Communities

through Library-based Literacy Initiatives: A Case Study in Assam. Journal of Community Development and Education, 5(2), 45-58.

4. Das, A., & Dutta, R. (2019). Fostering Social Cohesion through Library Discussions: Case Studies from Assam. Community Development Journal, 54(3), 398-414.

5. Gogoi, B., & Borkotoky, K. (2018). Libraries as Drivers of Socio-Econom-ic Change: Case Studies from Assam. International Journal of Information Dissemination and Technology, 8(3), 210-225.

6. Rahman, S. (2020). Adapting Libraries to the Digital Age: A Study of Tech-nological Initiatives in Assam. Journal of Information Technology in Li-braries, 38(2), 67-82.

7. Saikia, P. (2019). Role of Libraries in Enhancing Educational Opportunities for Marginalized Communities in Assam. International Journal of Library and Information Studies, 7(4), 112-125.

8. Website: Kalita, Mainisha. (2019, July 5). Prerona Puthibhoral: An influ-ential rural library in Assam that inspires its members to combine book reading with collective labour/NERZINE. https://www.nezine.com/info/jZZbzg5a3dzRGQ3NmQ0dWNsUXpmQT09/prerona-puth-ibhoral:-an-influential-rural-library-in-assam-that-inspires-its-mem-bers-to-combine-book-reading-with-collective-labour.html (Access on 24/02/2024 at 3.49 pm.)

CHAPTER 3

Strategic knowledge Management practices in Modern libraries: Navigating the 21st century landscape.

Rajshree Dutta
LIS Intern, Central Reference Library, Kolkata
MLIS, PGDCA
rajsheedutta35@gmail.com

Abstract

This study focuses mainly on the topic of knowledge management. This article discusses the properties of knowledge management and the technology used to implement it within libraries. Knowledge management refers to the exchange of knowledge within and beyond an organisation. Knowledge management involves producing, capturing, and exploiting knowledge to improve organisational performance. Knowledge acquisition is the foundation of knowledge management in libraries. This article looks at Knowledge Management as an essential tool that can help libraries better adapt to the new requirements of the digital era and meet the needs of its users. Academic institutions have significant opportunities to use knowledge management strategies to assist in all aspects of their mission.

Keywords: KM, Library & Information Science, KMS, Librarianship, Technology, Knowledge resources, Human resources.

1. Introduction:

This is the age of knowledge and information explosion. Successful libraries and information centres rely on their staff's expertise in information to serve their users. The term "document management" has been replaced by "information management," and the field is transitioning to "knowledge management" altogether. As knowledge drives social progress, society's focus on information and knowledge grows, as do people's desires. Shortly, libraries will need to focus on managing knowledge effectively. Libraries should prioritise knowledge management by conducting effective research and development, creating knowledge bases, exchanging and sharing knowledge among staff, training staff, and facilitating the explicit processing of implicit knowledge.

As globalisation and competition expand, organisations seek innovative strategies for competitive advantage. These organisations aim to utilise a diverse set of resources. Today, knowledge, an intangible asset, is valued more than traditional resources like capital and labour. Knowledge management is a growing discipline that involves identifying, capturing, developing, storing, applying, sharing, and updating knowledge to enhance organisational performance.

2. Objectives:

- ✓ Examine the concepts of knowledge and KM.
- ✓ Implications for the library and information science professions.
- ✓ The advantages and constraints of library digitisation.
- ✓ To examine the impact of technology on KM.

3. Methodology:

This study will adopt a descriptive research design to examine modern libraries' strategic knowledge management practices. Descriptive research provides a comprehensive overview of the current state of knowledge management practices, allowing for the collection of both qualitative and quantitative data to address research questions effectively. Relevant documents such as strategic plans, policies, and reports related to library knowledge management will be analysed to supplement primary data and provide contextual information.

4. Literature Reviews:

Harineeswaran, Nithyanandam and Muthu (2015), in the article "Knowledge, Management, Components, Steps, Tools and Their Strategies for

Modern Academic Libraries, focus on the advancement of Information Technology (IT) and its applications in libraries and information centres. The concept of document management has evolved into information management. This has led to a shift towards knowledge management.

Singh (2005), in his article "Knowledge Management and its Use in Libraries", describes various aspects of knowledge management and its applications. The document describes in detail the value of knowledge to an organisation. The importance of librarians and information professionals in organisations' knowledge management is demonstrated.

Jain (2020), in his article "Knowledge Management in Libraries and Information Centers: A Bibliometric Perspective", provides a bibliometric perspective on the literature on knowledge management (KM) in libraries for the past 21 years (1998-2019) web-based scientific collection bibliographic database. This study uses bibliometric and citation analysis methods to explore library knowledge management research profiles and trends.

Eighty-three sources were retrieved through the Web of Science core database using "Knowledge management, library, information centre, librarian, and information specialist". Husain & Nazim (2013), in the article "Knowledge Management Concepts of Library and Information Science Professionals", this study attempt to collect and critically evaluate research on conceptual knowledge Management concepts (KM) of library and information science (LIS) professionals. It is based on a review of published works in GC and library science. Based on an extensive literature review, this study lays the foundation for future research on the challenges and opportunities in implementing knowledge management (KM) in libraries.

Ebisi&Arua (2018), in the article "Knowledge Management in 21st Century Libraries", this article addresses the concept of knowledge management and what libraries can do to improve knowledge management activities. in all significant areas of library service and the challenges of such efforts. Kumara & Narasimhaiah (2019), in the report "Knowledge Management Concepts in Library and Information Services at Central Forest Library: A Case Study", present research on libraries and services information of the Central Forest Library of the Forest Department of Karnataka. The growing need for knowledge management has changed every aspect and function of libraries. Knowledge management requires systems that process information more efficiently, convey information quickly, and connect information to individuals and activities.

Poonkothai (2016), in their paper "Knowledge Management as an Important Tool in Library Management", looks at Knowledge Management as an essential tool that can help libraries better adapt to the new requirements of the digital era and meet the needs of its users. Academic institutions have significant opportunities to use knowledge management strategies to assist in all aspects of their mission. Jain (2022), in their paper "Knowledge Management of Libraries in Present Scenario", states that knowledge management is a big concern today. Professionals frequently deal with evidence-based knowledge and problem-based learning. Librarians play an important part in clinical practice decision-making. The article focuses on knowledge management's principles, tactics, components, and barriers, emphasising society.

Asogwa (2012), in their paper "Knowledge Management in Academic Libraries: Librarians In The 21st Century", explores librarians' contributions to knowledge management and their consequences for academic librarians. A survey of relevant literature on libraries and knowledge management identified current trends and future opportunities for librarians and information science practitioners. Evidence suggests that knowledge management encompasses all human and organisational activities, including libraries and archives. Reddy (2017), in their paper "Knowledge Management in 21st Century Academic Libraries", This paper provides expertise management tools for 21st-century academic libraries. Research suggests that knowledge management affects all human and organisational life aspects, including libraries and information. Academic librarians can use knowledge management to develop employees' expertise and strengthen user relationships.

5. Concepts of knowledge management

The concept of "Knowledge Management" was introduced and popularised in the business sector during the final decade of the twentieth century. The importance of knowledge in the "global economy" of the "knowledge age" was first recognised by the corporate sector. Organisations can acquire a competitive advantage in the new knowledge economy by developing and continuously renewing relevant and strategic information.

- Create repositories of knowledge and information, often in document form.
- The goal is to promote accessibility and knowledge transfer, focusing on connectivity and access.
- Create a knowledge environment that is more conducive to the effective production, transfer, and use of knowledge.
- This involves addressing organisational norms and values related to knowledge.
- Treat knowledge as an asset and recognise its value to the organisation.

Knowledge management solutions have expanded to other organisations, such as government agencies, R&D departments, universities, etc. Librarians and libraries have long been considered the experts in information management.

6. Knowledge Management in the Library

Information technology is a library knowledge management tool, and knowledge acquisition is the starting point for library knowledge management.The application of information technology expands the scope of knowledge acquisition. The goal of knowledge management in libraries is to promote knowledge innovation.

As a learning company, it should give strong leadership in knowledge management. Librarians are critical in developing systems and policies that leverage an institution's knowledge base. As information custodians and disseminators inside institutions, librarians significantly contribute to effectively implementing knowledge management programmes.

Knowledge innovation is the core of the knowledge economy society.

It is Used to collect, process, store, and distribute knowledge and information. Libraries play a crucial role in advancing scientific knowledge and innovation. Libraries actively contribute to scientific research. Library work is part of knowledge innovation. Libraries should prioritise the dissemination and transformation of knowledge.

Knowledge management aims to foster relationships between libraries and users to improve the sharing and circulation of knowledge.

Libraries in the knowledge economy will seek to develop and apply information resources, build virtual libraries, and protect intellectual property rights in the digital age, laying the foundation for innovation. Implementing knowledge management in libraries improves traditional library activities, such as collecting, processing, disseminating, storing and using information, to provide multidisciplinary services to meet library users' personal and professional needs. Nowadays, the information management function has evolved into that of knowledge management programs in that it involves the discovery, collection, production, resolution, storage, and sharing of knowledge. Librarians and information staff must manage relationships with external providers of information and expertise, including negotiations.

7. Advantages of Knowledge Management

7.1 Efficient Information Retrieval: Knowledge management improves cataloguing and indexing, allowing users to access relevant information more quickly.

7.2 Improved Decision-Making: Organised knowledge enables librarians and users to make more informed decisions about resource purchase, collection development, and research.

7.3 Enhanced Collaboration: Knowledge management promotes collaboration between librarians and patrons by fostering sharing of thoughts and resources, resulting in a more dynamic learning environment.

7.4 Optimized Resource Utilization: Librarians can better understand resource utilisation patterns, allowing for more strategic allocation and optimisation of library materials.

7.5 **Adaptability to Technological Changes**: Embracing knowledge management helps libraries keep up with technological changes, ensuring their value in the digital age.

7.6 **Personalized User Experiences**: Libraries may provide patrons with a more personalised experience by learning their preferences and requirements and tailoring services, recommendations, and resources accordingly.

8. Disadvantages of Knowledge Management:

8.1 **Implementation Challenges**: Implementing knowledge management systems in libraries can encounter resistance and hurdles, such as staff training and adapting to new technologies.

8.2 **Resource Intensiveness**: Establishing and maintaining good knowledge management processes necessitates significant resources, both in terms of time and money, which some libraries may find challenging.

8.3 **Data Security Concerns**: Managing and sharing sensitive information in a knowledge management system may create data security and privacy issues, necessitating strong safeguards against unauthorised access or data breaches.

8.4 **Resistance to Change**: Library personnel or users may resist new knowledge management approaches, mainly if used to traditional procedures, resulting in a sluggish or partial shift.

8.5 **Knowledge Silos**: In some circumstances, knowledge management systems may unintentionally generate silos by isolating information within specific departments or among particular staff members, preventing cross-functional cooperation.

8.6 **Maintenance Challenges**: Over time, knowledge management systems may face difficulties maintaining current and relevant content, necessitating continual efforts to ensure the information stays correct and helpful.

9. Impact of technology on knowledge management

Technology has had a transformational impact on knowledge management, transforming how organisations acquire, organise, and exploit information. In a world of rapid change and digital growth, incorporating technology into knowledge management procedures has become critical to remaining competitive and promoting creativity. One of the most significant contributions of technology to knowledge management is increased information accessibility. Traditional ways of keeping knowledge in physical documents or localised databases had limited accessibility. However, with the introduction of cloud computing and online platforms, information has become more accessible to people across borders. Cloud-based knowledge repositories enable teams to access and contribute to shared data, reducing geographical boundaries and encouraging collaboration. Collaboration has evolved significantly in response to technological advancements. Digital communication tools, project management platforms, and collaboration software have allowed team members to engage more seamlessly. Virtual teams can collaborate synchronously or asynchronously, exchanging insights and updates in real-time. This speeds up decision-making processes and ensures that pooled knowledge is used efficiently, resulting in more informed and strategic outcomes.

Automation is another critical component of technology's influence on knowledge management. Organisations may use AI and ML to automate data analysis, classification, and predictive modelling. This allows for faster discovery of patterns and trends within large datasets, delivering significant insights to decision-makers. Automation saves time and eliminates the chance of human error, ensuring that knowledge repositories are accurate and reliable. Real-time updates have become a feature of current knowledge management systems. Instead of depending on static texts, organisations can create dynamic knowledge bases that evolve as new information is discovered. This dynamic aspect is vital in rapidly changing businesses like technology, healthcare, and finance. Real-time updates ensure decision-makers get the most up-to-date and relevant information, increasing the organisation's agility and adaptability.

Technology integration has streamlined information sharing inside organisations while facilitating external knowledge acquisition. Organisations can access external sources of knowledge by conducting web research, monitoring social media, and participating in industry forums. This more significant viewpoint improves internal information vaults, allowing for a more complete understanding of market trends, client needs, and industry changes. Furthermore, technology has played an essential role in developing an innovative culture within organisations. Cross-pollination of ideas is often the source of innovation, and technology facilitates this by connecting disparate teams and allowing for the exchange of insights. Platforms for idea generation, virtual brainstorming sessions, and collaborative innovation technologies enable employees to contribute to the organisation's knowledge pool, promoting continual improvement and creativity.

The impact of technology on knowledge management is significant and diverse. From improving accessibility and collaboration to automating processes and providing real-time updates, technology has become an invaluable ally in exploiting and optimising organisational knowledge. Embracing technological innovations enhances productivity and decision-making and enables organisations to prosper in a constantly changing commercial world.

10. Conclusion

Knowledge management focuses on delivering relevant information to the appropriate people at the right time. This may appear simple, but it requires a solid connection to company strategy, knowledge of bureaucracy information, developing techniques that span organisational capabilities, and ensuring that organisational personnel regularly support initiatives. Knowledge management might encompass new knowledge creation or focus simply on sharing, storing, and improving information. Refer to my knowledge control definition for a more extensive discussion and description. Knowledge management involves discovering, acquiring, sharing, and applying knowledge. Librarians can utilise Knowledge Management to strengthen their standing in management and provide additional services. Knowledge management consists of discovering, acquiring, sharing, and applying knowledge. Librarians can utilise Knowledge Management to enhance their standing in management and provide additional services. To be effective, organisations must prioritise strategic goals, engage people, and use technology as a tool for purpose. Knowledge management can play a significant role for libraries in the educational community. We hope that knowledge management will play a significant role in guiding Indian educational institutions in the future.

Knowledge management is an effective instrument for driving innovation and reengineering an organization's daily tasks. The rapid growth of knowledge makes it challenging for experts to record and transmit information to those who need it. Emerging technologies can help with this. The importance of knowledge management in academic libraries cannot be overlooked.

References

1. Jain, P., & Mutula, S. (2008). Libraries as learning organisations: implications for knowledge management. Library Hi Tech News, 25(8), 10-14.
2. Jotwani, D. (2008). Best Practices in a Modern Library and Information Centre Case of Central Library, IIT Bombay.
3. Marwick, A. D. (2001). Knowledge management technology. IBM Systems Journal, 40(4), 814-830.
4. MMcElroy, M. W. (2010). The new knowledge management. Routledge.
5. McInerney, C. (2002). Knowledge management and the dynamic nature of knowledge. Journal of the American Society for Information Science and Technology, 53(12), 1009-1018.
6. McInerney, C. (2002). Knowledge management and the dynamic nature of knowledge. Journal of the American Society for Information Science and Technology, 53(12), 1009-1018.

7. Subramanian, R., &Meyyammai, R. (2019). Library Collection Development And Management Practices In Academic Libraries With Special Reference To Modern Era. Think India Journal, 22(10), 5392-5401.

8. Teng, S., &Hawamdeh, S. (2002, June). Knowledge management in public libraries. In Aslib Proceedings (Vol. 54, No. 3, pp. 188-197). MCB UP Ltd.

9. Wiig, K. M. (1997). Knowledge management: an introduction and perspective. Journal of Knowledge Management, 1(1), 6-14.

CHAPTER 4

Managing Information Centres and Libraries Using Open Source Software

Dr. HARIKRISHNAN CA
Librarian, ISRO/VSSC/SCS, Trivandrum, Kerala, India.
harikrishnan.harikrishnan@gmail.com

Abstract

Open-source software is dominating the infrastructure of present-day libraries. These software are more secure, stable, flexible, auditable and reliable than other commercial software. This paper describes, in brief, library automation software like Evergreen, Koha, and New Gen Lib, as well as digital library software like EPrints, DSpace, and Greenstone. Some of the useful library management applications, such as Drupal, Joomla, CUFTS, and CORAL, are also explained in this paper.

Key Words: Evergreen, Koha, New Gen Lib, EPrints, DSpace, Greenstone, Drupal, Joomla, CUFTS, CORAL.

1. Introduction

The Term Open Source Software was coined by Eric Raymond. The word "Open Source" means software free of cost and has the source code. However, the term Free software was given by Richard Stallman in 1984. This software can be obtained free of cost. Free software provides only executable files to the end user. Anyone can use the executable file but cannot modify the software.

Open-source developers give importance to quality. Library and information centres that manage information sources require high-quality and sophisticated software. The high cost of this type of software prevents most libraries and information centres from using them. To deal with this issue, different organisations, individuals and NGOs have developed and distributed software free of cost. Such software is known as Open or Free Software. Now, in this digital era, free software is readily available online. Anyone can download it and use it easily.

2. History of Open Source

The open-source movement was started by Richard Stallman, who founded the GNU project in the 1980s. Free software foundation was done in 1985. Linus Torvalds developed the Linux kernel in 1991. Later, in 1998, Eric Raymond formed the Open Source Initiative.

3. Factors which resulted in the success of open-source software (Figure 1)

3.1. Openness

Openness is an important feature of the Open source software. The source code is freely available. It permits anyone to modify the software, thereby making allowances for increasing its efficiency.

3.2. Reliability

Open-source software is reliable. It can be downloaded free of cost from the internet. Many NGOs and other organisations support open-source software with free online services.

3.3. Flexibility

Flexibility is another important feature of open source software. It does not require any licensing fee. Once obtained, it can be installed any number of times and in as many locations as required.

3.4. Quality

The effective modifications made by the users make the software a quality software.As the source code is freely available, anyone can improve its efficiency and quality by modifying the software according to their needs.

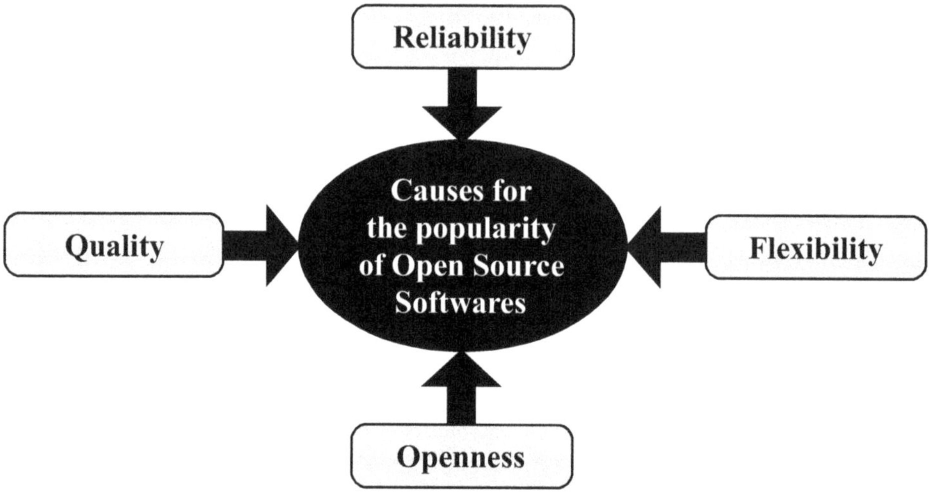

Figure 1.Reasons for the popularity of open source software.

4. Open Source Software for Libraries and Information Centers

4.1 Library Automation software

4.1.1 Evergreen

Evergreen is software that was developed for small and large libraries and information centres. The Evergreen software is freely licensed. It can be downloaded free of cost from the internet. It can be modified to meet the user's requirements.

Features of Evergreen

- Acquisition
- Administration
- Cataloguing
- Circulation
- Client
- OPAC

4.1.2 Koha

Koha is one of the most popular library automation software used in libraries. It was created by Katipo Communications Ltd, New Zealand. The main feature of this software is that it can be customized depending on the user's needs.

Koha Module

- Acquisition
- Cataloguing
- Serial Management
- Patron
- Circulation
- Koha-Reports
- Administration
- Tools
- Web OPAC
- Dual Database Design: Text-based and RDBMS to handle the transaction load of any library.

4.1.3 NewGen Lib

NewGenLib is also an automation software created by Kesavan Institute of Information, Knowledge Management, India and Verus Solutions Pvt Ltd. It is licensed under GNU GPL. Presently, more than 3000 information centers and libraries worldwide use this software. It is efficient and easily manageable.

Features of New Gen Lib

- Networking-Hierarchical and Distributed networks
- Scalable, manageable and efficient
- Completely web-based functional modules
- It is easily extensible
- It supports many languages

4.2 Digital Library Software

4.2.1 EPrints

EPrints is a software for creating online archives by Southampton University, United Kingdom. It supports self-archiving of e-prints. It can be configured as an institutional repository. It is licensed under the GNU General Public License. It can support multiple archives on one server.

4.2.2 DSpace

The development of DSpace software is a combined effort of the HP labs and MIT Libraries. It helps the information centres collect, index and spread the latest scholarly information. It is typically used for building an institutional repository.

4.2.3. Greenstone

Greenstone Software is one of the most popular software for developing digital libraries. It is promoted by the Digital Library project research group in New Zealand at the University of Waikato. It is sponsored by the UNESCO. It is licensed under the GNU General Public License.

4.3 Useful Library Management Applications

4.3.1. Drupal

It is a content-management software developed using PHP. It is licensed under the GNU General Public License. An important characteristic of Drupal is that it provides a user interface for adding, editing, and publishing content. It is a software used by many websites.

4.3.2. Joomla

Joomla is also a content-management software. It has won many awards. It can be used for all types of websites like corporate or portals, websites of Schools, websites of churches, personal home pages, etc. The core Joomla framework enables developers to make a lot of modifications to its effective use.

4.3.3. Cufts

This software was created in the University Library of Simon Fraser. It is designed to host multiple libraries as separate sites. CUFTS is based on Perl. Though it has been designed for use in a consortia environment, it can also be used by individual libraries. CUFTS is an Online serial management system.

4.3.4. Coral

This resource management software was created by the University of Notre Dame's Hesburgh Libraries. It is a good customisable software. It is simple software that allows modules to be installed independently. It is licensed under a GPL v.3 license.

5. Conclusion

Open-source software is free of cost. So, the money otherwise spent on purchasing other proprietary software can be used to purchase books, journals, etc. Library automation is a great financial burden for small libraries, but developing open-source software has helped automate small libraries without any financial investment. In conclusion, open-source software has helped a lot in managing the information resources of big and small libraries and information centres. Open-source software has attracted most library and information science professionals due to its numerous benefits and useful features. Open-source software has become so popular that most libraries use and benefit from it worldwide.

6. References

1. EPrints WIKI (N.D).Retrieved from http://wiki.eprints.org/
2. Greenstone DevelopersGuide.(n.d).Retrieved from http://www.greenstone .org/developers-guide
3. Jayakanth,F (2002).Eprints.org Open Achieve Software(EAS): An Overview [Power Point slides].Retrieved from: http://www.ncsi.iisc.ernet.in/raja/opendl/overview.pdf

4. Bare,S.A (2012).An evaluation of open source software for building digital libraries.Retrieved From: http://117.240.228.70/handle/10603/3731
5. Greenstone Overview (2012) Retrieved from- http://www.greenstone.org/manuals/gsdl2/en/html/Chapter_overview_of_greenstone.htm
6. Witten, I.H., Bainbridge, D., & Boddie, S.J.(2001, January).Power to the people: end-user building of digital library collections. In Proceedings of the 1st ACM/IEEE_CS joint conference on Digital libraries (pp.94-103).ACM.
7. DSpace System Documentation (2011) Retrieved from https://wiki.duraspace.org/display/DSDOC18/DSpace+System+Documentation
8. Open Achieves Initiative. (2012). Retrieved from http://www.openarchives.org/
9. Bradley, K, Lei, J, & Blackall, C.(2007).Memory of the World: Towards an Open Source Repository and Preservation: Recommendations on implementing an Open Source Digital Archival and Preservation System and Related Software Development. United Nations Educational, Scientific and Cultural Organization.
10. Bass,M.J.et al.(n.d).DSpace-A Sustainable Solution for Institutional Digital Asset Services-Spanning the Information Asset Value Chain: Ingest: Manage, Preserve, Disseminate: Internal Reference, Specification, Functionality,version2002-03-01.Retrieved from http://libraries.mit.edu/dspace-mit/technology/functionality.pdf
11. Reddy,Raghunanadha T (2013).Open source software's and their impact on library and information center:An Overview. International Journal of Library and Information Science.Vol.5 (4), PP.90-96, May, 2013.Available at http://www.academicjournals.org/IJLIS

12. Kaul, Sangeet (2014) Managing Libraries through open source software packages [PowerPoint slides].NACLIN 2014, December 9-11, 2014, Pondicherry.
13. Tramboo,Shahkar, Humma, Shafi, SM &Gul,Sumeer(2012).A study on the Open Source Digital Library Software's: Special Reference to DSpace, EPrints and Greenstone: International Journal of Computer Applications (0975-8887) Volume59-No 16, December 2012
14. Open Source Initiative http://opensource.org/osd

CHAPTER 5

Library Services Marketing using Digital Tools

Sonal Singh
Professor & Dean- Faculty of Arts
School of Studies in Library and Information Science
Vikram university, Ujjain, M.P.
E mail drssonal@rediffmail.com

Richa Sharma
JRF
School of Studies in Library and Information Science
Vikram University Ujjain, M.P.
E mail s.richa1512@gmail.com

Abstract

The business is a for-profit operation that demands regular upgrades of its products and services for sustainability. Marketing is the process of selling through which products or services are promoted in the market to attract customers. Digital marketing is a marketing process which uses digital channels and platforms to promote products and services. Libraries are social institutions devoted to the intellectual upliftment of society. Twenty-First Century libraries are transforming into digital to fulfil users' demands through a single click via online platforms. Thus, the concept of Digital marketing can also be applied to libraries to promote the products or services. Digital marketing will benefit the users, keeping them aware of the library's products and services. At the same time, it will also help new users to connect to the library. Marketing is a boon for the library to be proactive, maximise the use of the library, fulfil its users' desires, and make people aware of the library services, thereby increasing community support and reputation. People also get information about the library's services and how they can benefit from them. Additionally, library users can be informed about new services and resources. Various online platforms, like social media, Facebook, WhatsApp, email, website advertising, webinars, etc., can be used for marketing library services using digital tools. These platforms can motivate users to take advantage of the maximum advantages of library services at their convenience. The study defines digital marketing from a library's perspective and further explores digital tools and techniques for promoting library products and services in the 21st century. Digital marketing of library services requires various strategies and faces various issmultiple challenges. The study also focuses on how digital marketing impacts a large user community.

Keywords: *Marketing, Digital Marketing, social media, Digital channels,*

1. Prologue

Business is a for-profit operation or activity. Any business is established to earn a profit, which may or may not be monetary. The role of business is to produce and distribute goods and services to satisfy a public need or demand. For a business to be sustainable, it demands regular upgrades of its products and services to satisfy needs of its customers. Thus, creating and maintaining demands, relevance, reputation, competition, satisfaction, etc is an everyday activity to attract new customers and keep existing ones. For this, a company needs to promos products and services to create a distinctive place in customers' minds. This process, which helps identify the market needs and plan a strategy leading to the survival of a business, is known as marketing. Marketing is essential to achieve true and long-lacerate success for the secured future of any business.

Today, marketing is the most vital and widely accepted management process for offering products and services relevant to the marketplace. It encompasses all the activities from concept origination to the consumer's satisfaction. Marketing is a form of communication between a business house and its customers to better unbetter to understand the customer's needs/problems/requirements deviating strategies to satisfy customers' needs and accomplish the organisation's goals. Thus, marketing refers to ascertaining consumer needs, converting them into products and services, and then moving the product or service to the final consumer. All those activities a company undertakes to promote the buying or selling its products or services are part of marketing. As a precious tool for any business, marketing helps to create brand awareness, drive profit and growth, acquire and retain customers and enhance engagements. Marketing has become the first choice of professionals as they can use and develop their creative skills. With the advent of Digital Marketing is gaining prominence over traditional methods with the advent of Information and Communication Technology (ICT) is nothing, but the digital face but the digital face of traditional marketing to achieve business goals through the internet by interlinking with digital social media like email, video, blogs, catboats, and display ads on various online platforms such as Instagram, YouTube many more. It can also be called online marketing and connects with the target audience via a screen to achieve the goals through digital means. Digitally channels and technologies to globally reach and influence potential target through online connectivity effective manner. Digital marketing has become an indispensable part of modern digital society to enhance their customers and to stay ahead customer's anklet. Digital marketing is a vast umbrella term that covers the use of digital channels, platforms and promote products, services or brands to consumers and businesses. It is a boon to communicate with remote customers using just a digital device such as a Smart phone or a lain a personalised and strategic manner. Digital marketing is a way to promote brands and products online and through other digital channels. Thus, digital marketing refers to advertising delivered through digital channels such as websites, social media, email and mobile applications.

2. Digital marketing channels

Digital Marketing Channels are the online platforms and tools to reach to the target audience and are considered as the officiate target audience and are considered to the public. They are also known as digital advertising channels and provide opportunity to sell products and build brand awareness. , and they provide opportunities, online platform, multimedia tools used by a business to promote products, server multimedia too business useless to promote products, services or brands to their target audiences enable the systematic exchange of customer feedback and intelligence, which may be used to create more customer-driven sales materials that support marketing and sales objectives alike. One or several channels may be used to deliver the portal message. Following are some of the popular and widely used digital marketing channels-

Website- is a digital space that explicitly provides information about a business or individual. It is the collection of web pages and related content over the internet and are identified by the same domain name internet contented about the brands.

Electronic mail- shortened must-have tool for educating transmitting and receiving messages on electronic devices via into, is a method of transmitting and receiving messages on electronic devices via the International community to share information, inducer-centric platforms and create a virtual community to share information, ideas, personal messages, etch, and services, and creating awareness about the brands. The major social media platforms are Instagram, Facebook, Whatsapp, LinkedIn, Twitter, You Tube etc.

PODCAST- is a digital audio program consisting of a series and You Tube that can be downloaded or streamed from the internet. It is much like a radio show with one major difference that it can be subscribed and can be listened anytime.

VsignificantT- is subscribed and be listened toured atom s the video version of the Podcast. It is also video podcast or blogging. It is a digital video file or a collection/serial of video files that are available for download via internet. Each individual recording available for internet download is she Internet we frequently updated web page used for personal commentary or business content. Blogs and e often interactive and includes sections at the bottom of individual blog posts where readers can leave comment include sections at the bottom of individual blog posts where readers can comments' appears first at the top of the web page.

Webinar- is an online interactive meeting- a presentation, selectors, workshop, etc. It is a virtual group event held over the internet and allows participants to join online from different locations to attend, comment, react and clarify doubts.

You Tube- is an online video sharing website also known as video on demand platform. It is the most important and profitable website and allows creators to upload and share video content.

World Wide Web- is the global network of information and resources and is commonly known as web or WWW or W3. It is a hypertext- based information system that enables content sharing over the internet. It refers to all the public websites or pages that users can access on their local computers and other devices through internet.

3. Need for digital marketing

Digital transformation is considered today as the essential business practice for improved productivity and efficiency. It provides a platform to expose the creativity and shine like a star among the competitors in the congested market. The need of digital marketing can be justified through following key points.

Wider Reach: Digital marketing has broken all the geographical barriers allowing a business to easily promote own products and services to global audience. With internet access and use of social media, brands can become known worldwide. The number of Internet users are constantly increasing, making it possible to reach more potential customers.

Cost Effectiveness: Digital marketing is more cost effective than traditional marketing methods, even small enterprises can run effective marketing campaigns with a limited budget.

Through advertising, social media promotion, email marketing etc. the product can be reached among more people at lower cost.

Targeted Marketing: On Digital platforms one can target specific groups on the basis of age, gender, location, interests, etc. This can increase the relevance and effectiveness of advertising.

Performance and Analysis: Digital marketing campaigns can be monitored and analysed accurately. One can learn which ads and strategies are most effective. There are various analytics tools available to measure and understand the results of efforts in digital marketing. This can improve the marketing strategy.

Brand Awareness: Brand identity can be enhanced through social media, websites and other digital platforms. This creates a good image of the brand among customers. Consumer can feel the direct connection with brand with increased level of trust.

Valuable Customer Data: Digital Marketing allows to collect important information about customer behaviour and preferences. Such data are helpful to improve marketing strategies.

4. Digital marketing and libraries

Digital marketing has played an important role in various sectors, and libraries are not an exception to it. Libraries can use digital marketing to more effectively promote their services and resources and also to attract the users. In digital age, effective marketing of library products and services has become extremely important for increasing the reach of libraries, and also to enable them to provide more effective and user-centric services. Marketing in digital mode includes various tools and techniques such as social media, email newsletters, websites, mobile apps, and search engine optimization (SEO). Using social media platforms such as Facebook, Twitter, Instagram, and LinkedIn, libraries can share information about their latest collections, programs, and services. By sending regular updates to the users through email newsletters, their participation in library activities can be increased. The use of websites and mobile apps allows users to browse online catalogues, reserve books, and access digital content. Additionally, libraries can improve their online visibility by using search engine optimization (SEO) techniques, allowing more users to take advantage of their services. By making effective use of digital marketing, libraries can not only provide better services to their current users, but also attract new users. Thus, marketing in digital mode can prove to be a powerful tool for libraries to broaden their reach and impact. Libraries can have a regular research analysis to understand the changing needs of users. It will help them to modify library products and services to suit to the changing needs of the users. The up gradation of services and products can again be brought to the notice of the users through digital marketing.

5. Six components (cs) of digital marketing model

By concentrating on six key components, the organizations navigate the complexities of digital marketing. In the digital era, these Cs are considered as the pillars upon which the digital marketing strategies are built. These are- Customer, Content, Context, Convenience, Consistency, and Collaboration.

Content – Content marketing refers to creation and sharing of valuable, relevant and consistent content for targeted audience online. When applied to libraries, the focus should be to deliver relevant products and services to the targeted users online.

Choice – It refers to provide products and services as per consumers' choice. When applied to libraries, the focus should be to acquire a wide range of products to fulfil users' demands with a feel of extreme satisfaction.

Customization – Each customer is unique with their sets of demands or needs. Customization refers to personalisation of content or products to individuals or groups. It plays an important role in increasing the efficiency and maximum optimisation of resources. When applied to libraries, the focus should be to provide some services to specific users' community. Selective Dissemination Information (SDI) is an example of customization.

Community – The consumers are classified into different groups on the basis of similar backgrounds and goals. It helps in understanding the needs of various groups of potential users. When applied to libraries, the focus should be to organize library services taking into account different users' communities because the needs of different user communities may be different from each other.

Cost Reduction – It refers to practice of minimizing organization's expenses. It helps in increasing profit margin. When applied to libraries, the focus should be to check the purchasing policies to take bulk discount and avoid unnecessary expenses on multiple copies, etc. As library is a service institution, reasonable fees should be charged for accessing the information of users because demanding higher fees can reduce the interest of users in libraries. If possible, librarian should deliver open access content among the users.

Convenience – It refers to providing a seamless and effortless experience for customers across all digital touch points. In today's fast-paced world, consumers value ease and efficiency. When applied to libraries, the focus should be on providing conductive environment for research and learning. Digital reference service should be provided. The efforts should be made to develop a user-friendly and mobile optimized library website.

6. Digital tools for library service marketing

Digital marketing tools are online applications that allow a marketing team to execute an effective strategy to sell goods or services. Digital marketing strategies can be especially important for libraries to make their resources and services accessible to maximum users. Following are some key digital marketing strategies for libraries:

Social Media Marketing: Use social media platforms like Facebook, Twitter, Instagram, You Tube, Pinterest and LinkedIn. Post regular updates and updates about library activities, Books and services. Share stunning library photos, book covers and event photos. Use interactive content like polls, quizzes, and live sessions to engage with users. Upload videos of Library tours, Book reviews and Workshops.

Email Marketing: Send regular newsletters that feature information about new collections, upcoming events and services and new offers. Create personalized email lists and communicate personally with your members.

Website and Blog: Create an attractive and user-friendly website. Share information about library activities, new books, cataloguing services and reading recommendations through blog posts.

SEO and Content Marketing: Use SEO strategies to get your website ranked higher in search engines. Create high quality content that is valuable to users. Identify the keywords that your target users are searching for and include them in library websites and blog post. Run library advertisements on Google so that more and more people can know about the library.

Online Events and Webinars: Organize webinars and online workshops on various topics. Promote these events through social media and email. Host online events to discuss books, interact with authors and workshops, broadcast events live on Facebook, You Tube, and Instagram.

Promotion of Digital Resources: Promote the use of e-books, audiobooks, online journals, and databases. Provide information about resources available to students and researchers.

7. Strategies for digital marketing of library products and services

Understanding target users: First and foremost step is to identify and understand the target users of library. Their needs, preferences, problems, information seeking behaviour, etc. should be analysed and accordingly, strategies should be planned to promote library collection.

Push the users towards Library Website: maintain the library website and encourage users to visit the website, and provide information about library activities and services and collection to the users through the website. Provide them open access content.

Display Advertising: Display Advertising involves online banners and video ads on social media platforms to increase library services awareness, including programmatic display and native advertising, similar to digital sponsorship.

Website Optimization: Library's website should be user-friendly, mobile-responsive, and optimized for search engines (SEO) to improve visibility.

Social Media Engagement: Presence on those social media platforms should be established where the target audience of library spends time. One should share updates, promote events, and engage with followers to build a community.

Analytics and Data Analysis: Web analytics tools should be used to track website traffic, user engagement, and conversion rates. Trends, preferences and areas for improvement should be identified by analysing data. Accordingly, digital marketing strategies should be adjusted.

8. Impacts of digital marketing among users' community

- Users get aware about the importance of library due to which the use of Library increases.
- Digital marketing ensures that library services are accessible to users with disabilities by providing alternative formats and assistive technologies.
- Digital marketing enables libraries to gather feedback from users in real-time, allowing them to assess the effectiveness of their services and make improvements accordingly.
- Users can access library services from anywhere at any time through digital channels, enhancing convenience and accessibility.
- Digital marketing helps libraries reach a wider audience, making users aware of the services, resources, and events available to them.

9. Challenges before digital marketing of library products and services

Limited Budget: Libraries often have constrained budgets, making it challenging to allocate funds for digital marketing efforts.

Target Audience: Identifying and reaching the right audience amidst the vast online landscape can be difficult, especially when trying to engage both existing patrons and attract new users.

Content Creation: Generating engaging and relevant content consistently can be demanding, especially for libraries with small staff or limited resources.

Measuring Impact: It can be challenging to measure the effectiveness of digital marketing strategies in terms of increasing patronage, usage of services, or overall engagement.

Technological Barriers: Libraries may face technological barriers such as outdated systems or limited IT expertise, hindering their ability to implement and leverage digital marketing tools effectively.

Competition: Libraries compete with various other sources of information and entertainment online, making it challenging to stand out and capture the attention of their target audience.

10. Conclusion

Twenty First Century libraries are transforming into digital, to fulfil users' demand through a single click via online platforms. Digital marketing is gaining popularity due to its ability to reach target audiences, drive sales and increase revenue. Digital marketing is considered today as a powerful tool for libraries to promote their products and services to a wider audience. It is useful for initially identifying current and potential users and also in developing a relationship with them. By leveraging social media, email campaigns, search engine optimization, and other digital channels, libraries can effectively reach and engage patrons, increase awareness of resources, and ultimately enhance user experiences. Embracing digital marketing strategies enables libraries to adapt to changing user behaviours and preferences in the digital age, ensuring their relevance and impact in the community. Overall digital marketing empowers libraries to effectively promote their services, engage with their community, and adapt to the evolving needs of their users in the digital age.

References

1. https://www.smartinsights.com/marketing-planning/marketing-models/digital-marketing-models-6cs-online-customer-motivation/attachment/6-cs-digital-marketing-model/
2. www.smartinsights.com
3. https://www.spiralytics.com/blog/digital-marketing
4. https://digitalvidya.com
5. https://www.indiamart.com/proddetail/digital-marketing-course.
6. http://en.wikipedia.org/wiki/Digital_marketing

CHAPTER 6

Leading Retailers in the US: A Study of Business Impacts on Sustainable Development.

Ansh Sehgal
MBA 1st year student, IITM
E-mail: anshsehgaldelhi@gmail.com

Sarthak Tyagi
MBA 1st year student, IITM

Priya Gupta
MBA 1st year student, IITM

Abstract

A growing understanding of how businesses can contribute to the transition to a more sustainable future has led to many large corporations developing corporate sustainability strategies and policies to manage their environmental, social, or economic effects. Despite this, primary research on how companies address and contribute to sustainable development challenges must be a particulate study in the environmental studies curriculum. This review aims to showcase how five top US retailers evaluate their sustainability strategies and outcomes, as well as some severe reflections on the role of retail businesses in sustainable development. The paper notes that all five selected retailers publicly declared their commitment to sustainable development. Despite this, the authors assert that the retailers' commitment to sustainable development is primarily driven by business needs and efficiency gains, aligned with current business models prioritising growth.

Keywords: The US retailers, Sustainable development, Strategy, External assurance, Economic growth, and Environmental studies curricula.

Introduction

The significance and contribution of businesses to sustainable development are increasingly acknowledged. The SDGs are part of the United Nations agenda to tackle global challenges such as poverty, inequality, and climate change. Environmental degradation, prosperity, peace, and justice are all examples of this phenomenon. The United Nations Global Compact asserted that achieving these objectives requires unprecedented effort from all sectors of society. Still, it highlighted the crucial role of business in the process. Specifically, more and more large corporations have developed corporate sustainability strategies and policies. These strategies and policies address environmental, social, and economic issues, such as climate change, water conservation, waste management, natural resource conservation efforts, employee health and well-being, diversity and equality of opportunity, responsible sourcing, and local economic development. However, research on how companies contribute to sustainable development faces several obstacles, such as the difficulty of negotiating access, the size and geographic scope of large companies, and issues with measurement and metrics. Possibly more fundamental, tensions exist between methodologies that see challenges to sustainable development as socially constructed and those that focus on the material realities of environmental and social problems.

However, due to the growing significance of businesses' involvement in sustainable development, it is imperative to incorporate these areas of study into environmental studies curricula. An exploratory review paper argues that corporate annual sustainability reports provide an accessible means of exploring the current business contribution to sustainable development, and this is in response to the need for examinations of corporate donations for pedagogical purposes. Two primary objectives of the paper are to showcase the sustainability strategies and achievements of five prominent US retailers and to offer essential insights into the contributions of retailers and businesses to sustainable development. Its contribution is intended to shed light on the sustainable development achievements of several prominent US retailers and to inspire environmental studies scholars and students to investigate and analyse contemporary business practices related to sustainability.

The primary portion of the paper commences with a concise examination of sustainable development and corporate sustainability literature, along with an explanation of its reference point and research methodology. A review of selected retailers' sustainability reporting process and achievement prompts critical reflections on their contributions to sustainable development.

Literature Review: Sustainable Development and Corporate Sustainability

The concept of sustainability is not new. For example, Du Pisani shows that "the idea of sustainable development has developed over the centuries in opposition to the idea of progress." He also concluded: "Concern that current and future generations will not be able to sustain a sustainable lifestyle has inspired the idea that will pave the way for the emergence and international adoption of sustainable development." The idea was popular in the 20th century. It happened again. It began to attract attention in environmental literature in the 1970s. For example, Barr says that "one of the most important and difficult questions of the twenty-first century" is "how to encourage the behavioural changes necessary to create a stable life."

The most widely used definition of sustainable development is "development that meets the needs of today without compromising the ability of future generations to meet their needs". However, this concept is difficult to define and contains many different and contradictory meanings. In particular, there is a definition that acknowledges that all humans live in a world with weak systems and natural resources. Many definitions aim to encompass social and economic goals and meet people's needs reasonably.

Also, Hudson believed the meaning was from 'yellow blue-green' to dark 'black-green'. In the past, Hudson said that "focusing on remedial processes in the current relationship is important about trade-offs between economic and environmental goals, with the market being the main allocation mechanism", while for the latter, "Prioritization". Preservation of nature is essential." - Best'. Hudson also stated that the core concept of sustainable development "originates from the blue-green discourse of ecological modernization" and that "the creation of capital, the creation of profit and ecological stability are common goals." He also contrasted this view with the "green" view, which "requires a decline in living standards and a major change in the relations of production." Similarly, people often distinguish between "weak" and "strong" sustainability. Roper believes that "weak sustainability is important for economic development, whereas strong sustainability subordinates' businesses to the natural environment and people." This was recognized years ago as investors, consumers, governments, interest groups, and the media became increasingly involved. More aware of business's environmental, social, and economic impacts, many companies have begun to develop sustainable development processes as the basis of their business strategies. For example, KPMG said: "Sustainability has become an essential part of successful companies worldwide. Although there is general agreement that corporate governance relates to environmental, social, and economic issues, there is little consensus on the definition of the term and many problems, such as sustainability. The element can be defined.

There are some definitions, but they seem to refer to business continuity. For example, Dyllick and Hockerts define corporate sustainability as "meeting the needs of the company's direct and indirect shareholders..." without compromising the ability to meet the needs of future stakeholders." There are also contexts where the goal includes environmental and social objectives, and these objectives are translated into business strategies. For example, van Marrewijk and Werre argue that: "sustainable business refers to the activities of the company that are voluntary by definition. Integration of social and environmental issues". In some respects, Amini and Bienstock combine these two methods and argue that sustainable business "involves the idea that to preserve values in the long term, an organization must take into account all the conditions in which it operates: economic, social and environmental".

People's interest and commitment to occupational safety have increased, and information security has emerged in many companies and organizations. Sustainability reporting is a general term for how a company or organization reports its environmental, social, and economic impacts on business and employment. Various factors appear to be important in explaining this difference. These include the need to comply with environmental and health laws and regulations, concerns about the cost and scarcity of natural resources; raising public and shareholder awareness of the importance of social finance, media response to various anticommercial activities increases in the scope of the group's activities; Many changes in culture and values are occurring in today's society. Many companies, in particular, are looking for ways to expand their public presence and demonstrate their commitment to sustainability to help differentiate themselves from competitors and enhance their reputation.

However, there are few published studies about specific companies' security strategies and practices. Stoughton and Ludema conducted a comparative analysis of three large but unnamed companies that were a "good model of security" for modelling how security occurs in business and personal actions, in organisations that are all considered "important for long-term growth." long-term success with a commitment to sustainability". Lock and Steele analysed the content of more than 200 business reports from 11 European countries to analyse reliability. However, a recent literature review does not include company-specific studies.

Meanwhile, Baumgartner and Ebner argue that "while many companies are investigating security management and publishing security information, the actual purpose of this effort is not clear," and they have often published some guidelines designed to help companies check whether their precise commitments are consistent. Through the implementation of sustainability strategies. Although research on a single company is limited, some studies focusing on specific businesses have been published. Bonilla-Priego et al. and de Grosbois reviewed the promotion of sustainability in the maritime industry. Jones et al. conducted a literature review on European food and beverage wholesalers' commitment to sustainability. Wagner explores ways to adjust the environment and business practices to improve companies' sustainability in the European paper industry. Jones et al. investigated the promotional strategies and successes reported by hotel managers worldwide. Increasing interest in sustainable development, in general, has led to many attempts to develop a theoretical framework linking nature and people, emphasising that social development and business cannot be viewed in isolation from the natural environment. Many authors adopt the stakeholder perspective to make progress. Simply put, the shareholder perspective is built around the belief that to be successful, companies must be responsive to the interests of shareholders and many stakeholders, including suppliers, customers, and people. Do better. From a different perspective, Amsler believes that "political contradictions and ambiguity in discourse support" can be used to create a "critical theory of stability." He added that the current debate should be "in line with general social criticism" and that the "interpretation of security" should be seen as "an invitation to explore the complex process of production, struggle, and competition into a future vision for justice.". Castro tried to lay the foundation for many theories of sustainable development by questioning the possibility of growth in the economy and arguing that the development of the economy depends on the continuity and inexhaustibility of trade.

Methodology and Research

To investigate the contribution of business to sustainable development, the US retail sector, which includes seven out of ten stores worldwide, was selected for the research study. On the other hand, "retailers act as guardians of producers and consumers" and therefore retailers can be seen in a mighty position, through their daily interactions, designed to stimulate growth in our way through personal actions. With vendors and their customers. For example, Durieu believes supermarkets "can influence changes in production methods and standards and re-freeze manufacturers to promote sustainable choices." The United States, on the other hand, is the world's largest economy and therefore faces significant challenges in moving towards a sustainable future. Specifically, five of the largest retailers in the United States, namely Walmart, Kroger, Walgreens Boots Alliance, Target, and Home Depot, were selected to illustrate how the retailers' advertising touts their commitment to sustainability. These five stores were chosen partly because they have a wide variety of products and stores, and partly because they publish annual sustainability reports that provide valuable information about their sustainability approaches.

Wal-Mart, an international retail company founded in Arkansas in 1962, is the world's largest retailer. The company operates supermarkets, discount stores, convenience stores, and retail stores, with a large online presence and over 11,000 stores in 29 countries. Founded in Cincinnati in 1893, Kroger operates wholesalers, retailers, and supermarkets in over 3,000 locations in 35 states. With two retail divisions, Walgreens USA and Walgreens International, and a wholesale business, Walgreen Boots Alliance is the largest retail, health hygiene, and lifestyle retailer in the United States and Europe. Home Depot is a home improvement retailer that currently operates in the United States but also operates in Canada, Mexico, and China. Target, whose store headquarters date back to 1902, is a discount retailer specializing in general merchandise with more than 1,800 stores in the United States. To some leaders in American retail, these five stores could exemplify new paths in their commitment to sustainability.

It promises growth and success, but advertising on company websites has become the most popular and easy-to-use advertising method. With this in mind, the authors searched the Internet using the term "security training" and the names of five selected US vendors. This search was conducted in January 2019 using Google as the search engine. A recent sustainability report from a retailer was chosen for the study to illustrate the perspective the retailer currently reports on its approach to sustainability. The reports are extensive documents, with Walmart's report running to 232 pages, while the respective reports from Kroger, Walgreen Boots Alliance, Target, and Home Depot are 142, 92, 84, and 94 pages, respectively. The sources for these reports are listed at the end of this article and serve as evidence for this article. All quotes are from safety-related store information unless otherwise noted. When examining data on the stability of selected stores, the authors adopted a loose theory. They decided to challenge the main concepts and explanations by carefully examining the security statements of the selected companies' websites rather than using content analysis. The authors believe that this approach is fair in research studies where data and subjects are chosen as a sample and that the primary purpose is to examine how retailers promote their sustainability commitments rather than provide insight into comparing such contributions. The research is based on data from the public register, and the authors acknowledge that they may have obtained permission from this data without contacting the selected retailers.

Suppliers' Commitments and Achievements

All five selected retailers reported their commitment to sustainability, mainly in the details of their overall business agreements provided below. For example, Walmart "provides safe, affordable food and other products to people worldwide." Doing so improves job opportunities, the environment, safety, and local communities, and creates value for our business and people." Similarly, Kroger said: "Our 2020 sustainability goals help us prioritise our resources and efforts to be a sustainable and responsible company." This ranges from healthcare and climate change prevention to diversity and inclusion."

Commitment to sustainability is seen in environmental, social, and economic initiatives. Environmental problems include climate change and greenhouse gas emissions, water and energy conservation, waste management and recycling, sustainable production, protection and preservation of natural resources, and reduction of environmental pollution. For example, the Mission announced in addressing climate change weather: "To see that we all have the responsibility to address the effects of climate change, we are setting scientific security goals that will help us create good business and build a prosperous environment." Additional targets state: "To combat the impacts of climate change and work to make our business sustainable, we aim to reduce greenhouse gas emissions and improve the strength of our business". Walmart says, "We want to be part of the solution by working to reduce emissions in our operations and supporting emissions reductions across global value chains." Walmart believes companies can play a role in combating climate change by reducing greenhouse gas emissions. Our investments in renewable energy and efficiency reflect this belief. These actions are good for our business, good for our customers, and good for our environment. "

Water and waste management were reported as priorities for all five stores. For example, Home Depot reported: "We work with our suppliers' products to ensure products reflect our conservation values and help customers use less water." "We estimated that "Our products helped our customers save 79 billion gallons of water last year." Walmart recognized that "water scarcity has become a significant problem in many communities where our customers, partners, and suppliers live" and reported plans to measure and control water use in its operations and to purify and recycle water. Walgreen Boots Alliance said, "We are committed to reducing waste at our largest operations (US stores)," while Kroger said, "We are committed to reducing waste by reducing waste in landfills." Change to zero-waste Company "Better use" by 2020.

The sustainability reports of some stores include commitments to protect natural resources. For example, Home Depot shows its commitment to "sustainable forests" under the title "Using the world's resources wisely" and announces that the company has been working to protect endangered forests and ensure that trees meet the needs of forests since 1999. Future generations. More broadly, Walmart acknowledges that "our environmental impact extends well beyond our retail operations to include the products we provide to consumers with food, clothing, electronics, electrical and many other goods" and has announced that it has pledged to help reduce the cost of agriculture. For a factory to the customer. "

In addressing social issues, several themes were identified in the retailer's sustainability reports, including accountability, Food safety, seller's performance, diversity and equality, Training and Development, health and safety, working with local communities, and charitable donations. For example, Walgreens Boots Alliance reported "early employment programs, job support, and training" and efforts to address youth unemployment in Chicago. Home Depot is committed to "creating a rich work experience that prepares employees and managers for success, serves customers, and provides growth opportunities." The Mission says, "Mission is everything, and so are our members." As we advance, we will continue to invest in our approximately 350,000 employees and create quality jobs that enable them to thrive".

Kroger asserts: "We put our customers and communities at the centre of everything we do." Because we care, we continually improve upon acquisitions and more to make our communities better places to live and work. Being a reliable partner to our community is our top priority. "In announcing its commitment to customers, Kroger says, "With a focus on health and nutrition, we encourage our customers to add healthier and healthier products to their carts, including organic products, to improve their health." Walmart states that "developing communities within society" As part of its belief that "the local communities where our stores are located and where our customers and employees live are the foundation of our business," Walmart, in particular, describes its plans as "alleviating hunger," "disaster relief," "supporting communities," and "supporting veterans and military families." For example, Walmart, which focuses on disaster relief, reported its efforts to support communities affected by hurricanes in Florida and Puerto Rico, earthquakes in Mexico, and floods in China.

Clarification of business issues is often limited but includes job creation, local economic development, shareholder relations, the member's production value, and business management. For example, under the banner of "we deliver economic growth", the Mission states that "by investing in where we live and work, we come to the voluntary creation of communities beneficial to the future". Add Mission [32] says, "We now want to go further and think carefully about how our business can lead to economic growth" and "We want to bring our mission to the community we have and how investment can help the economy grow." Walmart reports its work in "developing a local and inclusive base" and training "more than 1 million small and medium-sized farmers." When it comes to corporate governance, Home Depot has stated its commitment to "delivering long-term shareholder value". It describes how its audit committee operates, which "oversees the company's critical financial and compliance risks."

In sustainability reports, retailers describe their successes while trying to meet their commitments in various ways. Often achievements are represented by a short description that includes or is accompanied by some simple explanations. For example, Walmart provides essential information showing that by the end of 2017, 28% of its electricity came from renewable energy, 78% of its global waste turned into landfills, and 34 million acres had shrunk. For fertilizer optimization plans. While Walgreens is often singled out for its lack of long-term data in stores' sustainability reports, Walgreens has provided some comparative data, including 2016 and 2017 CO2 emissions, waste disposal, and supplier statistics. The Sustainability Report includes measures to measure the achievement of commitments and goals. For example, the target reported progress against 32 goals in 2017, including water management, recycling, deforestation, and recycling, and discussed plans to drive security strategies. Similarly, Walmart has been providing progress metrics on keeping its promises since 2018 across various processes, including business development for suppliers, encouraging engagement, energy, trash, and animal disposal.

As announced by some retailers, sustainability focuses on the role of innovation and technology and improving the business cycle to support and encourage the transition to the future. For example, Kroger announced its "new food development" that "converts food waste and wastewater into renewable energy through anaerobic digestion" and that the company is "considering using this technology for other technologies." Walmart has emphasized its role in supporting innovation in its suppliers and ordering processes, changing its use of renewable energy, testing innovation in e-commerce, and investing in innovation to eliminate crime within its ranks. chain. The mission claims that "innovation is a key part of our growth" and charts the development of "business accelerator capital" aimed at bringing "new technologies, experiences, products, and solutions" to retail Many retailers have expressed their new commitment to the circular economy. For example, Mission (2018) announced: "Our desire to create a comprehensive strategy that builds on the many studies we have done to date to address the environmental impacts of our business, including our efforts to reduce waste, invest in renewable energy, and invest in sustainable energy." Similarly, Kroger reported that the company "has been effective in promoting a circular economy across our businesses" and that "key points" here include "eliminating waste and pollution, preserving products and information, and recreating "natural systems". Walmart believes: "Today we deeply understand the challenges and engage suppliers and consumers in finding a circular economy where products are produced, consumed and renewed in a continuous cycle." In addition, Walmart has moved from a "grab-and-go approach where resources are kept in production, and we want to help create a more circular economy by transitioning to one where materials and other materials finally return to production," he says. Economic flow'.

Discussion

Five stores that chose to go public show their commitment and success, thus making sense of the business Copy seeking security in some business transactions offers a good deal. Developed. However, there are some issues worth discussing. First, when retailers talk about their commitment to sustainability, sustainability becomes less clear. Instead, retailers' sustainability is often based on business performance and driven by business needs and significant environmental and safety concerns. The aim is to preserve the value of natural ecosystems and increase efficiency in a wide range of economic, social, and environmental issues, rather than reduce the demand for natural resources. Of course, retailers always talk about sustainable businesses and the protection and development of natural and social resources.

So many of the environmental measures offered by retailers aim to reduce CO2 emissions and improve energy use, for example, while also helping to reduce operating costs. Similarly, a store's commitment to employees, such as focusing on health and safety, empowerment, performance, and development, can contribute to employee stability, safety, integrity, and performance. Banerjee believes that "despite their rhetoric, discourses of citizenship, responsibility, and security are defined by narrow commercial interests" and that these "influence external stakeholders".

The importance of value creation is discussed in the Second Vendor Report. Although the question of "creating value for whom" was raised by Haksever et al., traditionally value creation has been accepted as one of the main objectives of the business. points out whether the company should create more value for its members or everyone. When addressing the issue of profitability, many marketers have identified shareholders and stakeholders, which seem to reflect the concept of shared value, where Porter and Kramer describe policies and practices that "increase the competitiveness of the company" and "also address the business." social relations of the communities in which they operate". So, Crane et al. pointed out some weaknesses and disadvantages in creating joint models. More specifically, Crane et al. argued that the model "ignores the rigor of social and economic goals," "does not do justice to issues of economic adjustment," and "as a perspective on the role of business in society." For example, in examining the first question, Crane et al. noted that "no matter how creative decision makers are, many corporate decisions regarding social and environmental issues will appear in reality rather than as a potential win-win." Therefore, Crane et al. suggest that this problem is "a constant struggle between businesses and their stakeholders for limited resources and recognition."

Third, although retailers discuss many environmental, social, and business aspects in their sustainability reports, many of their statements are unconvincing. So, the preface to this article saying, "We put our customers and communities at the centre of everything we do" and "We work to help reduce our impact from farm to factory to consumer", means little. I'm not "happy". Similarly, retailers' demands to encourage turnover and find more business opportunities can best be viewed as wishful thinking, with initial tidbits of safety information on achieving success proving such claims. ers.

More systematically, there is also the issue of independent verification of the data provided to demonstrate the success of this process. Some stores have allowed independent organizations to verify information in safety reports, but this practice is not shared. For example, Walgreens Boots Alliance enlisted Deloitte to produce a sustainability report covering 13 "environmental indicators", including carbon dioxide emissions from various sources, electricity use, and waste disposal, as well as "provider companies" meters "and" offices appointed. In contrast, Kroger claims that "we pursued a variety of external concepts to build our security concept" and that these integrations "provide a third perspective on our trust study," but no data on security performance is available. Defined independently. Walmart only said, "We did not seek outside insurance for this report." Failure to publish independent, external verification may undermine the effectiveness and reliability of the process. However, these five stores are all large, complex, and powerful organisations, and they store and store data and information in different areas across all devices, behind which it is difficult to grant outside access.

Finally, there are general issues regarding the tension between sustainability and economic growth. Looking ahead, the data security market shows continued growth and business expansion. In some ways, this reflects the general position of the export sector, as Sir Terry Leahy, chief executive of Tesco, then the UK's largest retailer, said he contributed "agree" at the launch of the Global Coca-Cola Retail Research Council Forum. as stated in the report. At the time, he believes, his company was "seeking to create a movement that would show that eating, going green, and growing was possible." This approach is based on the general belief that continued economic growth will be accompanied by more efficient use of resources. This trend is seen as relative or implicit decoupling (relative decoupling refers to using fewer resources per unit of economic growth, while absolute decoupling refers to reducing all resource use) leading to many sustainable development and size points. Most business ideas today. However, Wiedemann et al. argued that "trade progress alone is smaller than reported or even non-existent," which would ultimately lead to the concept of sustainable development.

Seeking alignment and economic growth through better use of resources, some major retailers have emphasized the role of technological innovation output and greater adoption of business plans in their business. Most business approaches to security are based on the "orthodoxy" that "achieving security is a business problem" and requires "better knowledge, motivation, and legacy urine technology" [40]. Schor notes that "much of the health literature focuses on technological solutions" and that "proponents of technological solutions argue that smarter design and technology can reduce or even prevent the consumption of ecological products and eliminate toxins." Clark and Dixon said that "it has long been recognized that sustainable development requires the promotion of appropriate science and technology" and that it is widely accepted that technological development provides the means to improve production. However, Alexander states that technology's ability to solve the environmental problem on Earth "is negative and will cause greater harm to the planet, its ecosystems, and us." Specifically, retailers have embraced the idea of proving business continuity despite environmental concerns such as overexploitation of natural resources and destruction of highways. For example, Valenzuela and Boehmargue that "given the fact that environmental problems are associated with business crimes, the business cycle is an important factor for the construction of good growth economic development." Valenzuela and Bohm also argue that the concepts of circular economy and sustainable development are "controlled by political and economic elites who claim to achieve rapid economic growth by finding ways to be environmentally friendly and responsible." Valenzuela and Bohm pessimistically comment on their conclusion: "The closer we come to the ideal of a global economy, the more we are allowed to consume without moral leadership".

Conclusion

Five US retailers announced their commitment to sustainability and demonstrated this commitment across environmental, social, and business areas. However, the authors argue that marketers are determined and sustainability can be defined as the orientation of business needs. The aim is to preserve the importance and integrity of natural ecosystems and improve performance on a wide range of economic, social, and environmental issues, rather than reduce the demand for natural resources. At the same time, some critics believe that the security industry and its advertising methods are nothing more than so-called "greenwashing". It is essentially a farce that attempts to address the concerns of government, consumers, and pressure groups about the impact of business on the environment and social relations. Equally important, the authors argue that the promise of maintaining stability in the current business model of U.S. suppliers is in development and continues to represent a tenuous path to stability. Roper believes that weak sustainability represents "a compromise in effective cultural practices, in which values should change very little, but voluntarily interrupt the positive response, correct it and allow business to continue as usual."

This research study has implications for the US retail industry and retailers in other parts of the world. First, knowing that the US retail industry is on a long and challenging journey is essential. For example, the American Retail Industry Leaders Association claimed in its "2017 Retail Sustainability Management Report" that by 2012 "environmental and social considerations began to add markers of success to the report, including price, service, and quality." However, he argues that many retailers still have a long way to go in creating "a business case for sustainability." As part of this process, American retailers may consider making independent outsourcing more reliable and trustworthy in their advertising and marketing processes, empowering their determination to create a business cycle in their business models. Both action plans will have significant financial implications for retailers, and the transition to more efficient business models will require substantial changes in consumer behaviour and the standards used. While America's largest retailer has made a public commitment to sustainability, commitment will be limited to the market, and change will be slow and best measured.

Many developing countries face the same challenges, and supermarkets are committed to public safety and changing lives in the future. In Europe, for example, the European Commission is considering working with retailers to develop best practices for sustainable retail, with all initiatives Trading is voluntary and there is little or no regulatory enforcement. Retailers in developing countries will face increasing pressure to demonstrate their commitment to sustainability. However, government, media, and public attention to the environmental, social, and economic impacts of retailers' practices and existing business models is limited in many emerging markets. This is because the current focus is on economic growth and economic growth in particular. work. It seems unlikely that government policy or legislation on retail security will be introduced. Overall, data on the stability of five U.S. exchanges provide a rich and accessible source of information for researchers interested in investigating how businesses seek security support. On the other hand, these reports provide helpful and detailed information on the progress of environmental, social, and economic activities that retailers are asked to implement how retailers are aware of sustainability issues, and how they are responding to them. a way for them. On the other hand, the report also offers researchers a vital opportunity to analyze and evaluate the firm's commitment and success, and to interact with the firm to analyze the complexity of collaboration in business. While this compendium focuses on the retail industry, companies in many other vital sectors report publicly on their sustainability commitments and achievements and provide rich and valuable information for environmental research.

References

1. https://www.unep.org/explore-topics/green-economy
2. https://www.greeneconomycoalition.org/news-and-resources/the-5-principles-of-green-economy
3. https://sustainabledevelopment.un.org/index.php?menu=1446
4. https://corporate.enelx.com/en/question-and-answers/what-is-green-economy
5. https://www.oecd.org/greengrowth/whatisgreengrowthandhowcanithelpdeliversustainabledevelopment.htm
6. https://sustainabledevelopment.un.org/topics/greeneconomy
7. https://www.investopedia.com/terms/g/greeneconomics.asp

CHAPTER 7

Professional Development Pathways for Library Professionals: Challenges and Opportunities

Dr Vijetacharya Malviya
Librarian, United Institute of Medical Sciences, Prayagraj, Uttar Pradesh
Email: vij0092@gmail.com

Introduction:

The panorama of library science and the job of library professionals are constantly changing, driven by technological breakthroughs, alterations in user behaviour, and shifting information landscapes. This dynamic climate needs continued professional development for library workers to remain relevant and practical. Implementing professional development routes presents difficulties and possibilities for library professionals, institutions, and stakeholders engaged in this field.

Professional development pathways allow library workers to learn new skills and knowledge, keeping them current in a continuously evolving information ecosystem. Adapting to technological improvements, such as digital librarianship, data management, and digital preservation, is essential in today's libraries. Library professionals might improve their job prospects through well-organised professional development programmes. Obtaining advanced training and certifications can result in promotions, increased income, and the chance to take on leadership positions and specialised tasks within and outside their existing organisations. Professional development frequently entails engaging with colleagues, authorities, and industry leaders. This networking can facilitate partnerships, the exchange of best practices, and the development of innovations in library science. Networking also provides opportunities for mentorship, which is extremely useful for personal and professional development. Library professionals can provide better services to users if they have up-to-date knowledge and abilities. Professional development ensures that library services meet the changing demands of their communities, whether through more effective information management systems, creative educational activities, or improved digital collection access.

Access to necessary funding is a significant obstacle to the widespread adoption of career enhancement programmes. Financial limitations can restrict the availability of training sessions, particularly in smaller libraries or those located in poor areas. Furthermore, it may be challenging for library employees to participate in professional development due to time constraints, given their frequently hectic schedules. Professional development programmes have a problem due to the fast rate of technological advancements. Constant curriculum and material updating are necessary to keep training current and relevant, and this can be resource-intensive. Demonstrating the influence of professional development on library services and customer satisfaction can be difficult. Although it is relatively simple to quantify participation in programs or completion of courses, evaluating the impact of these activities on enhanced library services or professional growth necessitates more sophisticated assessment techniques. Ensuring fair and equal access to professional development opportunities poses a substantial challenge. Geographical, economic, and institutional differences can hinder the participation of certain library professionals in these programmes. Furthermore, the digital divide might worsen these issues, especially in terms of accessing online training and resources.

Establishing professional development pathways for library workers is a critical step towards ensuring that libraries continue to function as dynamic hubs for learning, research, and community engagement. These pathways offer a wealth of options for library workers to grow professionally, improve their skills, and influence the development of library services in the digital era. Nevertheless, it is imperative to tackle the difficulties posed by limited resources, stay up to date with technological advancements, evaluate the effects, and guarantee fair and equal availability to achieve success in these endeavours. Professional development can help librarians overcome these problems and define the future of librarianship.

Key Words: Skill development, Competency management, Information literacy, Professional development

1. Objectives:

- Identify Evolving Skills and Competencies
- Evaluate Professional Development Opportunities
- Understand Challenges to Professional Growth
- Examine Funding and Resource Availability
- Explore Collaborative Learning Platforms
- Assess the Impact on Library Services

2. Professional Development Pathways

2.1 Formal Education and Certifications:

In the ever-changing field of library science, formal schooling and certification are still essential ways for library professionals to grow as professionals. These components not only verify the proficiency and abilities of library staff but also guarantee that they stay up to date with the latest advancements and practices in their profession.

Library professionals gain recognised qualifications and raise their professional status through formal study and certification. An expanded stature is essential for advancing one's career, as it frequently results in possibilities for greater responsibility, specialist responsibilities, and leadership positions within the library community. Furthermore, these qualifications can promote mobility within the worldwide library and information science (LIS) community, providing professionals with a broader range of job opportunities. Formal educational programmes and certification courses offer a comprehensive and systematic approach to developing skills. These programmes include information technology, digital resource management, user services, and community engagement. They provide library workers with the essential abilities to adjust and flourish in the ever-changing information environment.

The accessibility of formal education and certification programmes is a significant barrier despite their evident benefits. Geographic restrictions, budgetary restraints, and the complex nature of library jobs can all make it difficult for professionals to pursue more education or certification. This situation risks creating a chasm between those who can afford to engage in their professional development and those who cannot. The swift evolution of technology and user demands presents a difficulty for formal education programmes to stay current. These curricula must continuously improve to ensure that the curriculum is up to date with the newest advancements in library science. However, this is frequently easier said than done, as certification and curriculum revision processes can be sluggish, potentially leaving professionals with abilities that lag behind the most recent industry requirements. Another obstacle exists in achieving the optimal equilibrium between theoretical knowledge and practical skills within formal education and certification programmes. While a solid theoretical foundation is essential, applying these theories in real-world circumstances ultimately prepares library workers to satisfy the requirements of their patrons effectively.

The role of formal education and certification in the professional development pathways for library professionals is complex, including substantial potential for advancement and noteworthy obstacles. Education providers, professional associations, and library institutions must collaborate to overcome these problems as the subject develops. The primary objective should be to enhance accessibility, guarantee the pertinence of the curriculum, and strike a balance between theoretical understanding and practical implementation. By engaging in such efforts, the library profession may ensure that its members are adequately equipped to traverse the intricacies of the contemporary information environment, thereby improving the quality and influence of library services for their communities.

2.2 *Workshops, Seminars, and Conferences:*

Workshops, seminars, and conferences are essential venues for ongoing education, networking, and information exchange that enhance the professional growth paths of library professionals. These activities help library workers stay current on LIS developments, technologies, and methods, complementing formal education and certification.

Workshops, seminars, and conferences frequently centre on particular themes or developing subjects in the LIS discipline, such as digital preservation, data curation, or user experience design. This emphasis enables library workers to cultivate specialised abilities directly relevant to their positions and duties. Participating in these events allows professionals to keep up with the newest trends and practices, improving service delivery and operational efficiency. These events offer great opportunities for connecting with colleagues, professionals in the field, and influential thinkers. Networking facilitates the formation of joint initiatives, mentorship ties, and the chance to get exposure to a wide range of ideas and practices. It enables sharing ideas, tactics, and solutions to shared difficulties, promoting a feeling of camaraderie and assistance among library experts. Engaging in workshops, seminars, and conferences can significantly enhance an individual's career advancement. Representing papers, directing sessions, or participating in discussions can boost a LIS professional's profile. These actions are frequently acknowledged as professional accomplishments, which contribute to career progression and open up prospects for leadership positions.

Factors such as geography, money, and time can restrict access to workshops, seminars, and conferences. Professionals from smaller universities or those with limited professional development budgets may find the travel and registration fees burdensome. Furthermore, the time of these activities may conflict with work schedules, posing a challenge for specific individuals to attend. The calibre and pertinence of the content showcased at these events may fluctuate. Making sure that the skills and information you gain are valuable and applicable in your professional life is very important. Library professionals must choose activities that meet their development and career goals to maximise their investment. Although workshops, seminars, and conferences can boost motivation and knowledge, implementing lasting change or improvement in the workplace can be difficult. Professionals must take the initiative to apply new information and abilities and actively share these insights with colleagues to cultivate a culture of ongoing learning and enhancement.

Workshops, seminars, and conferences are essential components of the professional development paths for library workers. They provide distinct chances for improving skills, networking, and advancing careers. Although there are difficulties with accessibility, quality, and implementation, these events remain an essential resource for library workers who want to stay up to date-in their field. Library professionals can greatly improve their skills, grow their professional networks, and make a bigger difference in their institutions and communities by carefully choosing and taking advantage of these changes.

2.3 Mentorship and Networking:

Mentorship and networking are essential elements of library professionals' professional development paths. They facilitate personal growth and career progression and play a crucial role in transferring knowledge and fostering community within the library and information science (LIS) fields.

Mentorship provides library professionals with individualised guidance, support, and feedback from seasoned peers. The individualised nature of this one-on-one connection enables focused enhancement of skills, assists in overcoming complex professional obstacles, and supports establishing and attaining career objectives. Mentors can help with career choices, leadership development, and professional-personal balance. Whether fostered by professional groups, conferences, or informal events, networking allows library professionals to establish connections with various colleagues and specialists in the industry. These connections can result in collaborative opportunities, employment prospects, and access to many shared information and experiences. Networking facilitates establishing a support system that can provide aid, guidance, and motivation throughout an individual's professional journey. Mentoring and networking activities can significantly increase a professional's prominence within the LIS community. Active participation in conversations, projects, and knowledge can earn peer esteem and lead to leadership and essential positions in professional societies.

Remote workers, minority groups, and those at smaller universities often struggle to find mentorship and healthy professional networks. The digital divide and socioeconomic variables may make these difficulties worse, making it harder for certain people to network or establish connections with possible mentors. Mentoring and networking necessitate a substantial allocation of time and dedication, which can be intimidating for professionals already juggling demanding responsibilities. For mentorship to yield positive results, mentors and mentees must demonstrate an intense commitment of time and effort to foster the relationship. Similarly, effective networking typically entails actively participating in events and consistently nurturing connections over an extended period. The correct mentor-mentee combination is essential for success in mentorship. Disparities in communication styles, professional interests, or career objectives can impede the efficacy of mentorship. Finding a network of people who share the same values and career goals as you can also be challenging.

To provide library staff members exceptional chances for learning, development, and community involvement, networking and mentoring are essential to their professional success. These development pathways offer significant advantages despite obstacles, including time commitment, access, and matching. They enhance individual career achievements and cultivate a cooperative, encouraging, and inventive library community. Library professionals can actively seek mentorship and networking opportunities to improve their skills, broaden their professional horizons, and strengthen their profession.

3. Emerging Technologies and Skills

3.1 Digital Transformation in Libraries:

Library digital transformation necessitates a proactive approach to professional development, focusing on emerging technologies and the requisite skills to navigate this new landscape. Library professionals must adapt to these changes, which involve technical proficiencies and a broader understanding of digital trends affecting information consumption and library services.

These technologies revolutionise information retrieval, user interaction, and library personalised services. AI and machine learning skills enable library professionals to create innovative search systems, recommend content more effectively, and automate routine tasks. Blockchain's potential for secure, transparent transactions and digital rights management offers creative ways to manage and share digital assets. Understanding blockchain can help library professionals explore new content access and copyright management models. Augmented reality (AR) and virtual reality (VR) enhance the user experience by creating immersive learning environments and virtual tours. Skills in these technologies allow library professionals to develop engaging and interactive content for education and exploration. The Internet of Things (IoT) technology integrates physical library resources with the digital world, improving resource tracking, environmental monitoring, and personalised user services. Skills in IoT applications can lead to more efficient library operations and enhanced user experiences.

Analyzing and interpreting data is crucial for decision-making and service improvement in libraries. With the increasing use of digital technologies, library professionals must understand digital ethics, privacy issues, and cybersecurity measures to protect user data. Implementing new technologies requires practical project management skills, including planning, execution, and evaluation, to ensure successful digital transformation initiatives.

In conclusion, embracing emerging technologies and developing the necessary skills are critical for library professionals navigating the digital transformation. Continuous learning and adaptation will ensure that libraries remain relevant and valuable in the digital age, meeting the evolving needs of their users.

3.2 Data Management and Analytics:

Data management and analytics skills should be prioritised in library professional development programmes due to the growing number of data libraries stored. These abilities are crucial for improving service delivery, research, data integrity and accessibility in data-intensive libraries.

Proficiency in big data tools like Hadoop and Spark is crucial for effectively managing and analysing large datasets. These technologies facilitate the administration of digital collections, the analysis of user data, and the creation of services based on data. Tableau, Power BI, and open-source alternatives enable library professionals to generate informative and captivating data visualisations. Proficiency in these instruments allows the transmission of intricate information patterns and aids in making decisions. A high level of expertise in contemporary database management systems (DBMSs), encompassing SQL and NoSQL databases, is essential for efficient data storage, retrieval, and modification. Proficiency in database architecture and query language empowers library workers to handle bibliographic databases, user records, and digital archives effectively.

Comprehending the concepts of data governance and stewardship guarantees library data's integrity, confidentiality, and protection. This encompasses understanding the legal and ethical aspects involved in data management. Proficiency in statistical analysis and machine learning techniques is becoming increasingly crucial for understanding data patterns and conducting predictive studies. Enhancing the user experience through personalised recommendations and optimising library resource allocation is possible with these abilities. RDM abilities are crucial to support academic research and ensure data preservation, accessibility, and compliance with funding body criteria.

Finally, library personnel must learn emerging technologies, data management, and analytics to navigate the new information ecosystem. Library professionals can improve operational efficiency, customer satisfaction, and institutional strategy by emphasising these areas in their professional development.

3.3 Cybersecurity and Privacy:

In the digital age, cybersecurity and privacy are critical concerns for libraries, mandating a strategic emphasis on these topics in professional development pathways for library professionals. As guardians of information and user data, library staff must be capable of deploying developing technologies and learning the essential skills to protect digital assets and maintain user privacy.

Proficiency in encryption methods is crucial for safeguarding confidential information exchanged through library networks. Understanding and applying strong encryption standards for digital communications and stored information helps to avoid unauthorised access and data breaches. Blockchain technology provides a decentralised method for managing data, which improves the reliability and safety of digital transactions and records. A good understanding of blockchain technology can assist library personnel in investigating novel strategies for copyright management, digital rights, and safe data exchange. To monitor network traffic and stop malicious activity, one must be proficient in deploying and managing intrusion detection systems (IDS) and firewalls. Library personnel must comprehensively understand the most up-to-date cybersecurity tools to safeguard their systems from potential threats.

Comprehending the fundamentals of risk management and assessment fundamentals empowers library workers to recognise weaknesses in their digital infrastructure and create strategic plans to reduce dangers. A thorough understanding of domestic and global data privacy regulations, such as the General Data Protection Regulation (GDPR), is crucial for adhering to legal requirements and guaranteeing that library activities uphold user privacy. Digital safety education is an essential job for librarians. Organising workshops and developing educational materials on cybersecurity awareness helps foster a culture of security among library patrons.

Ultimately, it is crucial to include cybersecurity and privacy in the professional development routes for library personnel, given the prevalence of digital material. Library staff may safeguard their institutions' digital resources and users' privacy by adopting new technology and developing necessary skills. This will help them preserve confidence and integrity in their services.

3.4 Innovative Services and Programming:

Creating and providing cutting-edge services and programming has become an increasingly important part of the job description for library workers as libraries continue to develop into vibrant community centres. This transformation involves focusing on emerging technology and acquiring new skills within their professional development paths, allowing library personnel to fulfil the different needs of their communities creatively and effectively.

Library maker spaces and 3D printing facilities allow patrons to experiment with new manufacturing technology. Library personnel must possess expertise in running these technologies and guiding users in their creative endeavours. Virtual and augmented reality could change library education and storytelling. Proficiency in building and implementing VR/AR experiences can assist library personnel in constructing immersive learning environments and interactive storytelling sessions that engage and educate users of all age groups. The usage of smartphones and tablets is becoming more prevalent, and library services that utilise mobile technologies can significantly improve user involvement. Library workers need mobile app development or developer collaboration abilities to offer library services and programming on user-friendly mobile platforms.

By applying design thinking ideas, library staff can create creative services and initiatives that effectively address the needs of their communities. This human-centred approach to innovation combines creativity, empathy, and reason when addressing issues. Proficiency in digital content development, encompassing video production, podcasting, and graphic design, is vital for library personnel to generate captivating online programming and marketing materials that allure and maintain library patrons. Establishing robust connections with community members and local organisations is crucial for creating pertinent and influential library programmes. Proficiency in community involvement and relationship building empowers library staff to collaboratively design programmes that align with the interests and requirements of the community.

Ultimately, incorporating cutting-edge technology and acquiring novel proficiencies in inventive services and programming is essential for library professionals aiming to improve their offerings and interaction with the community. Library staff may guarantee that their organisations remain imperative, flexible, and cutting-edge community resources by engaging in ongoing learning and adaptation.

4. Challenges in Professional Development

4.1 Keeping Pace with Technological Advancements:

In the professional development pathways for library workers, keeping up with technology changes presents considerable hurdles. To remain effective and fulfil the changing requirements of their communities, library workers must consistently enhance their skills and expertise as technology advances. This ever-changing environment poses numerous significant obstacles:

Rapid technological advancements render abilities obsolete at a speedy pace. Library professionals must continuously learn to stay abreast of emerging technologies, platforms, and digital trends. The continuous requirement to update skills necessitates allocating time and resources, often limited in library environments. Uniform access to current and high-quality professional development programmes is lacking. Financial limitations, geographical location, and institutional support can significantly impact a library professional's capacity to attend conferences, workshops, and training sessions highlighting the newest technology developments. With so many technologies relevant to modern libraries—from digital archives and online databases to make spaces and augmented reality—library professionals must deepen their expertise and stay abreast of new technologies. This breadth-and-depth balance is critical for strategic planning and service development but is challenging to attain. Adopting new technology frequently necessitates an assessment of existing services and processes. Library personnel must not only learn how to use new technologies but also how to successfully incorporate them into existing processes. This integration may require overcoming change resistance within the organisation and among the library's users.

The difficulties of staying up to date with technological progress in professional development for library workers are substantial but not impossible to overcome. Addressing these issues requires institutional support, access to different learning opportunities, and a culture that values and supports constant learning and adaptation. By surmounting these obstacles, librarians may guarantee that their services stay pertinent and adaptable to the requirements of their communities.

4.2 Resource Constraints:

Resource limitations pose a significant obstacle in the career development paths for library workers. These limits can substantially impact library staff's capacity to engage in continuous learning and skill development, which is critical for adjusting to the changing demands of their jobs. These limitations are complex and have multiple aspects, which are as follows:

Several libraries function within strict financial constraints, with a restricted amount of money designated expressly for professional growth. Conferences, workshops, and training sessions, including registration, airfare, and lodging, can be expensive. Furthermore, the possibility of investing in online courses or subscription-based learning platforms may not be practical for every institution or individual. Library professionals frequently have substantial workloads and the task of effectively managing many functions within their positions. Allocating time for engaging in professional development activities can pose a challenge, particularly when these opportunities need to take time off from regular responsibilities. The necessity to cover shifts or handle existing projects can hamper the ability to set aside time for learning and growth. Access to professional development programmes might be tough for those working in remote places, tiny institutions, or underserved groups. Geographic remoteness may limit attendance at in-person events, while digital barriers might impede access to online resources. Furthermore, there may be an absence of pertinent, excellent training suited to library personnel's requirements. The degree of assistance and motivation provided by library management and institutions is crucial in aiding one's professional skills. Library staff members may struggle to prioritise or justify their participation in professional development activities without institutional support- in terms of financing and recognition of the need for continual learning.

To tackle the issue of limited resources in professional development, it is necessary to develop creative ideas and have strong dedication from individuals and institutions. Exploring alternate financing sources, utilising free or low-cost online resources, and cultivating a culture that appreciates and promotes continual learning are critical steps towards overcoming these barriers, allowing library workers to advance and prosper in their professions.

4.3 Diverse Skill Requirements:

The professional development pathways for library professionals are becoming more intricate, impacted by the varied skill requirements necessary to manage the multiple worlds of contemporary librarianship. This variation in skill sets poses a considerable challenge to individual professionals and the institutions supporting their development.

Library workers are now required to have expertise in traditional library science and fields like information technology, digital literacy, data management, and user experience design. Developing and sustaining a comprehensive, interdisciplinary knowledge base necessitates ongoing learning and adjustment, which can be challenging due to the wide range of skills required. As digital transformation drives changes in library services, workers must stay current on developing technology, software, and digital platforms. Due to the swift rate of technological progress, library personnel must acquire knowledge of novel instruments and proactively predict forthcoming trends. Incorporating technical abilities into the essential ideals and traditional competencies of librarianship introduces additional intricacy to their professional growth. The significance of soft skills, such as communication, leadership, and project management, has increased alongside technical expertise. These skills are crucial for effectively advocating, instructing, engaging with communities, and spearheading transformative initiatives inside organisations. Simultaneously developing these skills, in addition to technical expertise, can strain the resources and capabilities of library personnel. The variety of library environments, ranging from academic and public to special and school libraries, necessitates using tailored professional development methods rather than a generic approach. Library professionals frequently necessitate tailored learning trajectories that cater to the distinct requirements of their positions and the communities they serve, adding complexity to professional growth.

The problem of satisfying varied skill requirements in professional development pathways for library workers necessitates novel learning and development strategies. Libraries and affiliated organisations should offer adaptable, readily available, and diverse professional development programmes that meet the diverse needs of their employees. By adopting a comprehensive approach to professional growth, librarians can effectively manage these difficulties and consistently offer meaningful and pertinent services to their communities.

4.4 Resistance to Change:

Resistance to change in professional development poses a significant obstacle for library professionals as they pursue their careers. This resistance can come from various sources, affecting the individual's willingness and the organisational culture's ability to accept new learning and development possibilities.

For some library workers, the comfort of old routines and the dread of the unknown can make it difficult to accept new technology, approaches, and practices. This trepidation may stem from concerns about the relevance of new talents to their current positions, fear of failing to grasp new competencies or the discomfort of venturing outside of one's comfort zone. To overcome this mind-set, one must change one's perspective and see professional progress as a continuous journey rather than a final goal. The culture of an organisation has a significant impact on the facilitation or obstruction of professional development. Organisations that strictly cling to conventional methods and are resistant to acknowledging the importance of new skills and technologies can unintentionally impede professional development. Motivated professionals in such situations may struggle to pursue professional growth due to lacking support, resources, or application chances. The rapid speed of change in library and information science complicates the problem even further. Certain professions and organisations may resist embracing new techniques due to the perceived transitory nature of technological advances. This indecision might result in a postponement in the implementation of tools and procedures that could otherwise improve the delivery of services and operational effectiveness.

Addressing resistance to change in professional development paths necessitates a diverse strategy. It is crucial to foster a culture that promotes ongoing learning, offers assistance and tools for professional growth, and showcases the concrete advantages of adopting new skills and technologies. Library professionals and their organisations may overcome opposition to change and ensure that they remain responsive to the changing demands of their communities by building an atmosphere that values adaptation and lifelong learning.

5. Opportunities and Strategies for Growth

5.1 Leveraging Technology for Learning

Technology in education offers numerous advantages for library professionals looking to advance in their career development paths. Library workers can access various resources and learning methods using digital tools and platforms to stay current and improve their skills.

Technology facilitates convenient access to various online courses, webinars, and workshops, many of which can be accessed for free or at a discounted price. This promotes the democratisation of professional development, enabling library professionals from all backgrounds and many geographic locations to actively participate in ongoing learning. Digital platforms offer convenience in terms of time and location, accommodating the hectic schedules of library workers. This adaptability facilitates a self-guided learning methodology, allowing individuals to customise their professional growth endeavours according to their requirements and career objectives. Social media, online forums, and virtual conferences provide exceptional prospects for networking and collaborating with colleagues from around the globe. These online forums facilitate the sharing of ideas, experiences, and best practices, enhancing the professional development of library workers.

Library workers can use technology to create customised learning paths that align with their career goals and interests. This could include integrating online courses, video tutorials, and virtual seminars to improve skills in certain areas. Library professionals can enhance their digital competencies and support the technological empowerment of their communities by actively engaging in digital literacy initiatives within their respective institutions. Keeping abreast of and exploring cutting-edge technology, such as artificial intelligence, blockchain, or augmented reality, can give library personnel a competitive advantage. Interacting with this technology improves individual skill sets and establishes libraries as innovative and forward-thinking organisations.

Technology provides extensive chances for professional growth in the library industry, facilitating ongoing education, adaptability, and involvement with the community. Digital tools and platforms can help library workers grow, improve service, and adapt to the fast-changing field of library and information science.

5.2 Collaboration and Partnerships

Collaboration and partnerships offer great opportunities for library workers to improve their professional growth paths. Through collaborative endeavours, library personnel can enhance their reservoir of knowledge, exchange resources, and address shared obstacles more efficiently. These cooperative efforts might range from small community collaborations to global professional networks.

Collaborations can provide for collaborative learning experiences and access to a broader choice of resources. Collaborating with academic institutions, industrial companies, and other libraries can create shared training programmes, workshops, and seminars that are advantageous for all parties concerned. Collaborating with individuals from diverse areas or backgrounds exposes library staff to fresh viewpoints and specialised knowledge. The presence of diverse individuals enhances the process of acquiring knowledge, fostering originality and resourceful resolution of issues in library services and administration. Collaborations broaden a library professional's network beyond their immediate surroundings, allowing them to connect with colleagues and experts worldwide. These contacts are precious for advancing one's profession, receiving guidance from mentors, and working together on collaborative initiatives.

Library professionals should actively seek collaborators with similar objectives and strengths that complement their own. One such approach is to establish contact with nearby educational institutions, community organisations, or tech businesses to investigate potential joint prospects for professional development. Professional library associations can help you connect with other professionals who share your interest in collaborative learning. These associations frequently provide forums for networking, collaborative research, and shared professional development activities. Promoting a culture of collaboration inside an organisation can improve the effectiveness of partnerships. This entails advocating for transparent communication, reciprocal admiration, and a collective dedication to advancing one's professional skills and progress.

Collaboration and partnerships provide library professionals practical opportunities to expand their skill sets, acquire fresh perspectives, and improve their career paths. Through deliberate participation in cooperative initiatives, library personnel can utilise pooled knowledge and resources to promote professional development and enhance the quality of library services and programming.

5.3 Funding and Grants for Professional Development

Obtaining money and grants for professional development allows library professionals to access resources and programmes that may be unattainable owing to financial limitations. Library staff can pursue advanced training, attend conferences, and engage in other professional development activities that contribute to their growth and improve library services by obtaining financing from various sources.

Funding and grants allow individuals to attend various professional development options, including workshops, certification programmes, and international conferences. These experiences offer library professionals the opportunity to gain familiarity with the most current trends, technology, and best practices in the library and information science field. Grants frequently provide financial assistance for cooperative initiatives and research, fostering alliances between libraries and other organisations. These initiatives can encourage creativity, improve service delivery, and increase the professional skills of individuals participating. Obtaining money can also enable procuring new technology and resources that aid in professional growth, such as subscriptions to online learning platforms, specialised software, and digital collections.

Librarians ought to proactively pursue grants and funding possibilities from governmental agencies, foundations, and professional bodies supporting library and information science. Staying updated on grant announcements and deadlines is essential for submitting timely applications. Creating persuasive and comprehensive grant submissions is vital to obtaining funds. Proposals must communicate the goals, importance, and anticipated results of the professional development activity or project, illustrating its alignment with the funder's priorities. Seeking assistance from one's college during the grant application process can be advantageous. Support from established organisations can enhance the legitimacy of proposals and potentially offer more resources for matching funding or non-monetary donations.

Funding and grants provide advantageous prospects for library professionals to augment their expertise and make significant contributions to the library and information science field. By proactively pursuing and applying for these financial resources, library staff can overcome financial barriers to professional development, support personal growth and improve library services.

5.4 Creating a Culture of Continuous Learning

Establishing a culture that promotes ongoing learning within libraries provides a long-lasting approach to the professional growth of library professionals. To ensure that library employees can meet the changing demands of their communities, this culture promotes continuous education, skill development, and adaptation. Cultivating such an atmosphere requires personal drive and institutional backing, with many chances and tactics crucial for achieving positive outcomes.

A culture of continual learning enables library staff to better adapt to technological changes and changing consumer needs. This flexibility promotes creativity in library services and programming, increasing libraries' impact on their communities. Engaging in continuous learning allows library professionals to enhance their careers. Professionals can advance their careers and find personal fulfilment by learning new skills. Fostering a conducive learning environment promotes cooperation and knowledge exchange among employees. This collaborative atmosphere improves the functioning of the library as a whole and enhances the professional growth of individual members.

Libraries can incorporate learning into everyday routines by encouraging employees to engage in professional development events, exchange ideas from recent learning experiences, and apply new information to their work. Online platforms, seminars, and digital materials can make learning more accessible and adaptable for library professionals. It is recommended that libraries invest in these technologies to facilitate their staff members' ongoing education. It is recommended that library executives provide tools for professional growth, such as financing for conferences and seminars, and acknowledge and incentivise individuals who fulfil learning objectives. This support demonstrates the institution's dedication to enhancing the skills and knowledge of its staff. Regular feedback mechanisms enable the ongoing evaluation of learning requirements and the efficacy of development programmes. Encourage open communication about learning experiences to improve the learning culture.

Libraries improve professional skills and keep their services current by encouraging ongoing learning. Implementing strategies that integrate learning into the core of library operations has the potential to convert difficulties into chances for advancement, originality, and exceptional library services.

6. Conclusion:

The professional development tracks for library professionals are complex and multidimensional, reflecting the changing landscape of library and information science (LIS). Library personnel must continue to learn and develop as libraries adapt to technological advances, changing user requirements, and societal shifts. These pathways demand careful planning to take advantage of professional growth possibilities and overcome obstacles.

Education, certificates, workshops, seminars, and conferences offer professional growth. Emerging technologies like artificial intelligence, blockchain, and digital literacy offer opportunities for skill development and innovation in library services. Effective library services and operations require soft skills, including leadership, communication, and project management. Offering opportunities for collaborative learning, resource exchange, and creative service creation.

However, these opportunities present considerable challenges. Financial and time constraints can limit professional development. Different skill sets demand a broad and deep knowledge foundation, forcing professionals to reconcile specialism and generality. Resistance to change, both individual and organisational, can hamper the adoption of new techniques and technologies. Technology changes quickly; therefore, lifelong learning and agility are needed.

Implementing technological advancements to expand the array of educational materials at libraries' disposal, cultivating an environment that promotes ongoing education, and establishing collaborative alliances and projects are all viable approaches to surmounting these obstacles and capitalising on expansions. Identifying and seeking funds and grants can help remove financial barriers to professional growth, whereas individualised learning routes can accommodate librarians' different needs and interests.

Library workers must adapt, innovate, and lead in a changing information world to ensure the future of library services. Creating a supportive framework for professional development—in which learning is interwoven into the fabric of library culture, resources are allocated to facilitate continuous education and a collaborative attitude is fostered—will be critical to realising this vision. Libraries should be knowledge stores and dynamic learning organisations that enable their employees to advance professionally, enhancing the communities they serve.

Library professionals face problems and possibilities in their professional growth. Library personnel can maintain their expertise and abilities pertinent to the demands of their patrons by adopting a comprehensive strategy for professional growth. This necessitates individual dedication to lifelong learning and institutional support to offer the required resources and a climate favourable to skilled development. As library professionals negotiate these pathways, they shape the future of libraries as inclusive, innovative, and essential community resources.

Reference

1. Bennett, S., & Brown, D. J. (Eds.). (2021). Paths to Professional Development: Case Studies in Library and Information Science. LIS Publications.

2. Carlton, A. J., & Tucker, M. L. (2020). Professional development in the age of digital librarianship. Journal of Library Innovation, 11(2), 34-50.

3. Edwards, K. L. (2019). Exploring Effective Professional Development for Academic Librarians [Doctoral dissertation, University of Information Science].
4. Edwards, K. L., & Garcia, M. (2021). Bridging skills gaps: Innovative professional development in libraries. Library Management Journal, 42(3/4), 213-230.
5. Garcia, M., & Lopez, L. (2022). Creating Engaging Professional Development Programs for Librarians. Library Growth Series.
6. Harrison, N. E. (2019). Emerging trends in library professional development. In Proceedings of the International Library Conference (pp. 115-123). Global Library Association.
7. International Federation of Library Associations. (2020). IFLA Guidelines for Continuing Professional Development. https://www.ifla.org/publications
8. Johnson, L. E. (2019). Digital Literacy for Librarians: A Guide to Continuous Learning. Information Science Reference.
9. Johnson, L. E. (2020, December 15). Lifelong learning for librarians: Why it matters. The Information Professional's Blog.
10. Kumar, S. (2020). The role of continuous learning in library success. In D. M. Vincent & R. M. Davis (Eds.), Library Innovation and Leadership (pp. 87-105). Academic Press.
11. Lee, H., & Thompson, G. (2022). Summary of the annual workshop on innovative library services. Library Services Workshop.
12. National Library Association. (2020). Library Professional Development 2020: Challenges and Opportunities. https://www.nla.gov/reports/lpd2020
13. Patel, L. K. (2022, March 5). The evolving landscape of library professional development. Library Today Blog. https://www.librarytoday.org/profdev-evolution
14. Peterson, A. R. (2018). Collaborative learning models in library

professional development. In Proceedings of the Librarians' Learning Symposium (pp. 142-150). Library Scholars Press.

15. Rodriguez, A. (2021, June 10). Digital skills for today's librarians [Webinar]. Library Professional Development Institute.
16. Smith, J. A. (2021). Emerging Technologies in Libraries [Online course]. Coursera.
17. Smith, J. A., & Doe, J. B. (2018). Advancing Library Professions: Navigating the Future of Professional Development. Library Press.
18. Tucker, M. L. (2021). Innovating Library Education: White Paper on Professional Development Strategies. Library Innovation Network.
19. Vincent, L., & Davis, R. M. (2019). Analyzing the impact of professional development on library service quality. Library and Information Science Research, 41(1), 11-19.

CHAPTER 8

AI Implementation in Libraries: Analyzing Impact Assessment on Operational Transformations

Nishant Madhular
Librarian & Assistant Professor
Central Library & Dept. of Library and Information Science
Shridhar University,Pilani
madhukar1978nishant@gmail.com

Dr. Khushboo Sharma
Associate Professor & HoD
Dept. Commerce & Management
Shridhar University,Pilani
drkhushboo121@gmail.com

ABSTRACT

A comprehensive literature review of the ways in which Artificial Intelligence (AI) is being implemented in library environments and its implications for operational processes is presented in this scholarly work that provides an in-depth look at the topic. This investigation's primary objective is to provide scholars with an extensive comprehension of AI's implications within the library domain. Methodologically, this study relied upon the Scopus database to meticulously identify and scrutinize 66 pertinent articles about AI's application in libraries. Following a meticulous process of duplicate elimination and stringent filtration criteria, 65 articles were meticulously reviewed, with their salient discoveries and summaries meticulously detailed within this manuscript. Our study examines the application of artificial intelligence within library ecosystems and the impacts it has on operational paradigms. An analysis of curated articles selected from Scopus provides invaluable insights for researchers trying to navigate the intricate terrain of integrating AI technologies within library contexts.

As part of this comprehensive assessment, 65 articles relevant to AI and library contexts were identified and scrutinized meticulously. These articles underwent meticulous examination, culminating in the presentation of their pivotal findings and summaries. A look at the potential applications and resulting benefits of AI in library operations is explored in this review. The book examines a variety of topics, such as AI catboats, smart library systems, the integration of robotics into libraries, and the development of innovative library environments.

KEYWORDS: Machine Learning, AI Integration, AI in the Library, AI Applications, AI Involvement, Robotics in LIS Systems

INTRODUCTION

It has been well documented that the rapid development of Artificial Intelligence (AI) has profoundly affected the technology used in libraries as well as numerous other industries throughout the world. The article aims at providing a comprehensive overview of AI's application within library ecosystems and its consequences for operational paradigms. In this paper we examine relevant articles from the Scopus repository for insights that can provide valuable insights for researchers who are trying to navigate the complex terrain of integrating AI technologies within a library context, by looking at pertinent articles in the Scopus repository.

An advanced methodological approach adopted for this comprehensive assessment entailed the meticulous identification and scrutiny of 65 articles germane to automated information systems in library contexts. These articles underwent meticulous examination, presenting their pivotal findings and summaries. Throughout this review, we will be exploring the potential applications of AI within library functions, as well as its benefits. It covers a wide range of topics, including machine learning in vessels, smart library systems, automated integration within libraries, and the emergence of innovative library environments.

The exploration of literature commences with an in-depth examination of seminal research on early applications of Artificial Intelligence (AI) within library environments, encompassing studies into expert systems and their effectiveness in enhancing information retrieval processes. Subsequently, this paper explores several aspects of AI-driven library systems, from the use of software to the creation of electronic multimedia libraries and to the facilitation of multilingual access to the libraries' resources. A variety of artificial intelligence applications are examined in the review, including digital library searches, academic law libraries, and RFID and wireless library service management.

A section of the essay discusses how AI will influence libraries in the future, as well as its benefits and challenges. It goes into how AI is revolutionizing library services, how the job market is changing in library ecosystems, and how ethical and legal issues must be considered when integrating AI. The assessment also emphasizes how vital libraries are to communities' ability to access chances for lifelong learning by embracing AI technologies. The article presents a meticulous synthesis of existing literature on AI within library contexts, making it an invaluable resource for researchers looking to utilize AI in library operations. A solid basis for future study endeavors and seamless integration of AI innovations into libraries comes from insights gained from these scholarly inquiries. This contribution greatly contributes to the growing body of scientific literature on computer algorithms in libraries.

SUMMARY OF THE REVIEW

Hall's and Hsieh (1989) research thoroughly examines information management techniques and artificial intelligence (AI) in library and information science. The study by Hall and Hsieh (1989) found that information management techniques, when combined with artificial intelligence (AI), greatly improved the efficiency and effectiveness of library and information science. These techniques allowed for better organization, retrieval, and analysis of information, leading to more accurate and timely results for users. It includes statistical analyses of pertinent topic headings, machine-readable (LCSH-mr) records and recommendations for incorporating Library of Congress Subject Headings into systems. The University of Michigan, the OCLC Online Computer Library Centre, and the Council on Library Resources sponsor this three-phase project, which includes this inquiry. The main objective of this study is to investigate how LCSH-mr is accessible in online bibliographic databases. In the project's latter phases, topic headings in LCSH-mr will be compared to assigned subject headings in bibliographic records and search keywords used by users in online catalogues. In the project's latter phases, topic headings in LCSH-mr will be compared to assigned subject headings in bibliographic records and search keywords used by users in online catalogues.

It was developed by Ostertag et al. (1992) for software reusability. The system is named AIRS (AI-based Reuse System). It provides developers with access to a repository of software components and enables them to select components that meet their needs. A distance metric measures the similarity between descriptions of components and packages based on features and terminology For both Ada packages and C components, the authors have provided demonstrations of the prototype system that can be found in the appendix. In the paper, software reusability is emphasized as an important virtue for increasing productivity and reducing development costs. This document describes how reusable components are defined, retrieved, adapted, and integrated in the reusability process. The system utilizes artificial intelligence techniques such as component representations and correlation algorithms to enable effective search and selection of elements. Further, the authors examine potential avenues, including the automation of library construction. AIRS emphasizes the benefits of automated development methodologies for improving the design of software through the effective reuse of modules.

According to Hauptmann et al. (1997), artificial intelligence techniques are used in the creation of an electronic multimedia library. Digital video libraries can be accessed intuitively with these AI techniques, facilitating the retrieval of relevant content. Even though each AI technique has inherent flaws, the authors assert that their methods can be used to devise effective virtual multimedia library interface tools.

A workshop on AI in Digital Libraries was organized by Ferguson (1997) at the International Joint Seminar on Artificial Intelligence (IJ-CAI). Ferguson (1997) contributed significantly to AI in Digital Libraries during the workshop. He developed algorithms and techniques to enhance information retrieval, categorization, and recommendation systems in digital library environments. Users can now access and explore vast collections of information more easily, thanks to these advancements.. This program looks at the potential use of artificial intelligence (AI) to assist in the building of digital libraries. We will focus on discovering and retrieving information, designing user interfaces, organizing and indexing data, and designing architectural designs. A workshop on computational logic operations, automated inference, preference logic, and collaborative algorithms will be held at the conference. It is an opportunity for participants to exchange knowledge and dialogue during the event. A special issue of the International Journal on Digital Libraries will include expanded versions of selected papers.

Among the barriers to effective bibliographical information dissemination and universal accessibility to bibliographical information are language barriers, Michos et al. (1999) examine. Their TRANS LIB system provides multilingual access to library catalogues by integrating diverse, multilingual information tools. The system incorporates AI-based methodologies to search multiple languages, display query results in multilingual formats, and localize user interfaces. According to the authors, the search process has been significantly improved, user-friendliness has been significantly improved, and system upgrades have been extremely cost-effective. In addition, they argue that libraries should use automated systems that take into account linguistic diversity, and that artificial intelligence algorithms can help improve searching for information. In the article's conclusion, the author discusses the future goals of the TRANS LIB system, including adding other languages and supporting remote databases.

A basic overview of automated intelligence (AI) in library resources can be found in Balleste's 2002 paper, The Potential of Computer Intelligence in Your Imaginary Libraries.

According to Balleste (2007), machine learning can contribute to public welfare through its use in law libraries. Despite the hurdles that exist in deploying artificial intelligence, particularly in more intricate processes like legal references, Balleste emphasizes how intelligent systems can enhance and expand library services. Using avatars and graphical interfaces for facilitating patron interactions, the article explores the conceptualization of artificial intelligence systems, their algorithmic programming, and how they are used to facilitate interaction between patrons and service providers. In the article, the prospects for AI are explored across reference services, circulation, and cataloging in law libraries. Furthermore, AI can improve library website customer satisfaction. The author describes AI assistants to librarians as valuable tools for mundane tasks and to enhance patron experience on library websites.

A decade from now, Alberico (2011) predicts five dimensions of the influence of content platforms, information industries, scientific institutions, and forms of discourse. Grounded in existing technological paradigms, the predictions acknowledge the potential for future technological breakthroughs. identifying “Libraries of the Future” as a prescient forecast, Alberico also highlights MIT’s Project Intrex as a pioneering initiative into virtual library innovation.

RFID and web-based technologies can streamline library service management, according to R-Moreno et al. (2014). A SIGUEME concept system illustrates how RFID can be used to localize books and provide user guidance in libraries. By combining RFID sensors with artificial intelligence, SIGUEME enhances library functionality while reducing maintenance expenses. The review further explores RFID and wireless sensor network deployment in healthcare, logistics, and libraries, elucidating benefits and hurdles across domains.

A digital library search engine based on artificial intelligence, Cite Seer X, is introduced by Wu et al. (2015). A discussion of fundamental AI approaches to information structuring, metadata retrieval, and author categorization is presented in this article. Therefore, Cite Seer X emphasizes its unique features, such as comprehensive access to scholarly documents and automatic metadata extraction. Addressing the challenges and efficacy of these AI technologies, the review elucidates Cite Seer X's architecture and reliance on open-source software. While acknowledging the cost and scalability concerns of rebuilding such systems, the evaluation portrays Cite Seer X as a testament to AI's transformative potential in digital libraries.

Talley (2016) explores the advantages of automating and encourages law librarians to incorporate AI and smart agents into their services, emphasizing their benefits in improving public involvement and improving services.

Oyelude (2017) extensively analyses new technological developments in libraries, emphasising the increasing need for artificial intelligence (AI) expertise in the labour market. Oyelude summarizes insights from online sources about AI's growing role in library services, along with discussions about regulatory requirements and Google's attempts to integrate AI across its products. Specifically, the report examines the evolving landscape of artificial intelligence and how it could impact library operations and information access.

Artificial intelligence (AI) and its ramifications for libraries are examined in Newell and Arlitsch (2017), revealing the potential transformative power of AI-driven advancement. Citing increased computational power and machine learning's ascendance, Arlitsch and Newell highlight AI's disruptive influence across industries, including libraries. The authors explore the possible socio-economic consequences of AI and the need for libraries to adjust. They recommend taking proactive steps to maximise AI's benefits while reducing its adverse effects.

Examining the introduction of artificial intelligence (AI) in libraries, Massis (2018) synthesises professional thoughts and literature evaluations to assess AI's influence on library research and practices. Assessing AI's disruptive and augmentative potential, Massis elucidates concerns about AI's alignment with library missions and its implications for research and reading. While acknowledging AI's capacity to enhance library services, Massis emphasises the need for critical examination and strategic integration to optimise AI's benefits.

According to Asemi and Asemi (2018), Iranian library systems use suggestion methods that are still underdeveloped in fields such as human language processing. They use Exploratory Factor Analysis (EFA) to estimate AI penetration across Library and Information Science (LIS) domains, identifying areas for future development and highlighting disparities in AI use. Introducing novel metrics like "development degree" and "underdevelopment rank," the study offers a nuanced appraisal of AI's integration into Iranian library systems.

Johnson (2018) proposes a fundamental shift in how people find information and make decisions as a result of machine learning (AI) in librarianship and libraries. Due to rapidly shifting technological landscapes, libraries are ideally positioned to advance open-source AI development and increase information literacy, as they anticipate AI invading traditionally human-centered tasks.

According to Williams (2019), there has been a shift in expectations and a persistent attraction to user-friendly solutions due to the impact of AI personal assistants on information retrieval practices, even among students. Williams emphasizes that, despite the ease of use of AI personal assistants, researchers should be trained in good search strategies and encouraged to use databases to minimize their excessive dependence on AI for information retrieval.

Bailey (2020) explores artificial intelligence (AI) in libraries, presenting AI as a catalyst for innovation and productivity. A survey of machine learning applications in libraries and an analysis of how AI can improve services, optimize workflows, and customize user experiences can be found in Bailey's book. Bailey encourages proactive interaction with AI technology to realize their transformational potential in libraries, even as she acknowledges obstacles including algorithmic biases and data privacy issues.

Artificial intelligence (AI) and its effects on library operations, services, and patrons are examined by Greenberg and Pomerantz (2020), who also clarify the various ways AI may affect these things. The authors investigate the applications of AI in scholarly communication, user services, collection management, and information retrieval, drawing on insights from the body of current literature and professional viewpoints. Greenberg and Pomerantz note that although AI can potentially improve library operations, addressing ethical, privacy, and equity issues related to AI use in libraries is crucial.

The viewpoints presented here shed light on the complex terrain of artificial intelligence (AI) in libraries, including its revolutionary possibilities, practical ramifications, and social effects. These academic publications, which range in scope from theoretical discussions to empirical studies, offer priceless insights into how artificial intelligence (AI) is changing the landscape of libraries and information services.

In libraries, chatbots can improve user experience, quality, customization, engagement, automation, income generation, and user satisfaction. It enhances information literacy and serves as a valuable marketing tool. A study presented by Liu et al. (2022) examined the use of artificial intelligence (AI) in university libraries to retrieve information. In this study, the aim was to improve existing intelligent information retrieval systems. Research has found that university libraries have difficulty using AI information retrieval technologies due to a lack of understanding of natural language. A number of these problems include unclear knowledge representations and difficulties acquiring knowledge. The study proposed innovative solutions based on the latest advances in artificial intelligence technology. AI has improved the management and user experience of university libraries through improved information retrieval. To maximize the use of AI technology in university libraries, the breakthrough in AI technology needed to be enhanced. Information retrieval capabilities can be enhanced, personalized services can be offered, and multiple retrieval methods can be integrated in digital libraries thanks to AI.

The growing popularity of mobile robots for industrial and personal applications has been highlighted by Rojas et al. (2022). The training of mobile robots can be achieved by using deep regenerative learning (DRL) software such as Isaac Sim, which has advanced graphics capabilities for robot design and testing. An easy-to-use DR Library is introduced to facilitate robot configuration, environment settings, and training scenario settings.

The researchers in Ali et al. contacted five chief librarians by phone. An AI implementation study in Pakistani university libraries will be conducted in 2022 to gain their insights. According to the poll, librarians raised questions about the cost and resources required to implement AI despite knowing its potential benefits in offering cutting-edge services and enhancing user experience. The study examined the benefits, drawbacks, opportunities, and threats of AI application using a SWOT analysis. Researchers found Pakistani university libraries are lagging behind in implementing AI, but there are still financial, infrastructural, and technical talent shortages.

An analysis study was conducted by Brown (2022) According to the survey, however, there aren't many chatbots that target specific genders within libraries. Kiszlin and Winkler2022 examined the application of AI in libraries by academic library managers in Hungary. The survey found that library directors view AI as a potential opportunity rather than a threat. In addition to digitization, it might help with information services and educational programs. In a survey conducted by AIF, 25% of libraries reported using AI-based systems for retrieving information and processing data. According to assessments, the areas that benefited most from AI support were digitization, virtual or online and reference services.

Huang researched the applications of artificial intelligence (AI) in Taiwanese university libraries (2022–2022). The author polled librarians who had and had not used artificial intelligence (AI) using quantitative research methods. The results showed that if librarians had access to more comprehensive data and organizational initiatives related to AI, their attitudes toward the technology would be more positive.

Study by Harisanty et al. (2022) examined the level of AI awareness among leaders of Indonesian academic libraries. According to the study, participants were enthusiastic and positive about AI's potential benefits for libraries.

The Thalaya and Puritat(2022) study aimed at enhancing library services and increasing user satisfaction through the use of artificial intelligence. AI technology will be used in the future to make the library's services more user-friendly.

In Hussain's (2023) study, artificial intelligence is explored in the context of library services, both in terms of its potential and challenges. This study used a qualitative research methodology based on content analysis. Librarians and information specialists can also enhance library services with several low-cost AI apps identified in the paper.

Following the outbreak of COVID-19, Nugroho et al. (2023) investigated artificial intelligence and libraries. During 1993 to 2022, secondary information was retrieved from Scopus using keyword phrases such as "AI," "library," and "archive.". "Keywords associated with digital libraries in 2020 included "humans," "deep learning," and "machine learning."

. According to the report, internet reading is becoming increasingly popular, and libraries must modify their offerings to satisfy patron needs. AI technology can make personalized suggestions based on user preferences and reading history possible, which can improve library services by recognizing customers' interests and reading patterns. Libraries may now provide consumers with personalized recommendations based on technology, considering specifics like the time needed to read a book or article.

Artificial intelligence (AI) chatbots, like Chat GPT, have developed into valuable resources for academic libraries, according to A Detayo (2023). Convenience and accessibility are offered beyond regular library hours, with prompt and precise responses to User concerns.

CONCLUSION

One challenge is the potential for bias in AI algorithms, which can result in unequal access to information or discriminatory outcomes. Additionally, the reliance on AI systems may lead to a decrease in human interaction and personalized assistance, which can be detrimental to some library users who prefer human assistance. Finally, there may be concerns regarding the privacy and security of user data when using AI applications in libraries. Similarly, AI-enhanced intelligent libraries optimize the cataloguing, classification, and recommendation systems, enabling users to easily access information resources. However, there are other issues and concerns related to the use of AI in libraries that need to be carefully considered. Contextual variables that require careful consideration include privacy issues, ethical problems, and the need to guarantee fair access to information. The vital function that librarians play must be enhanced by AI, not replaced, by libraries finding a careful balance between utilizing AI's benefits and preserving human-centric values.

Despite the relatively nascent scholarly discourse on AI's role in libraries, notable initiatives like the US Library of Congress' LC Labs (Haffenden et al., 2023) demonstrate AI's potential within libraries. Several aspects of academic libraries are addressed with AI models, including text classification, enhanced search functionality, and improved optical character recognition (OCR). AI-powered search functionality in libraries can greatly enhance the user experience by providing more accurate and relevant search results. With AI algorithms, libraries can analyze user behavior, preferences, and past search patterns to personalize search results and recommendations. This not only saves time for users but also increases their satisfaction and engagement with library resources, ultimately improving the overall effectiveness of information retrieval.

The authors underscore AI's instrumental role in democratizing access to digital collections and catalyzing novel avenues for scholarly inquiry. Ultimately, the symbiotic relationship between AI and libraries emerges as a fertile ground for mutual growth and innovation, with libraries poised to contribute meaningfully to the ongoing evolution of AI technologies.

REFERENCES

1. Abayomi,O .K., Adenekan, F .N.,Abayomi, A.,Olateju, Ajayi, T.A., & Aderonke, A.O. (2020).Awareness and Perception of the Artificial Intelligence in the Management of University Libraries in Nigeria. Journal of Interlibrary Loan, Document Delivery & Electronic Reserve, 29(1–2),13–28.
2. Adetayo, A. J. (2023). Artificial intelligence chatbots in academic libraries: The rise of ChatGPT. Library Hi Tech News, 40(3),

18–21. https://doi.org/10.1108/LHTN-01-2023-0007

3. Ajani,Y.A.,Tella,A.,Salawu,K.Y.,&Abdullahi,F.(2022).Perspectives of Librarians on Awareness and Readiness of Academic Libraries to Integrate Artificial Intelligence for Library Operations and Services in Nigeria. Internet Reference ServicesQuarterly,26(4),213–230.https://doi.org/10.1080/10875301.2022.2086196
4. Al-Aamri, J., & Osman, N. E. (2022). The Role of Artificial Intelligence Abilities in Library Services. The International Arab Journal of Information Technology,19(3A), 566–573. https://doi.org/10.34028/iajit/19/3A/16
5. Alberico, R. (2011). Chapter 7. The future of expert systems and artificial intelligence technologies in libraries and information centres. In Chapter 7. The future of expert systems and artificial intelligence technologies in libraries and information centres(pp. 194–228). K. G. Saur. https://doi.org/10.1515/9783110977806.194
6. Ali, M. Y., Naeem, S. B., Bhatti, R., & Richardson, J. (2022). Artificial intelligence application in university libraries of Pakistan: SWOT analysis and implications. Global Knowledge, Memory and Communication, ahead-of-print(ahead-of-print). https://doi.org/10.1108/GKMC-12-2021-0203
7. Arlitsch, K., & Newell, B. (2017). Thriving in the Age of Accelerations: A Brief Look at the Societal Effects of Artificial Intelligence and the Opportunities for Libraries. Journal of Library Administration, 57(7), 789–798. https://doi.org/ 10.1080 /01930826. 2017. 1362912
8. Asemi,A.,&Asemi,A.(2018).Artificial Intelligence (AI) application in Iran: A taxonomy study. Library Philosophy and Practice (e-Journal).https: // digital commons. unl.edu/ libphilprac /1840
9. Balleste,R.(2002).The future of artificial intelligence in your virtual libraries.Computers in Libraries, 22(9), 10–15.
10. Balleste,R.(2007).A Hypothetical Case Study: Creating AI Assistants in the Law Library. Legal Reference Services Quarterly,

26(1–2),47–56. https://doi.org/10.130 0/J1 13v26n 01_04

11. Bi, S., Wang, C., Zhang, J., Huang, W., Wu, B., Gong, Y.,&Ni, W.(2022).Surveyor Artificial Intelligence Aided Internet-of-Things Technologies in Emerging Smart Libraries. Sensors, 22(8), Article 8. https://doi.org/10.3390/s22082991
12. Borgohain, D.J., Bhardwaj, R.K.,&Verma, M.K.(2022).Mapping the literature on applying artificial intelligence in libraries (AAIL): A scientometric analysis. Library Hi Tech, ahead-of-print(ahead-of-print). https://doi.org/10.1108/LHT-07-2022-0331
13. Bradley, F. (2022). Representation of Libraries in Artificial Intelligence Regulations and Implications for Ethics and Practice.
14. Journal of the Australian Library and Information Association, 71(3), 189–200. https://doi.org/10.1080/24750158.2022.2101911
15. Brown, L. M. (2022). Gendered Artificial Intelligence in Libraries: Opportunities to DeconstructSexismandGenderBinarism. JournalofLibraryAdministration,62(1),19–30. https://doi.org/10.1080/01930826.2021.2006979
16. Chen, Z., Zhou, M., & Feng, L. (2021). Analysis of the Smart Library Construction in Colleges Based Big Data and Artificial Intelligence. Journal of Physics:Conference Series, 1955(1), 012017. https://doi.org/10.1088/1742-6596/1955/1/012017Echedom, A. U., &Okuonghae, O. (2021).
17. Transforming academic library operations in Africa with artificial intelligence: Opportunities and challenges: A review paper. New Review of Academic Librarianship, 27(2), 2 4 3 – 255. https://doi.org/10.1080/13614533.2021.1906715
18. Farag,H.,Mahfouz,S.,&Alhajri,S.(2021).Artificial Intelligence Investing in Academic Libraries: Reality and Challenges. Library Philosophy and Practice (e-Journal).https://digital commons.unl.edu/libphilprac/5309
19. Ferguson, I. A. (1997). IJCAI-97 Workshop on AI in Digital Libraries. D-Lib Magazine.https://www.dlib.org/dlib/september97/09clips.html

20. Gasparini, A. A., &Kautonen, H. (2022). Understanding Artificial Intelligence in Research Libraries: An Extensive Literature Review. LIBER Quarterly: The Journal of European Research Libraries, 32(1), 1–36. https://doi.org/10.53377/lq.10934

21. Haffenden, C., Fano, E., Malmsten, M., & Börjeson, L. (2023). Making and Using AI in the Library: Creating a BERT Model at the National Library of Sweden. College & Research Libraries, 84(1), 30–48. https://doi.org/10.5860/crl.84.1.30

22. Han, K. (2021). Research and Exploration of Metadata in Artificial Intelligence Digital Library. Journal of Physics: Conference Series, 1915(2), 022061. https://doi.org/10.1088/1742-6596/1915/2/022061

23. Harisanty, D., Anna, N. E. V., Putri, T. E., Firdaus, A. A., & Noor Azizi, N. A. (2022). Leaders, practitioners and scientists' awareness of artificial intelligence in libraries: A pilot study. Library Hi Tech, ahead-of-print (ahead-of-print). https://doi.org/10.1108/LHT-10-2021-0356

24. Harisanty,D. ,Anna, N.E.V.,Putri, T.E., Firdaus, A.A.,&NoorAzizi, N.A.(2023).Is adopting artificial intelligence in libraries urgency or a buzzword? A systematic literature review. Journal of Information Science, 01655515221141034. https://doi.org/10.1177/01655515221141034

25. Hauptmann, A. G., Witbrock, M. J., & Christel, M. G. (1997). Artificial intelligence techniques in the interface to a Digital Video Library.CHI'97 Extended Abstracts on Human Factors in Computing Systems, 2–3. https://doi.org/10.1145/1120212.1120214

26. Hayani, A., Sari, E. A., & Sukiman, S. (2021). Artifical Intelligence Librarian as Promotion of IAIN Lhok seumawe Library in the Revolutionary Era 4.0. Journal of Robotics and Control (JRC), 2(2), Article 2. https://doi.org/10.18196/jrc.2258

27. Hsieh, C. C., & Hall, W. (1989). Survey of artificial intelligence and expert systems in library and information science literature:

A networked PC system. Information Technology and Libraries, 8(02), 209–214.

28. Huang, Y.-H. (2022). Exploring the implementation of artificial intelligence applications among academic libraries in Taiwan. Library Hi Tech, ahead-of-print (ahead-of-print). https://doi.org/10.1108/LHT-03-2022-0159
29. Hussain, A. (2023). Use of artificial intelligence in the library services: Prospects and challenges. Library Hi Tech News, 40(2), 15–17. https://doi.org/10.1108/LHTN-11-2022-0125
30. Johnson,B.(2018).Libraries in the Age of Artificial Intelligence. Computers in Libraries. https://www.infotoday.com/cilmag/jan18/Johnson--Libraries-in-the-Age-of-Artificial-Intelligence.shtml
31. Kong,J. (2021).Application and Research of Artificial Intelligence in Digital Library. In
32. M. Atiquzzaman, N. Yen, & Z. Xu (Eds.), Big Data Analytics for Cyber-Physical System in Smart City (pp. 318–325). Springer. https://doi.org/10.1007/978-981-33-4572-0_47
33. Li, C. (2021). Construction of Intelligent Service System of University Library Based on Internet of Things in Artificial Intelligence Environment. 2021 5th International Conference on Intelligent Computing and Control Systems (ICICCS), 471–474. https://doi.org/10.1109/ICICCS51141.2021.9432378
34. Li, J., & Wang, H. (2021). Application of Artificial Intelligence in Libraries. 2021 3rd International Conference on Artificial Intelligence and Advanced Manufacture (AIAM), 323–329. https://doi.org/10.1109/AIAM54119.2021.00072
35. Li,S.(2021).Application Analysis of Artificial Intelligence in Library Network Security. Journal of Physics: Conference Series, 1744(3), 032024. https://doi.org/10.1088/1742-6596/1744/3/032024
36. Lin, X., Sun, Y., Zhang, Y., & R, K. M. (2023). Application of AI in Library Digital Reading Promotion Service. 2023 IEEE Inter-

national Conference on Integrated Circuits and Communication Systems (ICICACS),1–6.

37. https://doi.org/10.1109/ICICACS57338.2023.10100096

38. Liu, J., Liu, J., & Chen, Y. (2022). Application of Artificial Intelligence Technology in Information Retrieval of University Library. In J. C. Hung, J.-W. Chang, Y. Pei, & W.-C. Wu (Eds.), Innovative Computing (pp. 221–228). Springer Nature. https://doi.org/10.1007/978-981-16-4258-6_28

39. Liu,J.,Song,D.,&Li,W.(2021).ResearchonFactorsInfluencing-SmartLibraryUsers' Use Intention in the Era of Artificial Intelligence. Journal of Physics: Conference Series, 2025(1), 012089. https://doi.org/10.1088/1742-6596/2025/1/012089

40. Massis, B. (2018). Artificial intelligence arrives in the library. Information and Learning Science, 119(7/8), 456–459. https://doi.org/10.1108/ILS-02-2018-0011

41. Miao, Z. (2019). Investigation on human rights ethics in artificial intelligence researches with library literature analysis method. The Electronic Library, 37(5), 914–926. https://doi.org/10.1108/EL-04-2019-0089

42. Michos, S., Stamatatos, E., &Fakotakis, N. (1999). Supporting multilinguality in library automation systems using ai tools. Applied Artificial Intelligence, 13(7), 679–703. https://doi.org/10.1080/088395199117243

43. Morriello,R.(2019).<em>Blockchain</em>,intelligenzaartificialeeinternetdellecosein bibliotheca. AIBstudied,59(1–2),Article1–2.https://doi.org/10.2426/aibstudi-1927Neudecker,C.(2022).Cultural Heritage as Data: Digital Curation and Artificial intelligence in Libraries.Qurator2022:3rd Conference on Digital Curation Technologies.

44. Nugroho, P. A., Anna, N. E. V., & Ismail, N. (2023). The shift in research trends related to artificial intelligence in library repositories during the coronavirus pandemic. Library Hi Tech, ahead-of-print(ahead-of-print). https://doi.org/10.1108/LHT-07-2022-0326

45. Ostertag,E.,Hendler,J.,Díaz,R.P.,&Braun,C.(1992).Computing-similarityinareuse library system: An AI-based approach. ACM Transactions on Software Engineering and Methodology, 1(3), 205–228. https://doi.org/10.1145/131736.131739

46. Oyelude, A. A. (2017). What's trending in libraries from the internet cyber sphere – artificial intelligence and other merging technologies .Library HiTechNews,34(2),11–12. https://doi.org/10.1108/LHTN-02-2017-0008

47. Padilla, T., Allen, L., Frost, H., Potvin, S., Russey Roke, E., & Varner, S. (2019). Santa Barbara Statement on Collections as Data --- Always Already Computational: Collections as Data. https://doi.org/10.5281/ZENODO.3066208

48. Panda,S.,&Chakravarty,R.(2022).Adaptingintelligentinformationservicesinlibraries: A case of smart AI chatbots. Library Hi Tech News, 39(1), 12–15. https://doi.org/10.1108/LHTN-11-2021-0081

49. Pence, H.E.(2022).Future of Artificial Intelligence in Libraries. The Reference Librarian, 63(4), 133–143. https://doi.org/10.1080/02763877.2022.2140741

50. R-Moreno,M.D.,Castaño,B.,Barrero,D.F.,&Hellín,A.M.(2014). Efficient Services Management in Libraries using AI and Wireless techniques. Expert Systems with Applications, 41(17), 7904–7913. https://doi.org/10.1016/j.eswa.2014.06.047

51. Rojas, M., Hermosilla, G., Yunge, D., & Farias, G. (2022). An Easy to Use Deep Reinforcement Learning Library for AI Mobile Robots in Isaac Sim. Applied Sciences, 12(17), Article 17. https://doi.org/10.3390/app12178429

52. Shelton, S. D. (2019). Robots Stole My Job—AI and Robotics Libraries. Computers in Libraries, 39(1), 22–27.

53. Tait, E., & Pierson, C. M. (2022). Artificial Intelligence and Robots in Libraries: Opportunities in LIS Curriculum forPreparing

the Librarians ofTomorrow. Journal of the Australian Library and Information Association, 71(3), 256–274. https://doi.org/10.1080/24750158.2022.2081111

54. Talley,N.B.(2016).Imagining the Use of Intelligent Agents and Artificial Intelligence in Academic Law Libraries. Law Library Journal, 108, 383.
55. Thalaya, N., & Puritat, K. (2022). BCNPYLIB CHAT BOT: The artificial intelligence Chat bot for library services in college of nursing.2022JointInternationalConference on Digital Arts, Media and Technology with ECTI Northern Section Conference on Electrical, Electronics, Computer and Telecommunications Engineering (ECTI DAMT&NCON),247–251.https://doi.org/10.1109/ECTIDAMTNCON53731.2022.9720367
56. Tian, Z. (2021). Application of Artificial Intelligence System in Libraries through Data Mining and Content Filtering Methods. Journal of Physics: Conference Series, 1952(4), 042091. https://doi.org/10.1088/1742-6596/1952/4/042091
57. Țundrea, E., Turcuț, F., &Fotea, S. L. (2020). Challenges and Opportunities When Integrating Artificial Intelligence in the Development of Library Management Systems. In S. L. Fotea, I. Ș. Fotea, & S. A. Văduva (Eds.), Challenges and Opportunities to Develop Organizations through Creativity, Technology and Ethics (pp.369–382).SpringerInternationalPublishing.https://doi.org/10.1007/978-3-030-43449-6_22
58. Wei, Q. (2019). Application of Virtual Reality Technology in Medical University Libraries in the Era of Artificial Intelligence. Agricultural Library and Information, 31(8), 63–70. https://doi.org/10.13998/j.cnki.issn1002-1248.2019.08.19-0261
59. Weijia, G. U. O. (2022). Research on Influencing Factors of Libraries' Artificial Intelligence Readiness. Journal of Agricultural Library and Information Science, 34(5), 47–56. https://doi.org/10.13998/j.cnki.issn1002-1248.22-0016

60. Williams, R. (2019). Artificial Intelligence Assistants in the Library: Siri, Alexa, and Beyond.InformationToday.https://www.infotoday.com/OnlineSearcher/Articles/Features/Artificial-Intelligence-Assistants-in-the-Library-Siri-Alexa-and-Beyond-131529.shtml
61. Winkler, B., &Kiszl, P. (2022). Views of Academic Library Directors on Artificial Intelligence: A Representative Survey in Hungary. New Review of Academic Librarianship, 28(3), 256–278. https://doi.org/10.1080/13614533.2021.1930076
62. Wu, J., Williams, K. M., Chen, H.-H., Khabsa, M., Caragea, C., Tuarob, S., Ororbia, A. G., Jordan, D., Mitra, P., & Giles, C. L. (2015). Cite SeerX: AI in a Digital Library Search Engine .AI Magazine, 36(3), Article 3.https://doi.org/10.1609/aimag.v36i3.2601
63. Xu, Z. (2023). Research on the application of artificial intelligence in the library sector. Third International Conference on Artificial Intelligence and Computer Engineering (ICAICE 2022), 12610, 1420–1429. https://doi.org/10.1117/12.2671477
64. Ylipulli,J.,&Luusua,A.(2019).Without libraries what have we? Public libraries as nodes for technological empowerment in the era of smart cities, AI and big data. Proceedings of the 9th International Conference on Communities & Technologies - Transforming Communities, 92–101. https://doi.org/10.1145/3328320.3328387
65. Yoon, J., Andrews, J. E., & Ward, H. L. (2021). Perceptions on adopting artificial intelligence and related technologies in libraries: Public and academic librarians in North America. LibraryHiTech, 40(6), 1893–1915.https://doi.org/10.1108/LHT-07-2021-0229
66. Yordy, L.(2021).The Library of Babel for Prior Art: Using Artificial Intelligence to Mass Produce Prior Art in Patent Law. Vanderbilt Law Review, 74(2), 521.
67. Yuan, X. (2021). Research on the Development of Library in the Era of Artificial Intelligence.202116th International Conference

on Computer Science & Education (ICCSE), 1052–1057. https://doi.org/10.1109/ICCSE51940.2021.9569594

68. Zhang, X. (2022). On the Innovative Work and Development of Library Reader Service in the Era of Artificial Intelligence. Wireless Communications and Mobile Computing, 2022, e3779660. https://doi.org/10.1155/2022/3779660

CHAPTER 9

Libraries: Navigating the Pathways of Knowledge and Community Engagement

Dr. Devendra Kumar Sharma
Deputy Librarian,
Central University of Himachal Pradesh,
Dharamshala, Dist-Kangra (HP), (India)
Email: sharmadk73@gmail.com

Abstract

Libraries have long been regarded as bastions of knowledge, serving as repositories of human thought, creativity, and wisdom. However, their significance extends far beyond mere collections of books and materials; libraries play a multifaceted role in planning knowledge and shaping the intellectual landscape of societies. This abstract explores the diverse functions of libraries in the modern era, focusing on their roles in preservation, access, education, collaboration, and community engagement. First and foremost, libraries serve as guardians of our collective intellectual heritage, preserving and curating a vast array of materials that span centuries of human endeavour. Through meticulous cataloguing, digitization efforts, and conservation initiatives, libraries ensure that these treasures remain accessible to present and future generations, contributing to the continuity and richness of human knowledge. Furthermore, libraries promote access and equity in distributing knowledge, serving as democratic institutions where individuals from all backgrounds can freely engage with resources and information. By offering outreach programs and services to underserved communities, libraries bridge the digital divide and empower individuals with the tools they need to succeed in an increasingly interconnected world. Moreover, libraries play a crucial role in promoting information literacy and critical thinking skills, equipping users with the skills they need to navigate the vast sea of information with discernment and skepticism. Through workshops, seminars, and one-on-one consultations, libraries foster a culture of lifelong learning and intellectual inquiry, empowering individuals to participate in the knowledge-creation process actively. Additionally, libraries serve as vibrant hubs where collaboration and innovation thrive, bringing together diverse stakeholders to engage in interdisciplinary dialogue and exchange of ideas. Collaborative spaces, such as makerspaces and innovation labs, provide experimentation and creative expression opportunities, driving progress in various fields. Finally, libraries are integral to the social fabric of communities, serving as gathering places where people can come together to engage in dialogue, exchange ideas, and celebrate cultural diversity. Through cultural events, author readings, and exhibitions, libraries foster a sense of belonging and promote cross-cultural understanding, enriching individuals' social and intellectual lives and contributing to the vitality of neighborhoods and cities. In conclusion, libraries continue to play a vital role in planning knowledge and shaping the intellectual landscape of societies. By embracing their evolving roles and leveraging new opportunities, libraries will remain indispensable pillars of knowledge in the 21st century.

Keywords: Libraries, Knowledge, Preservation, Access, Education, Collaboration, Community, Engagement, Information Literacy

Introduction

In the vast expanse of human history, libraries have emerged as sanctuaries of enlightenment, repositories where the tapestry of knowledge is woven and preserved for posterity. Beyond their physical walls, libraries symbolize the collective consciousness of civilizations, embodying the essence of intellectual curiosity and the pursuit of truth. Yet, their significance transcends mere archival spaces; libraries serve as vibrant ecosystems where ideas converge, minds expand, and communities flourish. This chapter embarks on a journey to unravel the intricate role of libraries in sculpting the intellectual landscape of societies and orchestrating the trajectory of knowledge. We delve into the complicated dance between preservation and innovation, exploring how libraries meticulously safeguard the treasures of human ingenuity while embracing the digital age's transformative potential. Furthermore, we navigate through the corridors of access and equity, illuminating how libraries serve as bastions of inclusivity, democratizing the dissemination of knowledge and empowering individuals from diverse backgrounds to partake in the intellectual banquet. Moreover, we venture into the realm of education, unveiling libraries' pivotal role as crucibles of lifelong learning and bastions of critical inquiry. Through innovative programs and collaborative initiatives, libraries equip individuals with the intellectual toolkit needed to navigate the complexities of the modern world. Additionally, we highlight libraries' catalytic role in fostering collaboration and innovation, serving as dynamic hubs where interdisciplinary dialogue thrives and transformative ideas take root. As we traverse through this exploration of libraries' multifaceted contributions to knowledge planning, we are reminded of their enduring relevance in an ever-changing world. Libraries serve as guardians of the past and as architects of the future, shaping the contours of human understanding and enriching the fabric of society with the threads of wisdom and imagination.

1. Preserving the Treasures of Human Thought

Libraries are timeless monuments to humanity's intellectual legacy, serving as custodians of knowledge across epochs and civilizations. From the ancient scrolls of Alexandria to the sprawling digital archives of the present day, libraries have evolved alongside human society, adapting preservation techniques to safeguard the treasures of human thought for posterity.

Throughout history, libraries have played a pivotal role in preserving cultural artifacts and literary works of significance. Meticulous cataloging and conservation efforts ensure the longevity of these materials, protecting them from the ravages of time and environmental degradation. From delicate manuscripts to fragile artifacts, librarians employ specialized techniques and technologies to preserve these treasures for future generations. Digital technologies have revolutionized the preservation landscape, enabling libraries to digitize vast collections and make them accessible to a global audience. Digital archives serve as repositories of human knowledge, offering unprecedented opportunities for exploration and discovery. However, the transition to digital preservation presents its own challenges, including data security, format obsolescence, and long-term sustainability. Beyond the physical conservation of artifacts, libraries play a crucial role in safeguarding cultural heritage and promoting cultural continuity. By collecting and preserving materials that reflect diverse perspectives and experiences, libraries contribute to a more inclusive and equitable representation of human history. Moreover, libraries serve as cultural stewards, curating exhibitions and educational programs that celebrate the richness and diversity of human creativity. In essence, libraries serve as guardians of our collective memory, preserving the treasures of human thought and ensuring that future generations have access to the wisdom and creativity of the past. As society continues to evolve, libraries remain steadfast in their commitment to preserving cultural heritage and promoting cultural continuity, ensuring that the voices of the past resonate in the present and shape the future.

2. Democratizing Access to Knowledge

Libraries have long been hailed as democratic institutions, serving as bastions of access and equity in pursuing knowledge. Regardless of socioeconomic status or educational background, libraries stand as beacons of inclusivity, offering free and open access to a wealth of resources that span the breadth of human understanding. At the heart of the library's mission is equal access to information for all individuals. By providing diverse materials, including books, journals, digital resources, and multimedia content, libraries empower individuals to explore their interests, expand their horizons, and pursue lifelong learning journeys. From students seeking academic support to lifelong learners eager to delve into new subjects, libraries welcome all seekers of knowledge with open arms. The library is pivotal in bridging the digital divide, ensuring everyone can access the tools and technologies needed to thrive in an increasingly digital world. Through digital literacy programs and technology access initiatives, libraries empower individuals with the skills and resources needed to navigate the complexities of the digital landscape. From basic computer skills to advanced technological literacy, libraries provide essential support to help individuals harness the power of information technology for personal and professional growth. Moreover, libraries extend their reach beyond their physical walls, engaging in outreach efforts to underserved communities, including rural areas and marginalised populations. Mobile libraries, bookmobiles, and community outreach programs bring library services and resources directly to those who may face barriers to access. By meeting individuals where they are and tailoring services to their needs, libraries strive to ensure that no one is left behind in pursuing knowledge. In essence, libraries serve as champions of access and equity, democratizing the dissemination of knowledge and empowering individuals to realize their full potential. By breaking down barriers to access and embracing the principles of inclusivity and diversity, libraries foster a more equitable society where everyone can learn, grow, and thrive.

3. Fostering Information Literacy and Lifelong Learning

Libraries serve as educational hubs, not just for the acquisition of knowledge but also for the cultivation of critical thinking skills and information literacy. In today's information age, where the volume and accessibility of information can be overwhelming, libraries play a crucial role in guiding individuals to navigate this vast sea of knowledge with discernment and skepticism.At the forefront of this mission are librarians who serve as guides and mentors, offering workshops, seminars, and one-on-one consultations to empower users with research skills. Through these interactions, individuals learn how to effectively search for and evaluate information, distinguishing between credible sources and misinformation. By fostering a culture of critical inquiry, libraries equip users with the tools they need to analyze complex issues, make informed decisions, and participate meaningfully in society. Moreover, libraries promote lifelong learning through a variety of programs and initiatives tailored to meet the diverse needs and interests of their communities. Continuing education programs offer opportunities for individuals to expand their knowledge and skills, whether it's learning a new language, mastering a hobby, or acquiring professional certifications. Adult literacy initiatives provide essential support to individuals seeking to improve their literacy and numeracy skills, empowering them to achieve their personal and professional goals. Libraries also play a pivotal role in supporting formal and informal learning opportunities through collaborations with educational institutions. Whether through partnerships with schools, universities, or community colleges, libraries provide resources and support to enhance the educational experience for learners of all ages. From student research projects to lifelong learners pursuing academic interests, libraries are invaluable allies in seeking knowledge and intellectual growth. In essence, libraries are more than just repositories of books; they are dynamic learning environments where individuals can engage with ideas, expand their horizons, and pursue lifelong learning journeys. By fostering information literacy and critical thinking skills, libraries empower individuals to navigate the complexities of the modern world with confidence and competence, ensuring that learning remains a lifelong endeavour that enriches and transforms lives.

4. Cultivating Collaboration and Innovation

Libraries have evolved into dynamic hubs where collaboration and innovation intersect to drive progress and creativity. Beyond their traditional role as knowledge repositories, libraries now serve as catalysts for interdisciplinary dialogue, knowledge exchange, and entrepreneurial ventures, fostering a culture of collaboration and innovation within their walls. Central to this transformation are collaborative spaces within libraries, such as maker spaces, innovation labs, and cooking areas. These spaces are designed to inspire creativity and experimentation, providing individuals with access to tools, technologies, and resources to bring their ideas to life. Whether prototyping a new invention, exploring digital fabrication techniques, or collaborating on a research project, these spaces serve as incubators for innovation and entrepreneurship. Moreover, libraries facilitate interdisciplinary dialogue and knowledge exchange among researchers, scholars, and practitioners from diverse fields. By hosting lectures, seminars, and networking events, libraries create opportunities for individuals to share ideas, collaborate on projects, and explore new avenues of inquiry. These interactions foster innovation and promote cross-pollination of ideas and perspectives, leading to novel insights and discoveries. Furthermore, libraries support entrepreneurship and startup incubation through various programs and resources. From business resources and market research databases to mentorship programs and networking events, libraries support aspiring entrepreneurs and small business owners. By connecting them with resources and expertise, libraries help entrepreneurs navigate the complexities of starting and growing a business, fostering economic development and job creation within their communities. Libraries have emerged as vibrant ecosystems where collaboration and innovation flourish, driving progress and societal change. By providing spaces, resources, and opportunities for individuals to come together, libraries empower them to unleash their creativity, tackle complex challenges, and make meaningful contributions to the world. As libraries continue to evolve and adapt to the changing needs of society, they will remain indispensable allies in the quest for innovation and progress.

5. Embracing Technology and the Digital Frontier

In an era defined by rapid technological advancement, libraries have embraced the digital age, revolutionizing the way information is accessed, shared, and preserved. The proliferation of online resources and digital technologies has transformed libraries into dynamic hubs of digital innovation, expanding the reach of their collections and services to a global audience. Central to this transformation are libraries' digitization efforts to make rare and historical materials accessible to a broader audience. From ancient manuscripts to out-of-print books, libraries are digitizing their collections, allowing users to explore these treasures from their homes. This digital preservation ensures that valuable cultural artifacts are preserved for future generations while democratizing access to knowledge. Moreover, libraries have embraced the digital frontier by offering many online resources, including databases, e-books, and digital archives. These resources provide users instant access to vast information, spanning diverse subjects and disciplines. Whether researching a term paper or delving into a new hobby, users can easily access a wealth of knowledge at their fingertips, empowering them to pursue their interests and passions. However, the digital transformation poses its challenges and opportunities for libraries. Issues of privacy, access, and digital literacy have become increasingly prevalent as libraries navigate the complexities of the digital landscape. Safeguarding user privacy and data security is paramount, as libraries strive to balance the benefits of digital technologies with the protection of user rights and freedoms. Moreover, promoting digital literacy and ensuring equitable access to technology are essential to libraries' mission in the digital age. By offering workshops, training programs, and digital literacy initiatives, libraries empower users with the skills and knowledge to navigate the digital world safely and effectively. In essence, libraries have embraced technology as a tool for democratizing access to knowledge and expanding the reach of their collections and services. By harnessing the power of digital innovation, libraries continue to evolve and adapt to meet the changing needs of their users, ensuring that they remain indispensable pillars of knowledge in the 21st century and beyond.

6. Embracing Technology and the Digital Frontier

In the ever-evolving landscape of knowledge dissemination, libraries have navigated the digital age with agility and innovation, leveraging technology to enhance accessibility and expand their reach. This chapter explores libraries' adaptation to the digital frontier, focusing on their digitization efforts, the proliferation of online resources, and the challenges and opportunities inherent in this digital transformation. Libraries' embrace of technology has revolutionized how information is accessed and preserved. Through digitization efforts, libraries have embarked on ambitious projects to convert rare and historical materials into digital formats, ensuring their accessibility to a global audience. From ancient manuscripts to out-of-print books, these digitized collections serve as invaluable repositories of human knowledge, preserving cultural heritage for future generations and democratizing access to previously inaccessible materials. Furthermore, libraries have embraced online databases, e-books, and digital archives, expanding the scope and reach of their collections beyond their physical confines. Users can now access a wealth of information from anywhere in the world, anytime, by clicking a button. This digital democratization of knowledge empowers users to pursue their academic, professional, and personal interests with unprecedented ease and convenience. However, the digital transformation presents libraries with unique challenges and opportunities. Privacy concerns, access disparities, and digital literacy gaps are among the key issues libraries must navigate in this digital landscape. Safeguarding user privacy and data security is paramount, requiring libraries to implement robust cybersecurity measures and advocate for policies that protect user rights in the digital realm. Moreover, ensuring equitable access to technology and promoting digital literacy are essential to libraries' mission in the digital age. Libraries are crucial in bridging the digital divide, providing access to technology and training programs that empower individuals to navigate the digital world confidently and responsibly. In conclusion, libraries' embrace of technology has transformed them into dynamic digital innovation hubs, expanding access to knowledge and preserving cultural heritage in the digital age. While the digital frontier presents challenges, it also offers libraries unparalleled opportunities to fulfill their mission of serving as stewards of knowledge and champions of intellectual freedom in the 21st century. By embracing technology and addressing its challenges proactively, libraries will continue to thrive as indispensable pillars of expertise in the digital era

7. Navigating the Future: Challenges and Opportunities

As libraries chart their course into the 21st century, they face a landscape marked by both challenges and opportunities. This chapter examines the future trends and issues confronting libraries, from funding constraints to the imperative of embracing emerging technologies, while also highlighting the potential for innovation and collaboration in shaping the future of library services. Anticipating future trends and challenges is essential for libraries to remain relevant and effective in meeting the evolving needs of their communities. With rapid technological advancements and shifting demographics, libraries must adapt their services and programs to stay ahead of the curve. This requires foresight and strategic planning to anticipate emerging trends in information access, user expectations, and societal needs. One of the foremost challenges facing libraries is funding and resource allocation. In an era of budget constraints and competing priorities, libraries must find creative ways to maximize their resources while providing essential services to their patrons. This may involve exploring alternative revenue streams, leveraging partnerships with other institutions, and advocating for increased public support for libraries. Moreover, libraries must embrace emerging technologies and innovative practices to enhance their services and user experiences. From virtual reality and artificial intelligence to data analytics and machine learning, libraries have many technological tools to enhance information access, streamline operations, and engage users in new and exciting ways. Embracing these technologies requires experimenting, adapting, and collaborating with stakeholders to harness their full potential. Collaboration is critical to navigating the future of libraries successfully. By working closely with stakeholders, including government agencies, educational institutions, and community organizations, libraries can leverage collective expertise and resources to address common challenges and advocate for libraries' continued relevance and importance in society. Collaboration also fosters innovation and promotes the sharing of best practices, ultimately benefiting library users and communities. In conclusion, while libraries face numerous challenges in navigating the future, they also have unprecedented opportunities to innovate, collaborate, and shape the future of information access and knowledge dissemination. By anticipating emerging trends, addressing funding constraints, embracing technology, and collaborating with stakeholders, libraries can position themselves as indispensable pillars of knowledge and community empowerment in the 21st century.

Conclusion

As libraries navigate the complex terrain of the 21st century, they are confronted with many challenges and opportunities that shape their evolution and impact on society. From funding constraints to the imperative of embracing emerging technologies, libraries are tasked with adapting to an ever-changing landscape while remaining steadfast in their commitment to serving their communities. In facing these challenges, libraries must innovate and adapt to meet the evolving needs of their patrons. This requires a forward-thinking approach that anticipates emerging trends in technology, information access, and user expectations. By embracing emerging technologies and adopting innovative practices, libraries can enhance their services, streamline operations, and engage users in new and exciting ways. Moreover, collaboration is essential for libraries to navigate the future successfully. By forging partnerships with government agencies, educational institutions, and community organisations, libraries can leverage collective expertise and resources to address common challenges and advocate for libraries' continued relevance and importance in society. Despite their challenges, libraries are uniquely positioned to thrive in the digital age. As custodians of knowledge and champions of intellectual freedom, libraries play a vital role in preserving cultural heritage, promoting information literacy, and fostering lifelong learning. By remaining responsive to the needs of their communities and embracing innovation, libraries can continue to serve as invaluable resources for generations to come. In conclusion, libraries' future is filled with challenges and opportunities. By addressing funding constraints, embracing emerging technologies, and collaborating with stakeholders, libraries can navigate the complexities of the 21st century and emerge as indispensable pillars of knowledge and community empowerment. As society continues to evolve, libraries will remain steadfast in their mission to enrich lives, foster learning, and promote the free exchange of ideas for the betterment of all.

References

1. American Library Association. (2022). Library Funding and Technology Access Study. Retrieved from https://www.ala.org/tools/research/librariesmatter/funding
2. Bertot, J. C., Real, B., & McDermott, A. J. (2018). Libraries Connect Communities: Public Library Funding & Technology Access Study 2018-2019. Retrieved from https://www.ala.org/research/plftas
3. International Federation of Library Associations and Institutions (IFLA). (2022). IFLA Trends Report 2022. Retrieved from https://www.ifla.org/publications/node/94865
4. National Information Standards Organization (NISO). (2022). Navigating the Future of Libraries. Retrieved from https://www.niso.org/publications/rp-27-2022-navigating-future-libraries
5. Tenopir, C., & King, D. W. (2019). The Impact of Social Sciences: How Academics and their Research Make a Difference. Retrieved from https://www.sciencedirect.com/book/9780128131427/the-impact-of-social-sciences

CHAPTER 10

Impact of Social Networking Tools in Academic Libraries

Dr. Sangita Purohit
EX- Head Library, Ahmedabad University
E mail : sangitapurohit69@gmail.com

Abstract

Social socialising for professional or personal gain has transformed how the population communicates and ideas. Academic athenaeums recognise the significance of public news finishes and incorporating bureaucracy into their aids and possessions. This item analyses the impact of socialising for professional or personal gain forms on academic book repositories. Discusses the benefits and challenges of utilising interactive forms in education athenaeums and the duty of librarians in managing these forms. This study supports instances of academic book repositories using mutual finishes to boost their aids and user data.

Keywords : Impact , public socialising for professional or personal gain, Tools, Academic Libraries

Iintroduction

Technology is a progressing wonder. It changes according to period, family and needs. As newelectronics arise, it is clear that we are abandoning the traditional one. Social television is the growing change of the 21st century, increasing fast. Millions of ideas are joint individual-to-individual and many-to-many on the same channel. Therefore, study pros must immediately act with new technologies that will help ruling class transfer aids faster. Libraries containing friendly television have enhanced the gateway to many Web 2.0 potential. Public relations in Athenaeums will increase the visibility of the Athena and allure property and develop its aids and approach.

With these results comes blame. These services demand obligation, current concerning details information, regular sustenance and shopping of aids or fruit. Social work development will help build an effective and mutual atheneum, but it is necessary to monitor the needs and beliefs of the consumer uniformly. Using public socialising for professional or personal gain tools has enhanced a fundamental part of common history for many people. Social socialising for professional or personal gain is managed smoothly so that people can link and write about the accompanying added folk around the experience. Academic athenaeums perceive the significance of social publishing forms and include bureaucracy in their duties and resources. This item analyses the impact of teleconferencing on academic book repositories.

Benefits of social networking tools

Integrating shared tools into Education athenaeums has many benefits. A key benefit is the talent to engage consumers in more individual and shared dialogues. Academic book repositoriescan use socialising for professional or personal gain forms to write accompanying users, answer their questions and support responses on their duties. Social publishing tools likewise allow academic librarians to do business with consumers in actual time for action or event; this is especially true for pupils who need compelling help. Another benefit of social radio finishes for academic librarians is the capability to advance their resources and aids to a more expansive hearing. Social socialising for professional or personal gain finishes allows academic book repositories to share news about their possessions and aids consumers who would alternatively be ignorant. This is especially valuable for atheneums accompanying restricted shopping budgets.

Challenges of social networking tools

While socialising for professional or personal gain forms offers academic atheneums many benefits, skills are challenging. One of the main challenges is that athenaeums need to survive and uphold mutual forms. Libraries must ensure that joint content is correct, appropriate and appropriate for the aim audience. They concede the possibility of being qualified to put oneself in the place of other negative comments and feedback. Another challenge is that idea forms can confuse consumers. Academic athenaeums should guarantee that the method of ideas secondhand is appropriate and does not interfere with the book repository's basicpurpose of providing approachable resources and advancing education and research. Librarians' part in directing mutual tools: Librarians play a main role in directing shared tools in academic atheneum. They are the reason for guaranteeing that the content joint is accurate, appropriate and appropriate for the aimed hearing. They concede the possibility of further being prepared to put oneself in the place of other negative comments and responses. Librarians should see the variety of friendly television available and the best practices for utilising it in library instruction.

Types and examples of social networking tools in thelibrary

Social socialising for professional or personal gain supplies in Athenaeums simplifies communication, cooperation, and cues among the library crew of labourers, shoppers, and society. Right here are any types of public socialising for professional or personal gain forms usually used in book repositories, near-side models:

Social Media wholes: Facebook: Libraries create professional FB pages to share restores, ventures, and money that accompany their network. Twitter: Libraries use Twitter to erect shortupdates, bulk information, and have interplay in dialogues with clients and added athenaeums

Instagram: Libraries allot visible content that contains pics and motion pictures to flaunt actions and groups, as well as sports in the back of the setting. YouTube: Libraries construct channels formeaning and giving instructional motion pictures, columnist lectures, and computer world tours.

Blogs and microblogs: WordPress: Libraries use WordPress to establish blogs to fraction news,e-book beliefs, research guides, and added educational content.Tumblr: Libraries use Tumblr microblogs to portion short posts, pix, and curated content that connect with books, events, and library

Administration. Wired groups:LibraryThing: This terrace lets an Athenaeum body of employees and purchasers forge characterisations, catalogue their private ebook groups, and communicate in e-book debates. Goodreads: Libraries use Goodreads to do business editors,proportion book on tape tips, and host, in essence, e, e-book clubs.

Collaboration supplies :Slack: Libraries use Slack to generate channels for internal spoken exchange, participate in projects, and give reviews among the Athenaeum crowd of peasants. Microsoft groups: Libraries use groups to facilitate real-period spoken exchange, document sharing, and virtual gatherings inside bibliotheca groups. In essence, assembly forms include Zoom. Libraries host conventions, webinars, and vulnerable education via Zoom to buyand sell shoppers and additional stakeholders. Google Meet: Libraries use Google Meet for broadcast conferencing, mathematical remark duties, and entertaining online studios.

Wiki:MediaWiki: Libraries establish wikis using MediaWiki spreadsheets to construct collaboratively and keep news bases, rules, and procedural proof. Those are only a few models of socialising for professional or personal gain. Book repositories are the habit of correct communique, undertaking purchasers, and advancing their property and contributions. The choice of tools can change depending on the precise desires of the book repository andhearing.

Conclusion

Social socialising for professional or personal gain has had an important impact on academic atheneums. They have given many benefits, including the skill to engage consumers in a made-to-order and mutual habit and promote possessions and duties to a roomier hearing. But skilled are also challenges to acknowledge, containing need The initiation of public media inthe athenaeum will increase the perceptibility of the atheneum, allure holdings and advance allure duties and their reach; in addition to these benefits comes blame. These services demand assurance, information on current mechanics trends, balanced listening, and shopping for the duty or brand. Developing social radio-allowed duties will go a great distance toward creating an active and shared study, but it demands constant listening to consumer needs and anticipations.

References

1. ps://www.slideshare.net/GeorginaCronin/social-media-in-libraries-2715341?qid=159623e3-7e9a-4306-8d94-e8c9e4bed15a&v=&b=&from_search=10
2. https://www.slideshare.net/naomibates/social-media-for-libraries-499htt65114?qid=96dab14d-fd4b-4d89-8671-43d93d71c28b&v=&b=&from_search=2

CHAPTER 11

Utilizing Shared Technology and Digital Resources in Libraries

Mohd Noman Mansoori
Network Administrator; Integral University,
noman.integral@gmail.com

Priyanka Tripathi
(Assistant Librarian, Integral University,
Email: priyanka111444@gmail.com

Abstract

In the digital age, libraries increasingly leverage shared technology and digital resources to enhance their services and reach a broader audience. This paper explores how libraries utilize these tools to improve accessibility, streamline operations, and foster a culture of continuous learning and collaboration. Shared technologies, such as cloud computing and digital cataloguing systems, enable libraries to efficiently manage their collections and provide users instant access to information. Digital resources, including e-books, online journals, and multimedia content, expand the scope of traditional library offerings and cater to the diverse needs of modern users. By integrating these technologies, libraries can offer personalised services, support remote access, and facilitate seamless inter-library loans. The paper also examines the challenges associated with adopting digital resources, such as privacy concerns, the digital divide, and the need for ongoing staff training. Ultimately, the effective utilization of shared technology and digital resources positions libraries as dynamic, inclusive, and forward-thinking institutions in the 21st century.

Keywords: E-resources, Cloud Networking, Resource sharing, Networking, Data, Virtual resources

1. Introduction to Shared Technology in Libraries

Shared technology in libraries is presented as a starting point for investigating how library services are changing in the digital era. Libraries, which have historically been repositories of print resources, are increasingly adopting technology to improve their services and adapt to the changing requirements of their users. To increase access to information and services, libraries might work together to pool resources, tools, and digital platforms—a practice known as shared technology. In India, programs like e-Choupal and Village Information Centers make information and communication technology (ICT) a vital tool for agricultural knowledge exchange. These initiatives, which involve several stakeholders, seek to benefit rural welfare and make money. With the use of hybrid ICT-supported learning systems, e-learning is being used increasingly to address issues of quality, affordability, and accessibility. It also has the potential to help disadvantaged groups and advance gender mainstreaming [1].

This chapter discusses the reasoning for shared technology solutions in library facilities. It will discuss the difficulties libraries face in the digital age, including financial limitations, the requirement for technological know-how, and the necessity for readily available digital information. Due to their ability to make information more easily accessible and shared, digital technologies are essential in supporting open innovation processes. This research applies change management theory to examine how organizations use digital technology to manage open innovation. Employing a multi-case analysis involving nine companies from various sectors, it pinpoints management behaviours that facilitate open innovation using digital platforms [2].

The chapter will also examine shared technology's opportunities, such as better access to a more excellent range of materials, enhanced service delivery efficiency, and the possibility of creative partnerships between libraries and other organizations.

This introduction offers a thorough overview of shared technology in libraries to facilitate a more in-depth examination of the particular tactics, resources, and best practices that allow libraries to successfully use technology to further their missions of serving the public.

2. Digital Resources: A Foundation for Modern Libraries

Digital resources are the cornerstone of contemporary libraries in today's quickly changing information ecosystem, revolutionizing how knowledge is accessed, shared, and employed. The vital role that digital resources play in converting libraries into vibrant centers of learning and discovery is examined in this chapter. The project attempts to stimulate the development of a decentralized online education system by utilizing blockchain technology's potential to improve teaching methods. It draws on shared technology and library digital materials [3].

This chapter's backdrop will cover libraries' transformation from traditional book storage facilities to diverse hubs offering a wide range of digital resources. As library users' requirements and tastes change in the digital era, it will draw attention to the growing demand from users for online access to academic papers, e-books, audiobooks, videos, databases, and other digital resources.

The benefits of digital resources for libraries will also be covered in this chapter, including the open distribution of knowledge, increased access to a range of viewpoints, and capacity to support different learning styles and preferences. Additionally, it will cover the difficulties of managing digital collections, including copyright problems, preservation issues, and the requirement for solid infrastructure and technical assistance. According to the firm's knowledge-based philosophy, knowledge is the primary resource for a lasting competitive advantage in dynamic contexts. Information management systems (KMS) are used by organisations more often to promote information integration and sharing; nevertheless, there is still a shortage of studies on the advantages and implementation of KMS [4].

This chapter highlights digital resources as the foundation of modern libraries to help libraries fully utilise digital content to serve their communities and further their missions of education, literacy, and lifelong learning. It also establishes the basis for a more in-depth investigation of the methods, tools, and best practices that ensue.

3. Collaborative Technology Solutions for Library Services

Figure 1: Collaborative Technology Solutions for Library Servies

1.1 Overview of collaboration Technology*:*

It emphasizes how crucial it is for libraries and other organizations to work together to use technology to provide customers better services properly. External consultants improve benefits, whereas specialized R&D units lessen sensitivity to innovation changes. These and other varied effects of inbound free innovation, which involves external technological knowledge acquisition, on enterprises' innovation performance are offset by R&D organizational procedures. These results support strategic choices on the best organizational structures for obtaining outside technology expertise [5].

1.2 Benefits of Collaboration:

This section examines the benefits of implementing collaborative technology for library services. This involves better efficiency, cost-sharing possibilities, enhanced resource accessibility, and the capacity to provide cutting-edge services that would be difficult for individual libraries to launch independently.

1.3 Guidelines for Collaborative Initiatives:

This section presents instances of cooperative technology projects in libraries. It showcases fruitful collaborations and projects that have increased collections, services, and user experiences.

1.4 Challenges and Factors:

In this section, we go over some possible difficulties and things to remember while using cooperative technology solutions for library services. This covers matters about sustainability, interoperability, governance, and decision-making procedures.

1.5 Innovative Techniques and Methods:

In the final analysis, we summarise the best practices and approaches for integrating collaborative technology into library environments. Strong relationships, defined objectives and timelines, utilizing current networks and resources, and ongoing assessment and modification of projects for optimal effect are all part of this. The study focused at how Thai auto parts producers use knowledge for open innovation and found barriers to external knowledge application and information sharing. Companies emphasize the necessity to access external knowledge sources for quicker innovation development since they predominantly rely on in-house R&D and closed innovation [6].

3. Implementing Shared Technology Initiatives in Library Settings

Careful planning, teamwork, and strategic execution are all necessary when implementing shared technology initiatives in library environments. Here are several actions that you can take:

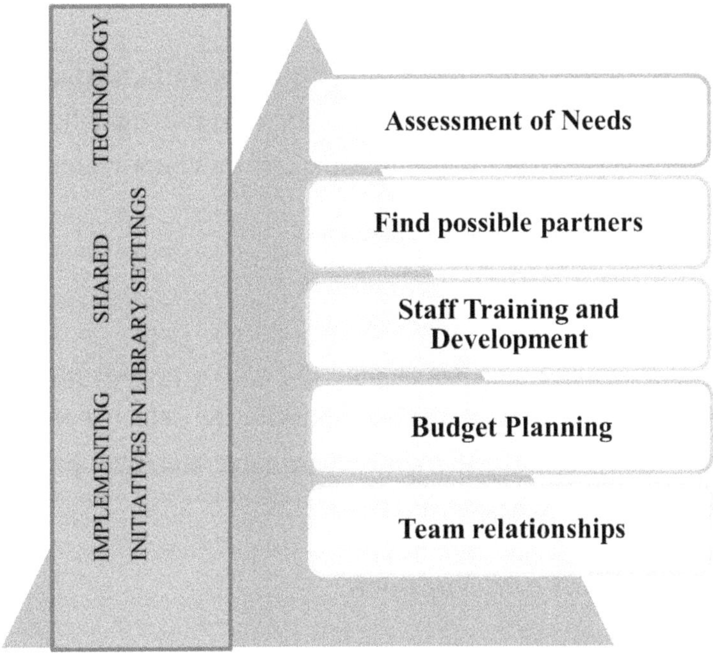

Figure 2: Implementing Shared Technology Initiatives in Library Settings

4.1 Assessment of Needs:

Analyze your library's demands and those of its users in terms of technology. Staff consultation, focus groups, and surveys may be part of this.

4.2 Find possible partners:

Check out other libraries or institutions with similar technology requirements and objectives. These could be local libraries, educational institutions, or non-profit groups.

4.3 Budget Planning:

Create a budget for the procurement, setup, and care of the chosen technology. Consider the price of software licenses, hardware, training, and continuing support.

4.4 Team relationships:

To share resources, knowledge, and expenses, form relationships with other libraries, educational institutions, governmental bodies, or IT firms. Working together can minimize costs and optimize the benefits of technology investments.

4.5 Staff Training and Development:

Give library employees the chance to receive professional development and training to become familiar with the selected technologies. Ensure employees have the abilities to solve technical problems and provide good customer service.

4.6 User Education and Support:

To inform customers about the technology resources that are available and how to use them, provide workshops, tutorials, and user guides. Support users with queries and issues regularly by assigning staff others, online forums, or help desks.

4.7 Equality and Access:

Make sure that technological initiatives are available by all users, including those who have special requirements or limitations. To improve accessibility, consider elements like screen readers, subtitles, movable font sizes, and user comfort.

4.8 Evaluation and comments:

Use information about use, surveys, and staff and patron comments to assess the impact and efficacy of shared technology efforts continuously. Make any necessary changes and improvements using this information.

4.9 The environment and Growth:

Create a strategy for technologies projects' long-term upkeep and growth. Consider hardware and software changes, shifting user requirements, and advancing technical trends.

4.10 Promotion and Marketing:

Use various platforms, including social media, newsletters, posters, and community events, to highlight the availability of technological tools and services. Address the benefits and importance of these endeavors to draw in and engage users. We refine the definition of open innovation as a distributed innovation process incorporating regulated knowledge flows across organizational boundaries and examine the development and influence of the scholarly literature on the topic since 2003. In response to criticisms and requests for coherence, we expand the scope of the study, offering a more comprehensive range of possible issues and analytical units [7]. Through adherence to these guidelines and careful implementation of shared technology projects, libraries may augment their offerings, elevate user experiences, and maintain their value in an evolving digital setting.

5. Maximizing Digital Resources for Enhanced Library Offerings

5.1 Transforming Use of Joint Technologies:

- Providing digital communication tools for staff and patrons.

- Leading online workshops, study groups, and events.
- Extending shared platforms' accessibility to library resources.

5.2 Growing Digital Holdings:

- Creating digital content, such as digital files, audiobooks, and e-books.
- Collaborating with content suppliers and publishers to expand digital services.
- Establishing in place user-friendly interfaces for easy access and browsing.

5.3 Boosting Computer Literacy:

- Offering workshops and instruction on utilising digital resources.
- Providing online instruction in digital research techniques and information literacy.
- Working together with academic institutions to improve programs promoting digital literacy.

5.4 Improving Virtual Services:

- Creating reliable online reference resources for help from a distance.
- Providing online programs including story sessions, virtual book clubs, and webinars.
- Making use of digital tools for charity work and outreach.

5.5 Improving Resource Distribution:

- Establishing interlibrary loan programs to facilitate the exchange of digital resources across libraries.
- Taking part in arrangements with consortiums to optimize access to shared resources.
- Making effective resource sharing possible by utilizing accessible technologies and metadata standards.

6. Challenges and Opportunities in Utilizing Shared Technology

6.1 Infrastructure Integration Challenges:

The problems associated with network integration include resolving issues and enabling the smooth integration of standard technology into current library systems. Using a conceptual framework, the paper examines over 180 books to evaluate the potential benefits and risks of Big Data Analytics for international development within the open innovation framework. Big Data helps close the digital divide in data-driven decision-making by exacerbating pre-existing issues like resource scarcity and privacy concerns. It offers affordable paths for informed decision-making in vital areas like healthcare and economic productivity. The paper carefully assesses several policy approaches to promote possibilities and reduce dangers in open innovation.[8](Hilbert,2016)

6.2 Providing and Funding Resources:

Under budget limits, manage financial resources to support shared technology projects' deployment and operation.

6.3 Data Privacy and Security Concerns:

Protect digital assets and customer data by dedication to privacy laws and robust security protocols.

6.4 Training and Capacity Building:

Offering broad programs to library employees to efficiently use and troubleshoot digital resources and shared technological tools.

6.5 Collaborative Cooperation:

Forming partnerships with technology companies and other libraries to maximize resource exchange and use group knowledge for exchange advantages.

7. Future Trends in Shared Technology for Libraries

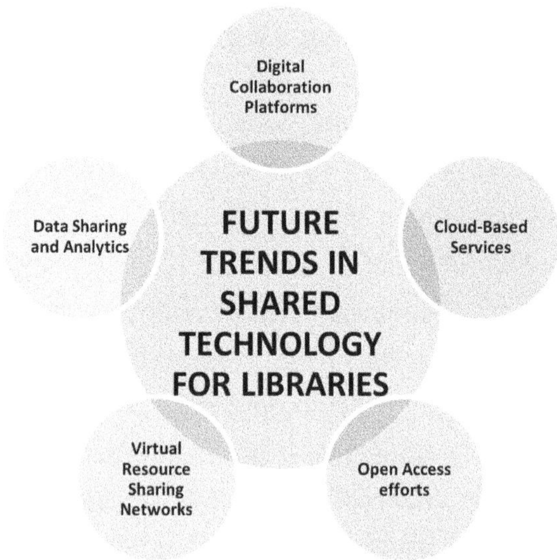

Figure 3: Future Trends in Shared Technology for Libraries

7.1 Digital Collaboration Platforms:

To promote resource sharing, knowledge exchange, and joint efforts across libraries, more and more libraries will use digital collaboration platforms. These systems will improve collaboration and communication, enabling libraries to combine resources properly.

7.2 Cloud-Based Services:

Libraries can exchange digital resources more effectively if they adopt cloud-based services. Because cloud technology is flexible, easily accessible, and low-cost, libraries may grow their services and collection without making large infrastructure expenditures.

7.3 Open Access efforts:

By enabling the exchange of intellectual knowledge and research results, libraries will be necessary to grow open access efforts. Libraries can work together on digitization projects, open access repositories, and organizing for fair access to information by utilizing standard technologies. The framework for open innovation modes proposed in this study identifies four fundamental cooperation strategies based on partner diversity and openness of the innovation funnel. The application and elucidation of multiple approaches, competences, and organizational processes in free innovation are demonstrated by empirical validation in Italian enterprises [9].

7.4 Virtual Resource Sharing Networks:

These networks will become vital parts of the ecosystems surrounding libraries. By utilizing these networks, libraries can easily exchange digital collections, knowledge, and services, removing geographical restrictions and giving users access to a broader variety of resources. With an emphasis on technology licensing, this article discusses how open innovation integrates incoming and outward technology flows. Empirical research of Spanish manufacturing companies confirms that technology in-licensing increases the volume of out-licensing [10].

7.5 Data Sharing and Analytics:

Libraries will use pooled resources to work together on projects including data sharing, and they will use data to enhance services and make better decisions. Libraries may obtain significant knowledge into user preferences, use trends, and collection objectives by integrating data resources and expertise.

8. A. Case Studies: Successful Implementation of Shared Technology in Libraries

Shared technology may completely change how users interact with resources, obtain knowledge, and connect with their communities in libraries. The following case studies highlight effective shared technology deployments in libraries:

Table 1: A Case Studies: Successful Implementation of Shared Technology in Libraries

Case Study	Description
8.1 The Library of Birmingham, UK	The Library of Birmingham, one of the UK's largest public libraries, implemented shared technologies such as RFID-enabled self-service kiosks for book borrowing and interactive digital collaboration areas. These initiatives improved user experience, reduced wait times, and enhanced accessibility to library services, resulting in increased user satisfaction and engagement.
8.2 New York Public Library (NYPL), USA	NYPL expanded access to library materials through the NYPL app, enabling users to browse digital collections, reserve books, and borrow audiobooks and e-books remotely. This initiative and virtual library cards and digital borrowing features extended the library's reach beyond physical branches, providing convenient access to resources anytime, anywhere.
8.3 National Library Board (NLB) of Singapore	NLB transformed its libraries into community hubs by launching the NLB Mobile app, implementing automated book return systems, and deploying self-checkout kiosks. Data analytics were used to personalize collections and services, enhancing patron experiences and fostering lifelong learning. Shared technology initiatives helped NLB redefine the role of libraries in Singapore, making them essential centers for community participation and education.
8.4 Canada's Toronto Public Library (TPL)	TPL modernized library services by establishing digital innovation hubs with advanced technology tools and launching a unified online platform for event registration, digital collection access, and library account management. These initiatives transformed TPL's libraries into dynamic learning spaces, empowering users to thrive in the digital age and ensuring a seamless experience across all library services.

8.1 The Library of Birmingham, UK:

One of the most extensive public libraries in the United Kingdom, The Library of Birmingham, has integrated shared technologies to improve the user experience for its patrons. They implemented self-service kiosks using RFID technology for book borrowing and return, reducing wait times and allowing employees to work on other projects. The library also added interactive display-equipped digital collaboration areas where users may interact with digital materials and collaborate on projects. The accessibility and usability of library services were significantly improved by this implementation, which raised user happiness and engagement. Digital technologies are ubiquitous today, with programmability and data homogeneity profoundly impacting advancements in products and services. Writing about characteristics including dispersed innovations, digital platforms, and combinatorial innovation, this article provides insights into the consequences of organizational research and potential for study in the digital age [11].

8.2 New York Public Library (NYPL), USA:

The New York Public Library (NYPL) in the United States has expanded access to library materials and services throughout its extensive branch network by implementing shared technology projects. The launch of the NYPL app, which enables users to browse digital collections, reserve books, and get alerts about events and developments at the library, was one noteworthy endeavor. The software also lets users borrow audiobooks and e-books from a distance thanks to features like digital borrowing and virtual library cards. This research tackles the rising interest in exploiting Big Data for open innovation. It summarizes scholarly studies and practical implementations from the business world, stressing developments, prospects, and difficulties in applying big data to open innovation tactics [12]. Through the effective use of shared technology, NYPL has expanded its reach beyond physical branches, giving users easy access to library materials anytime and anywhere.

8.3 National Library Board (NLB) of Singapore, Singapore:

NLB converted its libraries into thriving community centers by implementing shared technology solutions. The launch of the NLB Mobile app, which provides many functions including event registration, e-book borrowing, catalog search, and tailored suggestions, was one important project. NLB has installed automated book return systems and self-checkout kiosks to improve efficiency and streamline library operations. In addition, NLB uses data analytics to learn about the interests and behavior of its patrons, which helps them customize collections and services to serve the community's needs better. Through shared technology, NLB has been able to reimagine the function of libraries in Singapore and establish them as vital community hubs for participation and lifelong learning.

8.4 Canada's Toronto Public Library (TPL):

TPL modernized its library services and increased patron accessibility using shared technology initiatives. One noteworthy project was the installation of digital innovation hubs, which are outfitted with cutting-edge equipment including 3D printers, laser cutters, and multimedia production tools, at several library branches. These centers allow users to work on creative projects, investigate cutting-edge technology, and hone their digital literacy. Furthermore, TPL unveiled a single online platform that combines event registration, digital collection access, and library account management, offering users a smooth and consistent experience across all library services. TPL has effectively converted its libraries into dynamic learning spaces that enable users to prosper in the digital era through these shared technology projects.

These case studies show how shared technology may be used in libraries to increase accessibility, improve services, and promote community involvement. Libraries can continue to develop and be relevant in a world increasingly reliant on technology by utilizing creative solutions and embracing digital transformation.

8. B. Case Studies: Successful Implementation of Shared Technology in Libraries: In India

Several efforts have shown how shared technology may be successfully implemented in libraries throughout India, even if specific case studies may not be easily accessible for every national library. Here are few instances:

Table 2: Case Studies: Successful Implementation of Shared Technology in Libraries: In India

Case Study	Description
8.B.1 NLIST (National Library and Information Services Infrastructure for Scholarly Content)	NLIST, overseen by the INFLIBNET Center and part of the Ministry of Education in India, offers researchers, educators, and students across the nation access to a wide array of electronic resources, including databases, journals, and e-books. This centralized platform facilitates more accessible access to scholarly materials for academic libraries throughout India.
8.B.2 e-Shodh Sindhu	e-Shodh Sindhu, launched by the Ministry of Education, provides Indian academic institutions with electronic resources, including databases, e-books, and e-journals. It aims to support academic and research endeavors by simplifying access to scholarly materials for schools, universities, and research institutes in India.
8.B.3 DELNET (Developing Library Network)	DELNET facilitates resource sharing among member institutions in India through services such as interlibrary loans, document delivery, and access to a Union Catalogue of books, journals, and theses. This network enhances cooperation and resource exchange among libraries, leveraging technology to improve access to library resources.

8.B.4 Consortium for e-Resources in Agriculture (CeRA)	CeRA, established by the Indian Council of Agricultural Research (ICAR), provides member institutions in the agricultural sector access to electronic materials related to agriculture and related fields. Its goal is to facilitate academic research and learning by offering scholarly information through a unified platform.

8. B.1 NLIST (National Library and Information Services Infrastructure for Scholarly Content):

The National Library and Information Services Infrastructure for Scholarly Content, or NLIST, is a government of India effort run by the INFLIBNET Center and is part of the Ministry of Education. Through a single platform, it gives researchers, teachers, and students at colleges and universities throughout India access to intellectual content. Participating institutions can access various electronic resources, including databases, journals, and e-books, that are subscribed to by NLIST. Academic libraries in India now have much easier access to scholarly materials because to this common technological platform.

8.B.2 e-Shodh Sindhu:

The Ministry of Education, Government of India, launched e-Shodh Sindhu, a project akin to NLIST, intending to give Indian academic institutions access to scholarly materials. It makes accessing various electronic resources easier for schools, universities, and research institutes. Participating libraries may access databases, e-books, e-journals, and other resources through e-Shodh Sindhu, which promotes academic and research endeavors.

8.B.3 DELNET:

The Developing Library Network is an Indian library network that makes resource sharing easier for its member institutions. Interlibrary loans, document delivery, and access to a Union Catalogue of books, journals, theses, and other materials are just a few of its services. DELNET has played a pivotal role in fostering cooperation and exchanging resources across libraries, thereby improving the utilization of technology to augment access to library resources.

8.B.4 Consortium for e-Resources in Agriculture (CeRA):

Indian Council of Agricultural Research (ICAR) founded the Consortium for e-Resources in Agriculture (CeRA), a network of agricultural libraries in India. It gives its member institutions access to electronic materials related to agriculture and related fields. CeRA aims to enable academic research and learning in the agricultural sector by offering scholarly information through a common platform.

These projects show how shared technology platforms have been effectively adopted in Indian libraries to support academic and research activities, foster collaboration across libraries, and improve access to intellectual materials. Although comprehensive case studies may not always be accessible, these instances demonstrate how shared technology has affected the environment of Indian libraries.

9. Best Practices For Leveraging Digital Resources In Library Settings

9.1 Digital Resource Curation:

Implementing in place dependable processes to choose, arrange, and preserve digital materials to guarantee their applicability and accessible to library patrons. Combining knowledge management, dynamic capabilities, and capacity to absorb, this study offers a capability-based model for open innovation processes. It sheds insight on the interfirm variation in knowledge management and innovation performance by identifying six crucial "knowledge capacities" and suggesting "knowledge management capacity" as a dynamic competence [13].

9.2 User Training and Support:

Use of digital resources is providing instruction and continuous assistance to users so they can efficiently browse and make.

9.3 Promotion and Outreach:

Creating focused marketing plans to inform library users about digital resources and motivate them to use them.

9.4 Collaboration and Consortia:

Creating alliances and participating in consortiums to increase digital collections, pool resources, and bargain for advantageous licenses.

9.5 Data Privacy and Security:

Putting strict protocols in place to preserve customer privacy and keep digital assets safe from abuse or illegal access.

9.6 Continuous Evaluation and Improvement:

Monitoring how digital resources are used and impacting users, getting input from users, and making necessary changes to maximize their efficacy in serving users' requirements. The opinions and worries of IT professionals on Taiwan's adoption of cloud computing. The main issues are connection with company policies, development environments, and business needs, even though the benefits like computing power and cost savings are acknowledged. As a result, most companies are reluctant to adopt until security and uniformity concerns are resolved [14].

10. Conclusion:

In brief, the effective integration of digital resources and shared technology in libraries represents a significant advancement in service delivery and innovation. Libraries need to adapt to the changing information landscape to serve the various needs of their users and stay relevant in the digital era. They should embrace digital solutions and collaborative platforms. Shared technology may improve access to scholarly information, encourage collaboration across institutions, and support research. Examples include initiatives like NLIST, e-Shodh Sindhu, DELNET, and CeRA in India. To fully utilize technology's potential to advance library services, strategic alliances and resource sharing are essential. In the frame of the comcute volunteer and grid system, this article investigates the application of artificial intelligence approaches for managing large amounts of online data. It optimizes resource cost and load balance using a genetic programming calendar and presents Pareto solutions from numerical tests [15].

Libraries may maximize the use of digital resources by utilizing shared technology under the guidance of best practices that cover digital curation, user support, promotional activities, collaborative strategy, data security, and continuous development. In an ever-changing digital world, libraries must be adaptable and creative to overcome challenges and grab possibilities. Libraries may drive innovations, encourage lifelong learning, and guarantee equal access to knowledge for all community members by skillfully utilizing shared technology.

Reference:

1. Tiwari, S. P. (2008). Information and communication technology initiatives for knowledge sharing in agriculture. *Indian Journal of Agricultural Sciences, 78*(9), 737-747.

2. Urbinati, A., Chiaroni, D., Chiesa, V., & Frattini, F. (2020). The role of digital technologies in open innovation processes: An exploratory multiple case study analysis. *R & D Management, 50*(1), 136-160. https://doi.org/10.1111/radm.12313

3. Alam, A. (2022). Platform Utilizing Blockchain Technology for eLearning and Online Education for Open Sharing of Academic Proficiency and Progress Records. In *Smart Data Intelligence* (pp. 307–320).

4. Alavi, M., and Leidner, D.E. (1999). Knowledge management systems: issues, challenges, and benefits. *Communications of the AIS, 1*(2es), 1.

5. Bianchi, M., Croce, A., Dell'Era, C., Di Benedetto, A., and Frattini, F. (2016). Organizing for inbound open innovation: how external consultants and a dedicated R&D unit influence product innovation performance. *Journal of Product Innovation Management, 33*(4), 492-510.

6. Chesbrough, H.W. (2004). Managing open innovation. *The Journal Research Technology Management*, 23-26.

7. Chesbrough, H.W., and Bogers, M. (2014). Explicating Open Innovation: Clarifying an Emerging Paradigm for Understanding Innovation. Henry Chesbrough, Wim Vanhaverbeke, and Joel West, eds. New Frontiers in Open Innovation. Oxford: Oxford University Press, Forthcoming (pp. 3-28). Available at SSRN: https://ssrn.com/abstract=2427233.

8. Davenport, T.H. (1993). Process innovation: reengineering work through information technology. Harvard Business Press.

9. Lazzarotti, V., and Manzini, R. (2009). Different modes of open innovation: a theoretical framework and an empirical study. *International Journal of Innovation Management, 13*(04), 615-636.

10. Sikimic, U., (2016). Investigating the influence of technology inflows on technology outflows in open innovation processes: A

longitudinal analysis. *Journal of Product Innovation Management, 33*(6), 652-669.

11. Yoo, Y., (2012). Organizing for innovation in the digitized world. *Organization Science, 23*(5), 1398-1408.
12. Del Vecchio, P., (2016). Big Data for open innovation: Unveiling challenges and opportunities. Available at: http://www.continuousinnovation.net/events/cimworkshops /2016 /cfp-si-big-data-and-open-innovation.pdf
13. Lichtenthaler, U., and Lichtenthaler, E. (2009). A capability-based framework for open innovation: Complementing absorptive capacity. *Journal of Management Studies, 46*(8), 1315-1338.
14. Lin, A., and Chen, N.C. (2012). Cloud computing as an innovation: Perception, attitude, and adoption. *International Journal of Information Management, 32*(6), 533-540.
15. O'Leary, D.E. (2013). Artificial intelligence and big data. *IEEE Intelligent Systems, 28*(2), 96-99.

CHAPTER 12

Dusty to Digital:- Reimagining Libraries in the Era of NEP 2020

Ajay Saini
Librarian, Directorate of Education Delhi
ajjaysaini@gmail.com

Vikas Saini
Librarian, Directorate of Training and Technical Education, Delhi
vikashsaini2011@gmail.com

Abstract

This article focuses on the role of the library in the New Education Policy 2020. The NEP 2020 introduced many reforms in the Indian Education System, revamping the educational structure, including its regulation and governance, to create a new system aligned with the aspirational goal of 21st-century education. The policy bridges the gap between education and technology. The NEP encourages a peer review system of assessment by creating the National Assessment Center. This article explains the vision of a New Education Policy 2020. NEP 2020 focuses on digital education for the purpose of the digital repository and modernization of the library. This policy focuses on students as well as teachers for better results in the education system. This policy focuses on continued professional development (CPD) and career management and progression (CMP) for teachers. The objective of NEP is equitable and inclusive education that means learning for all. This policy aims to overcome the social status hierarchy associated with vocational education and requires the integration of vocational educational programs into central-stream education in all institutions. This paper highlights the main points of NEP 2020 and the role of libraries in NEP 2020.

Keywords: New Education Policy, School Education, Higher Institution, Library, Teacher, Infrastructure, Technology

1. Introduction

National Education Policy 2020 is the first Education policy of the 21st Century. It was launched by the Ministry of Education in India on 29 Jul 2020. The 1st National Policy on Education was formed by Govt. of India by Prime Minister Smt. Indira Gandhi in 1968, the 2nd policy by PM Sh. Rajiv Gandhi in 1986 and the 3rd one was presented in 2020 by PM Sh.NarenderModi. This policy focuses on school education, higher education and vocational education.

A committee under former cabinet secretary Sh. TSR Subramanian started the consultation process for the new education policy in Jan 2015. The draft of NEP was released by the Ministry of HRD with the vision "Nation Education Policy 2020 envisions an India-Centric Education System that contributes directly to transforming our nation, sustainably into an equitable and vibrant knowledge society by providing high-quality education to all."

This policy focuses on the global education development agenda reflected in the goal (SDGM) of the 2030 agenda for sustainable development, adopted by India in 2015- It seeks to "Ensure inclusive and equitable quality education and promote lifelong learning opportunities for all" by 2030. This requires the entire education system to be reconfigured. The policy focuses on developing good human beings capable of rational thoughts, actions, causes, compression and empathy, encouragement and resilience, scientific tampering, and creative imagination with sound ethical morals and values.

This article discusses NEP 2020 and the role of libraries in NEP 2020. In today's Era, libraries should focus on providing 24*7 hours access to their users. Libraries should be digitised to cater for the needs of their users. NEP 2020 focuses on the modernisation of libraries where the document should be in organised form &also available in digital form; there are concepts of digital library, mobile library, E-Documents, Equipment used in the digital world, etc. Now, the users can't wait for a long time. So, the concept of E-document solves this issue. Users can access its content, such as magazines, articles, books, papers, periodicals, etc.. at any time & it has all become possible due to the modernisation and automation of libraries.

2. Objectives of study

a. To discuss the primary purpose of the New Education Policy 2020.

b. To discuss the digitisation of the library system.

c. Role of Educational Software.

d. Library access is available to everyone from everywhere.

e. To discuss the role of teachers in the education system.

3. Research Methodology

This research article has been bought out on the hour of study and evaluation of recent research work published online, in journals and other sources. There are so many scopes and opportunities for libraries as per our NEP 2020 in India. This is an important and need of hour, attempt to understand and evaluate the use of libraries. This article has been written based on an evaluation of NEP 2020 introduced by the Ministry of HRD, Govt. of India. The data for this article was collected from the internet and other relevant sources. The data used in this article was first analysed and evaluated for getting a conclusion. The research done for this article is a descriptive study. This article discusses the role of the library in NEP 2020.

4. Main Purpose of New Education Policy 2020

The Modern Instruction policy's essential reason is to create an instruction framework that makes excellent and sensible human creatures able to informed thought and activity, having sympathy and mettle and setting up such an instruction framework where each student welcomes and cares to supply a secure learning environment, centring on conveying great physical foundation, such as buildings, seats, work areas, etc., and giving all hardware related to learning. All these qualities ought to be accessible in instructive institutions.

The worldwide instruction improvement motivation reflected within the objective (SDGY) of the 2030 motivation for feasible advancement, received by India in 2015, looks to "Ensure comprehensive and evenhanded quality instruction and advance deep rooted learning openings for all "by 2030 motivation for maintainable advancement.

There's a hole between the current learning preparation and results, and what is required must be bridged through the NEP 2020. It incorporates the nearby and worldwide needs of the nation, and it is all conceivable after perceiving, Distinguishing, and cultivating the one-of-a-kind capabilities of each understudy. NEP 2020 centers on no inflexible division between the subjects; presently, the understudies can select the subject of his/her choice from the stream of expressions, commerce & science. NEP 2020 emphasises conceptual understanding instead of repetition learning. It also centres on people's moral values and protected values like sympathy, regard for others, cleanliness, friendliness, equitable soul, open property, balance and equity. Before this, the centre was not on innovation; instructors utilised conventional instructing strategies. Currently, the world requests innovation in each segment of the economy. It is vital to utilize innovation in instructing and learning. These days, understudies depend on coaching culture since their instructors utilise innovation to clarify the concepts to understudies; if this innovation is accessible in schools & colleges, why do understudies select coaching classes? As we all know, instructors and staff are the heart of the learning preparation, so their enlistment, nonstop proficient improvement, positive work environment, and best Benefit conditions ought to be given. The instructive framework ought to have judgment, straightforwardness, and asset effectiveness through reviews and open revelations while empowering advancement and out-of-box thoughts through independence, excellent administration, and strengthening. NEP 2020 centres on a persistent audit of advance based on maintained investigations and customary evaluation by instruction specialists. There's a requirement for a significant venture in a robust, dynamic open instruction framework and the support and assistance of substantial charitable private and community participation.

5. Vision/focus on NEW Education Policy 2020

The Unused Instruction arrangement centres on economically changing India, that's Bharat, into an evenhanded and dynamic information society by giving high-quality instruction to all. NEP 2020 centres on making India a worldwide information superpower. This arrangement centres on Early Childhood Care and Instruction (ECCE). This approach centres on creating a profound regard towards crucial obligations and protected values, holding with one's nation, and a conscious mindfulness of part and duty in this changing world among the understudies. NEP 2020 must teach a deep-rooted pride in being Indian, not as it were in thought but in the soul, judgment skills, abilities, values, and miens and bolster dependable commitment to human rights, among the understudies. 10+2 structures in school instruction will be altered with a modern academic and curricular rebuild of 5+3+3+4. That centres on creating way better, general learning and well-being.

ECCE: Early Child Care and Instruction (ECCE) is the establishment of learning, and a child's total brain improvement happens sometime recently at the age of 6, so a solid environment ought to be given to small children. ECCE should be play-based, activity-based, dialect, coloured, drawing, portrayal, confusion, and coherent considering. It moreover centres on creating social capabilities, excellent conduct, affectability, affability, morals, individual and open cleanliness, collaboration and participation. The centre of ECCE will be to achieve ideal results in physical and engine improvement, cognitive advancement, socio-emotional-ethical improvement, social improvement, aesthetic improvement, communication with others, dialects, education, and numeracy.

NCPFECCE: National Curricular and Educational System for Early Childhood Care and Instruction is for children up to the age of 8, and it'll be created by NCERT in two parts, i.e., 0-3 a long time ancient and 3-8 a long time ancient. ECCE will include expressions, stories, verses, diversions, Melodies, and more. This will serve as a direct to guardians, Early Childhood Care, and instructive education. ECCE Comprises standalone Anganwadies, Which co-locate with essential schools, and pre-primary school/

sections cover the slightest age, 5 to 6, for a long time. This organising will enrol prepared specialists or instructors, co-located with existing essential schools and stand-alone preschools. Bal Vatika ought to be sometime in lesson 1 or a preliminary lesson. The Balvatika or preliminary courses should centre on creating cognitive, emotional, and psychomotor capacities and early proficiency and numeracy. The mid-day dinner ought to be expanded to preliminary classes in essential schools. Appropriate well-being checkup camps ought to be sorted out for children at standard intervals of time.

MHRD: The Service of Human Asset Advancement guarantees progression from pre-primary school to establishing instruction. The MHR will set up a National Mission on Establishment Education and Numeracy. The arrangement and execution of the early childhood care and instruction educational modules will be carried out with joint endeavours of MHRD, ladies and child advancement (WCD), well-being and family welfare (HFW), and tribal issues.

PTR: The pupil-teacher proportion ought to be kept up at 30: 1 and guaranteed at each school level. The Proportion of PTR ought to be 25: 1 for socio-economically impeded understudies. Instructors will be persuaded to be prepared, empowered, and bolstered with persistent proficiency advancement to affect foundational proficiency and numeracy. Educator opportunities ought to be filled as before as long as possible in a time-bound way, concentrating basically on provincial and impeded regions. The pupil-teacher proportion ought to be maintained for the advantage of understudies.

DIKSHA: Digital infrastructure for knowledge sharing requires Digital documents and digital media for students. A national repository of fundamental and numerical resources will be available on digital infrastructure for knowledge sharing. Technology helped to bridge gaps such as language barriers between teachers and students. The main focus of DIKSHA is to support teachers in the mission of attaining universal foundation literacy. During the coronavirus pandemic, the need for Digital Media arose, and it showed how proper digital education is in all schools/colleges. Office work was done on a digital platform at that time.

Knowledge of India: It will focus on the History of India, the Culture of all states, tribal knowledge & Culture, environment, etc. There should be special courses in tribal, ethno-medicinal practices, forest management, traditional (organic) crop Cultivation, natural farming etc. There should be elective competitions in schools to learn various topics and subjects. Video documentaries on inspirational luminaries of India, whether ancient or modern in any area, will be shown to students through the school Curriculum. There should be programs that include students' visits to different states to learn about the cultures of other states. Students will be taught all the essential human and constitutional values such as seva, ahimsa, swachhtasatya, nishkam karma, sacrifice, tolerance, diversity, pluralism, gender sensitivity, respect for elders etc.

PARAKH: Performance Assessment Review and Analysis of Knowledge for holistic development under the National Assessment Centre as a standard-setting body under MHRD established for setting norms, standards and evaluations for all recognised school boards of India. It will guide the State Achievement Survey (SAS) and undertake the National Achievement Survey (NAS) that will monitor the learning outcomes in the country. This will be set up according to the needs of 21st Century students and achieve the goal of NEP 2020. It will advise school boards regarding new assessment patterns; the latest research promotes collaboration between school boards. National Testing Agency will conduct high-quality standard aptitude tests and ordinary subjects in the sciences, humanities, language, arts and vocational exams. It will serve as a premier, expert, autonomous testing organisation to conduct the entrance exam. NTA will enable most universities to use a single standard entrance test.

CPD & CMP – Continuous Professional Development and Career Management and Progression, both programmes are related to teacher Continuous Professional Development program will give Continuous opportunities for self-improvement and to learn the latest innovations and advances to the teacher online platform will be provided to the teachers to share ideas and best practices. The teacher should offer at least 50 continuous professional development opportunities every year. CPD will cover leadership and management and a contest focusing on preparing and implementing competency-based education career management and progression programmes. It will recognise, promote and also give salary raises to the teacher for their outstanding work. A system of multiple parameters for proper performance assessment will be developed for the State/UT Governance based on the peer review attendance commitment hours of CPD and other forms of service to the school. It will ensure career growth in terms of tenure promotion, salary increases, etc., is available to teachers within a single school stage. Both CPD and CMP motivate teachers to give their best to students.

Three Language Formula: Language is a medium of communication between people. Young children learn and grasp non-trivial concepts more quickly in their mother language. The mother language of an area is the language that is spoken by the local communities. NEP 2020 prefers the mother language as a medium of instruction. If possible, then the Mother/ Local language shall continue to be taught as a language wherever possible. This should be followed in private and public schools. If gaps exist between the local language and the language of instruction between the teacher and students, they should be bridged. The three languages children will learn will be the choices of states and regions by the students. Indian language may be standardised across the country and should be respected and taught.

Focus on Gifted Students: Teachers should recognise the talents of students and foster such talents. As we know, every student has a talent that must be discovered, nurtured, fostered and developed. The NCERT and NCTE will form guidelines and procedures for educating gifted children. Schools should encourage topic-centred and project-based clubs and circles, like chess circles, language circles, yoga clubs, Eco-health clubs, etc. There should be coordination from school to local to state to national level for olympiads and competitions in various subjects to ensure that all students may participate at all levels. Public and private universities should conduct and encourage Competition or entrance exams for admission.

When Internet-connected smartphones and tablets are available in all homes and schools, online quizzes, competition assessments, study materials, and group activities should encourage the centre supervision of parents and teachers. Intelligent classrooms will be developed by the schools to enrich the teaching-learning process using online resources.

Focus on Technology/ Digital India: The Digital India Campaign transforms the nation into a digitally empowered and knowledge-based society. Technology plays a vital role in the educational process and outcome. The new technology involves artificial intelligence, machine learning, intelligent boards, adaptive computer testing for student development, and other educational software and hardware forms. An autonomous body, the National Educational Technology Forum, will be created to provide a platform for the free exchange of ideas on the use of technology to enhance learning, assessment planning, admission and so on, both for school and higher education. NETF will help in decision-making regarding induction development.

Function of NETF

(a) Give free, evidence-based exhortation to central and state Government offices on technology-based intercessions.

(b) To construct mental and organisation capacities in instructive innovation.

(c) To imagine key pushed ranges in this space.

(d) To verbalise unused headings for investigation and development.

Educational Software: An instructional computer program will be created and made accessible to undergraduates and instructors at all levels. The instructive program will be accessible in all essential Indian dialects. It'll offer assistance to the understudies of farther regions and DIVYANG Understudies. Educating learning e-content will be advanced and created by all states in all territorial dialects and by the NCERT, CIET, CBSE, NIOS, and other Government or private bodies and Teach. NEP 2020 was defined when unquestioning troublesome innovation (Manufactured Insights) was created. 3D/7D Virtual reality will point to offer PhD and Ace programs and multi-disciplinary areas AL+X. These courses may be accessible like 'Swayam'. Pondering current and moral issues will incorporate troublesome innovations such as those recognised by NETF/MHRD.

Digital Education: Advanced Instruction plays an essential part amid Plagues like the coronavirus. The NEP 2020 perceive the significance of innovation while recognising its potential dangers and unsafe advanced stages. ICT-based instructive activities must be advanced to meet the current and future challenges in giving quality instruction to all. The Computerized Isolate must be disposed of for the victory and completion of Computerized Instruction. Preparing ought to be given to instructors for their advancement so that they can be successful online teachers. It cannot be guaranteed that a great instructor in a conventional classroom will consequently be a great teacher in a web classroom. There's also an impediment to courses/ subjects like performing arts and science commonsense in online/ advanced instruction. There's a need to contribute to making an open, interoperable, evaluable, open computerised framework within the instruction segment so instructive programs will be made accessible on TV in different dialects to the students' needs.

6. Role of Libraries in NEP 2020:

New Education Policy 2020 promotes libraries and also focuses on library staff to meet its goal of building, developing, automation and digitisation libraries to cater to the needs of its users.

Automation of Library: The NEP2020 promotes the Automation of all Libraries. A library with a computer and library software or networks solves all users' queries in less time than traditional libraries. Providing library facilities in remote areas of the country, NEP 2020 promote access to libraries for the country's people.

There are many places where there is no library, and mobile libraries may solve this problem as they give library services to their users at their doorsteps. NEP 2020 focuses on SamagraShiksha, which means education for all, and the mobile library plays a vital role. A mobile library's primary purpose is to promote users' education and reading habits.

Digital Repository: A digital repository of consent includes the creation of coursework, learning games, augmented reality, and virtual reality developed focus. A reliable backup mechanism for disseminating e-consent to students will be provided.

Modernisation/digitisation of library: The NEP2020 recommends that all the vital and modernised libraries ensure an adequate supply of books that cater to the needs and interests of all students. Particular focus should be given to disabilities and other differently-abled persons to promote online accessibility of library books for the smooth functioning of libraries for all library staff. Libraries should modernized/digitised for the betterment of users as we know that there is a collection of more lakhs of books in higher institutions. It can be handled only with the help of library software. This type of library software/should be available in each library.

Libraries should focus on increasing the number of e-documents in the library. For example, a print journal will be accessible by one user at a time at a particular place. Still, if the library has an e-journal facility, it can solve many users' queries at any place at any time.

Print documents should be scanned and saved for future use in the library. NEP 2020 focuses on training library staff at regular intervals/periods so that the staff gets regular updates in the library's field.

Promote setting up rural libraries, strengthen existing libraries, set up reading rooms in disadvantaged regions, and open children's libraries and mobile libraries. NEP 2020 promotes setting up more schools for students in rural areas. Merit-based scholarships will be given to students in the weaker sections. Rural schools will have the provision of local houses near or in the school. Library facilities should be provided in every rural school, and if possible, a library will be made available for the familiar people on off days of school.

7. Conclusion

This article clarifies the focus of NEP 2020 and the part of the library in it. The NEP 2020 satisfied the unfinished motivation of the national approach to instruction in 1986, which was altered in 1992. NEP 2020 centers on building an instruction framework that creates great human creatures capable of judicious thought and activity, kindness and compassion, grit and strength, logical mood and imagination, and creative ability with sound ethical mornings and values. The objective of the national instruction arrangement is to construct an evenhanded, comprehensive, and plural society as our constitution imagines. The NEP 2020 take after Samagra Shiksha Abhiyan to form our nation self-reliant & satisfy the dreams of Aatm Nirbhar Bharat Abhiyan. This arrangement makes a more comprehensive, cohesive, and profitable country. The victory of this modern instruction arrangement will depend on how it is executed. This arrangement will advance our nation as a worldwide considered goal that gives premium instruction at a reasonable fetch. The NEP 2020 changes India into a dynamic information society and worldwide information superpower by making the instruction framework more all-encompassing, adaptable, multidisciplinary and suited to each student's current/present needs. The NEP 2020 centres on all instruction perspectives, from horticulture to artificial intelligence. It plans experts for each segment of our nation.

The NEP 2020 points to attaining integrity, transparency, and asset proficiency within the instructive framework through reviews and open divulgences, while empowering advancement and out-of-the-box thoughts through independence, excellent administration, and strengthening. This article clarifies the part of libraries in NEP 2020. The NEP 2020 advance libraries additionally centre on library staff to meet its goal of building, creating, mechanisation and digitisation libraries to cater to the desires of its clients. The NEP2020 advances the Automation of all Libraries. Moreover, libraries ought to be modernised/digitised to improve clients, as we know there's a collection of more lakhs of books in higher education. It can be dealt with with the assistance of a library computer program. The NEP 2020 emphasises digital India with a vision to convert India into a carefully enabled society and information economy; hence, NEP centres on advanced foundations to attain the specified future.

8. References

1. Asif, Md., & Singh, K.K.(2022).Libraries@ national education policy (NEP 2020) in India:IP Indian Journal of Library Science and Information Technology
2. https://www.ijlsit.org/html-article/16823
3. Sharma,K.(2022).New National Education Policy 2022: The Asian School.Dehradun India
4. https://www.theasianschool.net/blog/new-national-education-policy/
5. Rohatgi,A.(2020, August 07).NEP will play role in reducing gap between research and education in India PM . The Hindustan Times: India
6. https://www.hindustantimes.com/india-news/pm-modi-s-address-at-conclave-on-transformational-reforms-in-higher-education-under-national-education-policy-highlights/story-dehOW8q8ZRrONbbFSRjg0H.html
7. Chopra, R.(2020).Explained: India's National Education Policy, 2020. Indian Express: India
8. https://indianexpress.com/article/explained/reading-new-education-policy-india-schools-colleges-6531603/
9. Ministry of Education .(2020).Highlights of New Education Policy-2020
10. https://www.pib.gov.in/PressReleasePage.aspx?PRID=1654058
11. Ministry of Education, Govt. of India (2020). Nationl Education Policy 2020
12. https://www.education.gov.in/sites/upload_files/mhrd/files/NEP_Final_English_0.pdf

CHAPTER 13

Research Data Management

Dr.Anjali Srivastava
Assistant Professor, Sarala Birla University
Email:anjali.srivastava@sbu.ac.in

Abstract

In the digital age, the only thing that cannot be overestimated is the importance of correctly managing research data. The ever-growing scale and availability of digital data are a treasury of invaluable information that Internet users look for in making public policy decisions, scientific discoveries, or even doing business. For example, take the significant companies that collect customers' purchase history, demographics, or user interests; thus, they make a base for discovering possibilities for scientific research data. The scientists need to have an understanding of the data and how to make sense out of it. This chapter presents a thorough overview of research data management, including data analyses, uses, and performance metrics based on data sciences (Saura,2021). This chapter elaborates on the fundamental elements of data organisation and data handling in research. Concentrated on the drama of data-informed research techniques, this chapter examines ways to procure, deposit, and share research data properly. It highlights all the issues data collectors face and how data integrity, accessibility and resourcefulness contribute to their work. The course also discusses the robust technologies and devices to help professionals simplify data management tasks. It offers both intellectual perspectives and practical suggestions; therefore, it is a broad source for scholars, learners, and professionals who pursue enhancing their scientific data-handling skills. The chapter introduces data acquisition to the preservation, giving the reader a complete picture of the complex world that is the proper data storage and legislation. The article promotes responsible and efficient data stewardship.

Keywords: research data management, digital data, data analysis, data sciences, performance metrics

Introduction:

Understanding Research Data Management

Data resource management is a component. Every research project that aims for ultimate success should not be ignored. It is the process of the purposeful gathering of information, its structuring, registering, shelf storage and availability due to accuracy, uprightness, security, and convenience of access. Researchers use a multitude of sources and several collection methods such as keeping records, interviewing people, survey design, conducting experiments, observation techniques, and reading in their study. The quality of research data and its management throughout the research affects the conclusions that researchers come up with. Consider the possibility of incorporating the information given here if it is relevant.

Source: The knowledge of the various ways to conduct things using this approach is as vital as its deployment because the organisation may only apply the right system to manage its information resources if it is fully understood. The era of the digital age, where data volumes grow incrementally at an excruciating pace, calls for more organised and careful research data management.

An essential step towards providing research data integrity is proper records management that adheres to legal requirements and international standards. Moreover, it focuses on the characteristics of an accurate record, such as authenticity, reliability, completeness, and integrity. Proper research data management involves several key components: An excellent recommendation letter from a supervisor or a customer can significantly enhance my chances of being considered for the job.

File Naming Conventions: The development of a uniform file name format allows the researcher to search a specific file quickly without any difficulty.

Critical Principles of Managing Research Data

Managing research data effectively requires the following fundamental principles:

1. **Documentation and metadata:** Besides that, it is of utmost importance that you monitor entirely the activities being carried out, the specimens that have been chosen and any values involved in the data collection process. The documentation stage increases the understanding and the ability to reproduce findings, benefiting other researchers in the same field.
2. **Data Storage and Backup:** Data should not be lost due to corruption or damage. Hence, a good and reliable system to store all data, including sensitive ones, should be developed or enhanced. In order to keep data secured, if something happens to the system or there is some unexpected event, data should be backed up regularly.
3. **Data Security:** The study of computer systems must be protected from any unauthorised changes in the research data, including the deletion or alteration of it. Such an act can be done by using various security tools, such as providing access controls, large passwords, and encryption.
4. **Data Sharing and Accessibility:** Research data should be accessible to others. For researchers and experts, repositories could be open to the public or offer access upon request. The results of these studies thereby get validated due to attack by the scientific community and the outcome of the analysis presented to the public. Proper data management also implies determining clear rules and grants for sharing data at hand, including regulation of conditions under which data can be disclosed, access restriction level and signing obligatory data use accords or licensing procedures. Similarly, data-sharing procedures must consider ethical considerations, such as securing consent from participants and safeguarding the disclosure of sensitive or confidential data.

5. **Data Preservation:** For the long-term existence of research data to be guaranteed, it should not only be opened for future researchers but also be easily accessible and usable. This can be done by picking compatible data formats used widely, including a monitoring system that enables migration to subsequent storage media along with technological advancement, assigning persistent Digital Object Identifiers to datasets, and transferring data to trustworthy storage repositories.
6. **Data Management Planning:** Researchers should draft a data management plan upon commencement of their project; therefore, the critical item in the plan should be detailed guidance about handling data in every phase of the data life-cycle: collection, processing, analysis etc. (Brous et al., 2016). The above points can aid in ensuring that the researcher's data is well-managed and archived for future uses.
7. **Data Governance:** Accordingly, it is necessary to set a basis for data governance because it is the prerequisite to protecting the authenticity, security, and value of research data. Life is too short to devote our days to jobs we dislike or activities that do not light a fire within us. The awareness of the more used approaches to solving the information management problem is the preliminary stage in implementing the best mechanism. Data management encompasses all the activities to preserve data security and its proper usage. Moreover, it consists of delegation of duties and task assignments for data management, data safety measures to keep away from data unauthorised access or breach, and data quality measures to ensure accurate and precise data research. This can be achieved through specially designed data governance structures and principles.

   Example: In case they are relevant, consider incorporating the sources mentioned. You can learn more about safe driving practices and how to prevent distracted driving through educational campaigns and

Awareness programs, such as simulated or real-life scenarios, demonstrate the potential dangers and consequences of dangerous driving. Conclude a training program with data management principles repeated periodically. However, entities will probably create more issues connected with data security, data protection, data accessibility, data usability, data quality and so forth, among other data management issues.

8. **Data Sharing and Collaboration:** A significant part of contemporary research is collaborating while sharing data with co-researchers who can offer new ideas and insights. As a result, they may have to think about the most efficient way of exchanging data and other matters relating to it. This would necessitate using platforms or repositories facilitating simple access and sharing of data, such as cloud-based storage systems or online collaboration tools.
9. **Data Storage:** Ensuring that research data will remain accessible over long periods is very important. Scholars should also be very keen on their data storage settings and the techniques for keeping them going. The latter may involve backing up the data to make it easier for retrieval within future timeframes, using archival storage systems, and establishing metadata standards that would facilitate its discovery and use.
10. **Ethical considerations:** Research data management also includes ethical considerations that researchers must consider. The potential risks and benefits of their data collection, storage, and use will be assessed. This involves obtaining informed consent from participants, safeguarding the privacy and confidentiality of individuals participating in the research, and ensuring that data is used for the purposes for which they were intended, as well as within ethical guidelines and regulations.

Effective Strategies of Data Collection and Recording

For accurate and reliable research data, it is vital to have adequate data collection and recording strategies. These strategies begin with careful planning and designing methods of collecting data. Researchers should consider the types of questions they are seeking answers to and their objectives besides focusing on a target population or sample. They should also take any ethical considerations into account while securing appropriate measures for protecting the rights and privacy of research participants. Once the methods for collecting data have been identified, standardised procedures for conducting studies must be adhered to by researchers (Derry et al., 2010).

The data should be collected consistently and accurately using appropriate instruments and tools to make it possible. Besides, the researchers need clear guidelines for keeping, saving, and recording data. More specifically, it is about knowing which method of collecting data will be used, such as surveys or interviews, observations, or experimentation. These members also need to consider how this research data will be formatted. Consequently, the choice of correct formats can significantly affect the efficiency of data collection and recording processes. This means that while qualitative results may require audio or video recordings when collecting such information from respondents, quantitative information may necessitate structured survey questions or questionnaires. Factors like careful planning and standard operating procedures that ensure high standards during research activities and digital technology applications in enhancing efficient data recording during experiments are equally crucial in the research study. These could reduce time and errors related to human effort, streamline the storage process and permit better organisation (RDM). While conducting a study that complies with ethical codes, proper management should focus on maintaining effective document preservation methods (Johnson et al., 2020). These practices include data collection, storage, organisation, analysis, and sharing.

Research data management aims to ensure that the data collected is reliable, valid, and can be easily accessed and analysed. Furthermore, proper research data management helps maintain the research process's integrity and ensures that the findings are trustworthy and robust.

Data Storage Solutions for Researchers

Data storage is essential to managing research data; therefore, researchers must ensure that their data is secure and easy to access for analysis and other purposes. Researchers can keep their data in several ways: they might save it on external hard drives or personal computers. It can be noted that this method allows immediate use of the data but comes with capacity limits and security. Another possibility is cloud-based services such as Amazon S3, Dropbox and Google Drive, through which customers can choose scalable data storage options. These services offer large memory spaces and automatic back-ups, allowing customers to view their data from anywhere in the world with a network connection.

Institutional repositories: Several colleges and research centres have established safe online environments where scientists can share and preserve their data. Strict requirements are usually established so that these repositories remain available over time.

Data management systems: In scientific domains, specialised DMSs are pervasive. Advanced algorithms help process, organise, and present, among others. Examples of such systems include Open Science Framework (OSF), LabArchives, and REDCap.

Data Protection and Security

Regardless of the chosen storage option, researchers must focus on data protection and security. This can be achieved using encryption techniques, access controls and regular file backups. Proper data storage solutions are necessary to ensure research data's accuracy and integrity.

Privacy and Data Protection Factors

Privacy concerns and data protection issues play a crucial role in managing research data. Researchers should understand legal and ethical requirements concerning personal or sensitive information's collection, preservation or sharing. These directives may differ depending on the jurisdiction in question and particular areas of study. Researchers need to adopt several measures to protect both their privacy and their data. They include obtaining informed consent from subjects, de-identifying or anonymising whenever possible, storing data safely with restricted access controls and employing secure protocols for transferring and sharing such files. Therefore, researchers should use this approach to restrict sensitive information from unauthorised access.

This could include role-based access controls (RBAC), encrypting files during transmission or storage, and monitoring access logs for auditing purposes (Aczél et al., 2019).

Metadata and Data Documentation Essentials

In managing research data, it is essential to document details concerning the data correctly. This documentation comprises metadata that refers to any information describing different aspects of the data. It would include details such as study design, methods of data collection, variables and their definitions, formats of data and any other contextual information which might be relevant. Research data will be challenging to understand, interpret, and reuse without accurate and comprehensive metadata. Therefore, researchers should have a consistent and standard way of capturing or documenting the metadata. To do this, they can use tools for documenting datasets or templates and adhering to documented guidelines on how to document datasets.

Sharing and Disseminating Research Data

Sharing and disseminating research data is a critical concern in RDM. You contribute to a common knowledge pool by sharing your results with others. In addition, this allows for the validation of findings by other researchers who may wish to build on them further. However, works shared by one person with others attract privacy concerns over the content shared, data intellectual property rights, and potential misuse. To solve these issues, researchers must follow best practices associated with the sharing and dissemination of research data.

Legal and Ethical Aspects of Research Data Management

When dealing with research data, commercial and ethical aspects should be considered. This includes compliance with data protection laws, informed consent by the participants and proper handling of sensitive or confidential information. Researchers must comply with relevant legal and ethical frameworks surrounding their research, like institutional policies, data protection legislation, and guidance on research ethics (Aczél et al., 2019). This means they must implement appropriate procedures for managing their data that are compatible with these rules. If it does not happen, then the researcher could be implicated in a lawsuit due to the damage caused to this project's participants and the researcher's reputation.

Tools And Software For Managing Research Data

Researchers can use different tools and software options to help them manage their research data efficiently. These tools make organising, storing, analysing and sharing data easy. Some common examples of tools used for managing research data include:

1. **Data Management Platforms:** These platforms enable researchers to have a centralised system to store, retrieve and manage their data. They usually come with functionalities like versioning of data', 'permissions for sharing' 'and data security measures. Examples of data management platforms include Dataverse, Figshare, and Zenodo.
2. **Data curation tools** help researchers read their data for long-term preservation and reusability. They may have features such as data scrubbing, data reshaping and metadata creation. Among

the examples of data curation tools are OpenRefine, KNIME and Datamelt.

3. **Data analysis software:** This software assists researchers in analysing their research data, leading to significant findings. Among others, SPSS, R, Python, and SAS are some examples of software enabling data analysis.
4. **Data visualisation tools:** They allow for visualisation of the collected data to identify patterns, trends and causality relations. On this line, we have Tableau Software Incorporated's Tableau Public tool and Microsoft Power BI tool.
5. **Data encryption tools:** These tools can aid a researcher in protecting his/her research work against tampering or corruption by encrypting it. VeraCrypt, BitLocker, and GPG are examples of decryption programs researchers can use.
6. **Collaboration platforms:** These platforms promote collaboration among team members through sharing research information. Google Drive (formerly Google Docs), Microsoft SharePoint online (Office 365), and Slack are examples of such platforms that support collaborative research activities. Tools like these also enhance the integrity and security of one's own personal and academic works' online storage and facilitate teamwork during scientific investigations. As a result, data managers can save time processing large volumes of experimental results and reduce risks associated with losing important information about samples collected from different sources when sharing them with colleagues and the impact of their research.

Evaluating and Improving Data Management Practices

Research data management is growing in complexity; thus, researchers must consider their data management practices to improve them regularly. A tool that can be used for this kind of assessment is the KRDS Benefits

Framework and the Value-chain and Benefits Impact tool (Beagrie et al., 2012). The tools are designed to evaluate the benefits derived from keeping research data permanently. The KRDS Benefits Framework has a guide and worksheet for assessing benefits from research data curation activities. It helps determine the potential value and impact of researchers' data management practices, such as increased research efficiency, improved data quality, and enhanced collaboration.

On the other hand, The Value-chain and Benefits Impact tool enables researchers to look at the whole value chain of their data management activities and measure how well they have performed. It allows researchers to define quantitative metrics or qualitative indicators for measuring benefit impacts. Evaluation is used for strategic planning, organisational planning, and reporting purposes. These tools, therefore, enable scientists to recognise how effective their data management systems are and make decisions on which areas need improvement. The principal area where researchers can make improvements is through data visualisation. It is crucial to research data management since it enables the researcher to communicate complex datasets effectively.(Onukwugha et al., 2016). Still, assessing and enhancing data visualisation practices may pose significant challenges (Lam et al.,2012).

Chapter Summary:

The chapter presents an outline of research data management and the significance of efficient data management. It illustrates how diverse tools like open-source software and infrastructure allow for efficient data management. It stresses the importance of researchers continually evaluating and improving their ways of handling information to increase the worthiness and impact of their investigation(Saura,2021). Also discussed in this chapter are the KRDS Benefits Framework and Value-chain and Benefits Impact tool, which are considered indispensable materials in assessing benefits related to research data curation activities and overall implications arising from these activities.(Beagrie et al., 2012).

These tools can help researchers determine the potential worth and importance of their data management practices, such as improved research efficiency, better quality data and more collaboration. Also, it tackles the role of data visualisation in research data management and the challenges of assessing and improving practices in this area (Büyüközkan & Göçer, 2018). In addition, it highlights the significance of efficient data visualisation in comprehendible communication and analysis of intricate datasets. For research data management, this chapter is a one-stop guide that offers significant insights to researchers and provides them with tools to enhance their practices. The chapter on research data management gives a broad view of the need for effective data management strategies, which are today's prime necessity in relevance. It points out that researchers must continuously evaluate and improve their data handling processes to optimise their studies' impact and worthiness. One area researchers can focus on when they want improvement is the visual representation of information. Visualisation techniques are crucial in managing scientific information since they allow investigators to communicate effectively with each other when dealing with complicated sets of figures. Through a vivid mental picture, researchers can enhance the communication of their results and improve research presentation across different fields. Additionally, there is a discussion of data collection and collation challenges. This section emphasises why it is essential to know what data should be collected, how it will be collected, and what its quality is.

References

1. Aczél, B., Szászi, B., Sarafoglou, A., Kekecs, Z., Kucharský, Š., Benjamin, D J., Chambers, C., Fisher, A., Gelman, A., Gernsbacher, M A., Ioannidis, J P A., Johnson, E L., Jonas, K J., Kousta, S., Lilienfeld, S O., Lindsay, D S., Morey, C C., Munafò, M R., Newell, B R., . . . Wagenmakers, E J. (2019, December 2). A consensus-based transparency checklist. https://www.nature.com/articles/s41562-019-0772-6

2. Beagrie, N., Duke, M., Hardman, C., Kalra, D., Lavoie, B., Patel, M., Lyon, L., & Woollard, M. (2012, October 23). The KRDS Benefits Analysis Toolkit: Development and Application. https://ijdc.net/ijdc/article/view/219
3. Brous, P., Janssen, M., & Vilminko-Heikkinen, R. (2016, January 1). Coordinating Decision-Making in Data Management Activities: A Systematic Review of Data Governance Principles. https://link.springer.com/chapter/10.1007/978-3-319-44421-5_9
4. Derry, S J., Pea, R., Barron, B., Engle, R A., Erickson, F., Goldman, R., Hall, R., Koschmann, T., Lemke, J L., Sherin, M G., & Sherin, B. (2010, January 27). Conducting Video Research in the Learning

   Sciences: Guidance on Selection, Analysis, Technology, and Ethics. https://www.tandfonline.com/doi/abs/10.1080/10508400903452884
5. Johnson, J L., Adkins, D., & Chauvin, S W. (2020, January 1). A Review of the Quality Indicators of Rigor in Qualitative Research. https://doi.org/10.5688/ajpe7120
6. Lam, H., Bertini, E., Isenberg, P., Plaisant, C., & Carpendale, S. (2012, September 1). Empirical Studies in Information Visualization: Seven Scenarios. https://ieeexplore.ieee.org/document/6095544
7. Onukwugha, E., Plaisant, C., & Shneiderman, B. (2016, January 1). Data Visualization Tools for

   Investigating Health Services Utilization Among Cancer Patients. https://www.sciencedirect.com/science/article/abs/pii/B9780128021156000112?via%3Dihub
8. Saura, J R. (2021, April 1). Using Data Sciences in Digital Marketing: Framework, methods, and performance metrics. https://www.sciencedirect.com/science/article/pii/S2444569X-20300329?via%3d Ihub

CHAPTER 14

Education and Skill Development in India

Dr.Afshan Anees
Assistant Professor
Al-Barkaat Institute of Education, Aligarh
E-mail: afshan.anees1@gmail.com

Abstract

Education and skill development are pivotal components of India's socio-economic growth. Despite significant progress in expanding access to education, challenges such as quality, inclusivity, and relevance to the job market persist. The Indian education system comprises diverse institutions, from primary schools to higher education and vocational training centres. However, there is a notable gap between the skills imparted by educational institutions and the demands of the industry. This disconnect has resulted in high levels of graduate unemployment and underemployment. The government has launched several initiatives, such as the Skill India Mission and the National Education Policy (NEP) 2020, aiming to bridge this gap by promoting vocational training, digital literacy, and flexible learning pathways. The NEP 2020 emphasises a holistic, multidisciplinary approach and technology integration in education. The private sector and non-governmental organisations also play a crucial role in skill development through various innovative programs. To realise its demographic dividend, India must address systemic education and skill development issues, ensuring the youth are equipped with relevant and future-ready skills. The successful implementation of these policies and initiatives can potentially transform India into a global knowledge and skill hub.

Keyword: Skill India, Education, NEP 2020

Introduction

Education is an essential tool which is very useful in everybody's life. It differentiates us from other living creatures and makes man the most intelligent creature on earth. It empowers humans to face the challenges of life efficiently and intelligently. It effectively eradicates poverty and employment, improves the commercial scenario, and benefits the country's overall development. It is also responsible for modifying our lifestyle, providing career opportunities, making us better people, and enhancing our intellect and the ability to make the right decisions, which increases an individual's quality of life and growth.

Skill Development

Skills development is called to acquire the ability or capacity through sustained and systematic efforts to carry out complex activities, or job functions smoothly and adaptively. Skill education enhances students' employability and contributes to their personal and professional development.

Similarly, education inculcates skills, which also help make a person independent. Skill Development is the process of improving specific skills to be more efficient and effective when you perform a task. Those educated enough and with skill development won't depend on anyone else for their livelihood. They will be self-sufficient to earn for themselves and lead a good life.

In today's rapidly changing world, a good education alone is not enough to guarantee success. As the business world becomes more competitive, there is increasing emphasis on the need for individuals to acquire more skills than traditional education. Technical education is integral to school education because it provides students with the knowledge and skills to improve their prospects. Skill development can have a positive impact on academic success.

Instruction encompasses a solid potential to address these challenges by upgrading different abilities. Cognitive aptitudes matter, but social and passionate skills, such as tirelessness, self-control and flexibility, are fair as fundamental. These aptitudes must be cultivated for people and social orders to thrive.

Skill Development in Different Periods of Education

Ancient period:

Amid antiquated instruction, five unmistakable, well-known colleges like Takshashila, Nalanda, Vallabhi, etc. centred on the all-around advancement of understudies. Amid old times, understudies lived absent from their guardians; their instruction comprised physical instruction, mental instruction, legislative issues, financial matters, etc. A common misleading myth is that gurukuls provided education only in language, literature, religion, philosophy and ethics. In the early Vedic period, pupils were also trained in occupations based on their abilities, and the later Vedic period continued based on their classes.

This education was of the following types:

- Brahmins were trained in teaching, learning rituals, performing yajnas, etc.
- Kshatriyas were trained in politics and battle.
- Vaishyas were trained in agriculture, herding, precious stones and value estimation, cotton, spices, trade, etc.
- Shudras were meant to serve people. They were taught different activities like weaving, knitting, dyeing, architecture, drawing crafts, etc. They also entertained people with dance and music, for which their families trained them.

Medieval Period

Middle Ages roughly from the 5th century to the 15 century. English missionaries influence education during this period. Religious medieval education was the focus of instruction, emphasising the importance of Christian doctrine and moral values.

Vocational, technical and vocational education was provided during the Islamic period. Individuals acquire education based on their skills, abilities, and interests. During this period, individuals pursued some occupations, including silk weaving, carpentry, pottery making, dyeing, artwork, handicrafts, metal and gem working, and clothing and jewellery manufacturing. Jewellery, etc. The Mughal emperors were very interested in arts and crafts. Mughal paintings are still famous today. India's exquisite gold and silver fabrics, shawls, paintwork, and ornaments result from specialised, technical, and vocational education. People involved in manufacturing and producing these items must have sufficient knowledge and skills. They must know how to use machines and tools to create productivity. Professional education begins with the initiation of religious ceremonies. Military training and arts and crafts were the areas considered most important.

Skill Development During Modern Period

In the middle of the Middle Ages, the British invaded India and began to occupy it. Modern education was introduced in the British Empire. Over time, education began to develop and enter the contemporary era of science, technology and innovation.

Modern period

Skills development is a continuous process of identifying areas where your skills can be strengthened and actively acquiring new capabilities to meet the changing needs of the global landscape. Effective skill development progresses over time, ensuring you have the tools and knowledge you need to succeed. Skill development is a focus area of the Modi government's education agenda, with a significant allocation to initiatives such as the Skill India programme, Pradhan Mantri Kaushal Vikas Yojana, and the establishment of centres to develop multiple skills. These efforts aim to equip young people with the skills to thrive in the rapidly changing job market and contribute to India's economic growth.

Present status of Education and skill Development in India

India's education system is divided into primary, secondary, and tertiary. The primary level comprises grades 1-5, while the secondary level comprises grades 6-10. The tertiary level includes universities and colleges that offer undergraduate and graduate degrees.

At the primary stage and Secondary Stage

The Gross Enrolment Ratio (GER) in primary education in India is over 100%, indicating that more children are enrolled in schools than the age-appropriate population. However, the GER in secondary education is only around 77%, indicating that many students drop out after completing primary education.

The quality of education is also a concern in India, with many schools lacking basic facilities such as clean drinking water, toilets, and libraries. Additionally, the curriculum is outdated, and rote learning is prevalent. The lack of practical and vocational education limits students' employability, contributing to the country's unemployment rate.

At Tertiary Stage

Tertiary education in India has grown significantly, with over 1000 universities and 50,000 colleges. However, the quality of education remains a challenge, with many universities and colleges lacking the necessary infrastructure, faculty, and resources.

Obstacles to Effective Implementation of Skill Development in India

Skills development is also a significant challenge in India. While a vast talent pool exists, the workforce's employability remains low due to a lack of skills relevant to the job market. The skills gap is particularly evident in manufacturing, healthcare, and engineering industries, where the demand for skilled workers is high. Skills development is critical for the economic development of a country. It enables individuals to acquire the necessary skills and knowledge to succeed in the job market and contribute to the economy's growth. India has recognised the importance of skills development and has taken several initiatives to promote skill development in the country.

Despite these initiatives, skills development in India faces several challenges. The skills gap in the country is significant, with many industries struggling to find qualified and skilled workers. The lack of quality vocational education and training institutions limits students' access to relevant skills development programs.

Despite these initiatives, there are still several challenges in the field of skills development in India. One of the significant challenges is the lack of industry-academia collaboration. There is often a mismatch between the skills taught in educational institutions and the skills required by the industry. This results in a skill gap, where graduates are not adequately prepared for the job market.

Another challenge in skills development is the lack of access to training and development opportunities for marginalised communities. Women, people with disabilities, and people from disadvantaged backgrounds often face significant barriers to accessing training and development opportunities.

There have been three noteworthy challenges to abilities improvement in India: extending open segment collaboration with industry and the private segment, making pathways for worldwide portability and tending to women's moo support within the work drive.

Initiative taken by Govt. to Improve Education in Context to Skill Development

The government has launched several schemes and initiatives to promote skill development, such as the Skill India Mission. The mission aims to provide vocational training and skill development to millions of youth in the country. India has recently improved skills development, with several initiatives to bridge the skills gap. The National Skill Development Corporation (NSDC) was established in 2009 to promote skills development in various sectors, including manufacturing, construction, and healthcare.

The Skill India Mission, launched in 2015, aims to provide vocational education and training to 400 million people by 2022. The mission includes initiatives such as the Pradhan Mantri Kaushal Vikas Yojana (PMKVY), which provides skill training to youth and incentivises employers to hire skilled workers.

Higher education emphasises expanding access and improving quality. This included the establishment of the Indian Institute of Technology (IIT), National Institute of Technology (NIT) and Indian Institute of Management (IIM), leading to an exponential increase in the number of heads in the water.

Noteworthy changes have been started within the higher instruction segment to extend to and upgrade quality. Since 2014, momentous strides have been made in building up and updating head teachers, subsequently catalysing an exponential rise in the number of Indian Organizing of Innovation (IITs), National Establishing of Innovation (NITs), and Indian Establishing of Administration (IIMs) over the nation. Strikingly, six unused IIT organisations have been built up, and the Indian School of Mines (ISM), Dhanbad, has been overhauled into an IIT. The Lok Sabha passed the Establishing of Innovation (Alteration) Charge in 2016, encouraging the opening of seven unused IITs in different states and broadening access to quality specialised education. Additionally, seven unused IIMs have been set up within the past six years, with six commencing their Post Graduate Program in Administration in 2015 and IIM Jammu, set up in 2016, contributing to enhancing administrative ability over differing locales.

In a noteworthy improvement, 22 unused colleges have been built up within the Northeast region, marking a point of reference within the instructive scene of the range. Moreover, Ladakh has seen the foundation of its inaugural Central College, a critical step forward for the region's higher instruction division. Besides, setting up the first-ever legal college and a rail and transport college assist underscores the government's commitment to supporting particular instruction and inquiring about vital divisions. These activities point to upgrading instructive openings, advancing academic brilliance, and contributing to the general socio-economic advancement of the locales they serve.

The National Instruction Approach (NEP) 2020 has been a foundation in driving comprehensive changes in higher instruction, pointing to extend the net enrolment proportion (GER) to 50% by 2035. The College Gifts Commission (UGC), as the summit institution depended with defining and executing higher instruction arrangements, has initiated different activities to adjust India's instruction framework with worldwide guidelines and cultivate a culture of advancement and brilliance. Presenting a choice-based credit framework (CBCS) permits understudies to select courses and gain credits, advancing student-centric learning and intrigue thinks about. Moreover, the institution of a Scholastic Bank of Credit (ABC) will carefully store scholastic credits earned from perceived higher instruction educate (HEIs), encouraging consistent credit exchange and degree granting based on amassed credits.

Conclusion

Education is an essential tool which is very useful in everybody's life. It is also responsible for modifying our lifestyle, providing career opportunities, making a better person, and enhancing our intellect and the ability to make the right decisions, which increases an individual's quality of life and growth. It is also responsible for modifying our lifestyle, providing career opportunities, creating a better person, and enhancing our intellect and the ability to make the right decisions, which increases an individual's quality of life and growth. Skill education improves students' employability and contributes to their personal and professional development. Vocational, technical, and professional education was provided during the Muslim period. Effective skill development adapts with the times, ensuring you're equipped with the tools and knowledge necessary to succeed.

Effective skill development adapts with the times, ensuring you're equipped with the tools and knowledge necessary to succeed. Skills development in India faces several challenges

The government has launched several schemes and initiatives to promote skill development, such as the Skill India Mission.

References

1. Dewey, J. (1897). My Pedagogic Creed. The School Journal, LIV(3), 77- 80.
2. Durkheim, É. (1956). Education and Sociology. New York: The Free Press.
3. Chandra, Satish (2007), History of Medieval India, Orient Black Swan, Delhi.
4. Chaurasia, R.S. (2001), History of Medieval India: From 1000 A.D to 1707, Atlantic Publishers and Distributors, New Delhi.
5. Farooqui, S.A (2011), A Comprehensive History of Medieval India, Pearson, Delhi.
6. Khanna, M (2007), Cultural History of Medieval India, Social Science Press, New Delhi.
7. Rawlinson, H.G.(2001), Ancient and Medieval History of India, Bharatiya Kala Prakashan, De

CHAPTER 15

Role of Library and Information Centers in Promoting Knowledge

Vikash Kumar Singh
Librarian
Sainik School Tilaiya
(Under Sainik School Society, Ministry of Defence)
Koderma Jharkhand
Email: vksingh1718@gmail.com

Abstract

Libraries are meant for accessible and equitable access and dissemination of information and knowledge. Considering this, this paper discusses the role of the library system in various ways and means of knowledge and information dissemination to its wide variety of users. What factors affect patrons' information-seeking behaviour and their impact on knowledge sharing? The further paper discusses the role of libraries in knowledge promotion, the skills required for librarians and professionals that bring the world of knowledge and its users together, and the challenges of libraries and users while disseminating, searching and seeking information and expertise from various types of Modern and traditional libraries.

Introduction

Transmission of knowledge is one of the major activities of all kinds of libraries, irrespective of their type, collection, services or organisational attachment. They serve as repositories of information and provide various resources and services such as books, newspapers, magazines, journals, ICT-based information and multimedia resources, human experts, etc. All these resources help libraries transmit and disseminate knowledge and information to students, researchers, scholars, scientists, teachers, analysts, data managers and other unique and shared knowledge and information seekers. Libraries help them learn, research, intellectual development, etc. We know that libraries are involved in several activities with a prime aim to serve their users through their general functions such as dissemination of information, promoting education, promotion of culture, preservation of knowledge, assisting in research and development activities, providing aid to increase literacy and learning and widespread function to provide recreation. The best part of Libraries is that they provide resources and programs for individuals of all ages, ensuring that learning remains lifelong. Whether a child is learning to evaluate online sources or an adult is sharpening their research skills for a career, libraries support the ongoing development of these vital competencies. Historically, libraries have evolved into dynamic centres for promoting information literacy and critical thinking in the ICT era. They started offering education, became the centre of adult education, and have access to trusted resources and a supervised supportive environment for individuals to develop essential skills required for their growth and development. By allowing users to access digital resources conveniently, libraries empower individuals to make informed decisions, engage critically with information, and thrive in an information-rich world. In the ICT era, libraries became the centre of enlightenment, guiding individuals toward a brighter, more discerning future. We know that "Ideas can change a life" and that ideas are being generated and produced in places like libraries and learning centres, among various knowledge resources, leading to a knowledgeable society.

Scope of Study

This paper's scope is limited to the library system's impact, implementation, and role in promoting knowledge in society through various types of libraries, such as academic, research, and special libraries. The paper covers the role and impact of both ways of knowledge sharing, i.e. online and offline. This study looks closely at factors affecting knowledge dissemination among library users, the challenges and opportunities for libraries, and other possible ways for libraries and LIS professionals to promote knowledge in society. The paper will also analyse a few areas where libraries can help their patrons be more knowledgeable. Further, we will discuss some basic skills and expertise required to disseminate better services and knowledge to patrons and be helpful in re-engineering, re-branding, and new systems and services for modern and traditional Information users.

Research Method Used

The methodology used to write this review research paper is a literature search from primary and secondary sources of information related to Information dissemination, users' view to access libraries for knowledge and information requirements in various types of libraries. To collect comprehensive data and information on the research topic, online search form Internet resources are used widely along with the study of relevant books, available research papers of scholars, Government Documents, current updates from national newspapers and magazines and other available pertinent documents for the topic. Finally, the collected information, data, facts and figures were examined to critically analyse and bring out the focused outcome for this paper.

Factors Affecting Information seeking behavior in society

All over the world, libraries are committed to giving all free and evenhanded access to data, whether composed, electronic or varying media. They play a significant part in making proficient situations and advancing proficiency by advertising important and alluring perusing fabric for all ages and all proficiency levels and advertising grown-up and family education classes. They grasp social obligation to supply administrations that bridge social, political, and financial boundaries; customarily, they exert extraordinary exertion to amplify their administrations to minimise individuals. Libraries help find, utilise and decipher fitting data that opens up openings for long-lasting learning, education upgrade, educated citizenship, diversion, inventive, creative ability, personal inquiry about, essential considering, and strengthening in a progressively complex world. The information-seeking conduct of library clients and information searchers is affected by an assortment of components, which may briefly be portrayed within the taking after focuses

The information-seeking behaviour of library users and knowledge seekers is influenced by a variety of factors, including:

Information Needs: Users' specific information needs or goals heavily influence their seeking behaviour. Whether they seek information for academic research, personal interest, professional development, or solving a particular problem, the nature and urgency of their needs dictate the strategies they employ to find relevant information.

Demographics: Age, gender, education level, occupation, cultural background, and socioeconomic status can impact individuals' information-seeking behaviour. For example, younger users prefer digital resources and online search engines, while older users prefer traditional print materials or seek librarian assistance.

Technological Proficiency: Users' comfort level and proficiency with technology significantly affect their information-seeking behaviour. Technologically savvy users may rely heavily on online databases, digital resources, and search engines, while others may prefer traditional methods of accessing information, such as browsing physical library collections.

Information Literacy Skills: Users' ability to effectively navigate, evaluate, and utilise information sources is crucial in their seeking behavior. Those with solid information literacy skills may conduct thorough research, critically evaluate sources, and employ advanced search strategies. In contrast, others may struggle to locate reliable information or be susceptible to misinformation.

Access to Resources: The availability and accessibility of information resources within libraries and online impact users' seeking behavior. Users with limited access to libraries, internet connectivity, or subscription-based resources may face barriers in finding the information they need.

Time Constraints: Users' time constraints, such as deadlines for assignments or projects, influence their information-seeking behavior. Those with limited time may opt for quick searches or rely on readily available sources, while others may invest more time conducting comprehensive research.

Information Overload: The abundance of information in the digital age can overwhelm users and affect their seeking behavior. Information overload may lead to difficulty identifying relevant sources, decision paralysis, or reliance on superficial or biased sources.

Personal Preferences and Habits: Individual preferences, habits, and past experiences also shape information-seeking behavior. Some users may prefer specific formats (e.g., print vs. digital), sources (e.g., scholarly articles vs. popular magazines), or search strategies based on their preferences and previous successful experiences.

Social Influence: Peer recommendations, social networks, and recommendations from authority figures (e.g., professors and mentors) can influence users' information-seeking behaviour. Users may seek information based on recommendations from trusted sources or seek assistance from peers or experts in their network.

Cultural and Linguistic Factors: Cultural norms, language preferences, and socio-cultural contexts can influence how individuals seek and interpret information. Cultural differences in information-seeking behaviour may manifest in preferences for specific sources, search strategies, or communication styles.

Psychological Factors: Users' attitudes, motivations, and emotions also impact their information-seeking behavior. Factors such as curiosity, motivation to learn, fear of missing out (FOMO), anxiety about information accuracy, or perceived self-efficacy in finding information can influence how individuals approach information seeking.

Understanding these factors can help libraries and information professionals design services, resources, and interventions that better meet users' and knowledge seekers' diverse needs and preferences. By addressing these factors, libraries can enhance the effectiveness of their information and knowledge services and support users in achieving their information goals.

Role of Libraries in Knowledge Promotion

Libraries serve as invaluable institutions that democratise access and promotion to knowledge, foster intellectual inquiry and enrich communities with diverse educational and cultural experiences. They promote learning, which is one of the primary activities they do, and develop their infrastructure, staff, and expertise for the ultimate goal of providing the correct information to the right user at the right time and building a well-informed, knowledgeable and lifelong learner in society for the nation and world. In this way, libraries play a crucial role in promoting knowledge in society through various means. Here are a few points detailing their significance:

Access to Information: Libraries provide free or affordable access to various information resources, including books, journals, newspapers, and digital databases. They ensure that individuals from all backgrounds can access knowledge regardless of their economic status.

Library collaboration: Libraries collaborate with other institutions and community organisations to expand access to knowledge and resources, enhance educational opportunities, and address community needs effectively. Library partnerships and collaborative initiatives leverage collective expertise and resources to promote knowledge sharing and social impact.

Cultural Preservation: Libraries preserve cultural heritage by collecting, archiving, and curating materials that document the history, traditions, and achievements of societies. They safeguard rare books, manuscripts, archival documents, and artefacts, ensuring long-term preservation and accessibility for future generations.

Education Support: Libraries support formal education by providing resources for students and educators. They offer textbooks, reference materials, and study spaces conducive to learning. Additionally, many libraries provide educational programs and workshops to enhance literacy and academic skills.

Community Engagement: Libraries serve as vibrant community hubs where people gather for various activities, such as book clubs, lectures, workshops, and cultural events. They foster social interaction, intellectual exchange, and lifelong learning, enriching communities with diverse educational and cultural experiences.

Digital Literacy: In the digital age, libraries are crucial in promoting digital literacy skills. They offer access to computers, the internet, and software tools, enabling individuals to develop essential digital skills for work, education, and personal development.

Information Literacy: Libraries promote information literacy by teaching users how to evaluate, use, and communicate information effectively. Librarians offer guidance on conducting research, critically evaluating sources, and citing information ethically.

Innovation and Creativity: Libraries foster innovation and creativity by providing resources and support for entrepreneurship, creative endeavours, and collaborative projects. They offer maker spaces, innovation labs, and technology resources, encouraging individuals to explore new ideas, experiment with technology, and pursue creative expression.

Lifelong Learning: Libraries promote lifelong learning by offering educational programs, workshops, and learning opportunities for people of all ages and backgrounds. From early childhood literacy programs to adult education classes, libraries cater to diverse learning needs throughout the lifespan, promoting personal growth, skills development, and intellectual enrichment.

Intellectual freedom: Libraries advocate for intellectual freedom, privacy rights, and access to information as fundamental principles essential to a democratic society. They defend individuals' rights to access information freely, without censorship or restriction, and uphold privacy protections for library users.

Skills required to promote efficient knowledge-sharing

Nowadays, the role of libraries and proficient custodians is changing worldwide. They are now not detached attendants and preservers of books; instead, they have advanced to become facilitators of data and long-lasting learning openings with an accentuation on benefits, recognising client needs and communicating arrangements. Advanced libraries unfurl the community's learning potential by providing data on community issues, such as well-being, business, proceeding instruction, and neighbourhood history. This impartial getting to data is essential to empower taught and educated citizens to take part in a global community. There are many basic abilities custodians ought to have or create for viable information advancement and to maximise library utilisation.

Tech-savvy Professionals with emerging technological knowledge: Libraries should utilise more developing ICT instruments and advances. Libraries may advantage by utilizing ICT applications to supply clients with different quality administrations to create the communication, utilisation, and creation and dispersal of modern information. All sorts of library exercises can be done rapidly with the execution of ICT applications, which may lead the library into an energetic one.

Understanding of knowledge-sharing culture: One of the foremost fundamental perspectives of KM is to create a knowledge-sharing culture inside the organization since the extreme objective of knowledge-sharing is to disperse the correct substance to the correct individuals at the proper time. It empowers staff individuals to make speedy decisions and solve problems. LICs ought to empower their staff with motivation and motivating forces and orchestrate programs on knowledge-sharing societies. In expansion, devices such as substance administration instruments, knowledge-sharing devices, archive administration devices, entries, wikis, and information warehousing can be connected to quicken the speed of knowledge-sharing societies among staff individuals and clients inside and outside the LICs.

Availability to implement ICT infrastructure and application: Libraries continuously have to bargain with the client community to meet their day-by-day necessities and oversee their assets in a way that can be effortlessly available. The ICT framework of libraries offers great assistance. Building a vigorous foundation with developing library and ICT advances in Libraries is fundamental. Actualizing ICT applications would aid libraries in quickening information advancement and sharing.

Conduct of training Orientation/programmes/seminars/workshops and symposiums: The training programme can develop the quality of staff and professionals and create awareness among users. Therefore, Libraries should arrange more training, orientation programmes, workshops, and seminars to make well-trained staff and their users aware of their services.

Leadership qualities: Library management, especially the extensive libraries, demands leadership qualities. Hence, it is required to have leadership skills to manage and guide his team from time to time, as every library employee must be motivated towards his/her work to carry out responsibilities efficiently for the smooth running of the library and better knowledge sharing among its users.

Listening and communication skills: Library professionals must have good communication and listening skills. These skills improve understanding and self-confidence, as he/she has to interact with different types of users to identify the exact requirements and to make them present their requirements or queries happily to provide the required knowledge and information accordingly.

Interpersonal Skills: Librarians and LIS professionals must deal with people at all levels, including management, users, colleagues, vendors, etc. To deal with each one of them in an exemplary manner requires interpersonal skills. Building good rapport with all levels of users is crucial to making them comfortable with the information and knowledge gained.

Challenges of Libraries in Knowledge Promotion

Lack of Digital Literacy Training: In today's digital era, Digital literacy is indispensable. Libraries offer digital literacy training programs covering various topics, from online privacy and cyber security to responsible social media use. These programs empower individuals to navigate the digital realm with confidence, security, and ethics. Ultimately, digitally literate staff can better serve society through knowledge promotion and vice versa.

Lack of trained LIS professionals: Non-professional staff run numerous national libraries. It is accepted that any volunteer or instructor can oversee a library. However, the quality of a library's benefit depends on the proficient quality of its staff, which, in turn, depends on the quality and pertinence of the preparation they have gotten. Running a library with amateurish staff is like instructing without a proficient foundation, which leads to destitute information and data spread.

Infrastructural issues: Libraries must have well-equipped furniture, buildings, a sufficient collection of resources and journals, cosy reading or reference rooms, ICT facilities, online offline access, etc., to keep users motivated towards libraries and serve them better. Lack of such basic infrastructure facilities will result in low-quality services and less knowledge promotion.

Limited funds: Funding is a common problem for all libraries worldwide. Funding is very important to develop a sound library with sufficient collection, classification, preservation, and dissemination of library resources. Limited funding in libraries creates problems in promoting knowledge. The issue is more visible in developing countries struggling with their basic needs. The knowledge-seeking behaviour of users improves when they are being facilitated with their basic needs of food, shelter and clothes.

Lack of Inclusive Libraries: Still, there is a lack of libraries in India and in the world, barring a few to serve a variety of users. There is a lack of proper facilities for small children, differently able users, women having kids, old age users, etc. Most libraries do not have proper facilities and equipment for their special class of users, which restricts potential library users from visiting the library and gathering knowledge.

Technological gap between Users and staff and vice versa: Knowledge-sharing culture is exceptionally compelling not as it were for library staff but for clients, which can empower them rapidly and viably to discover significant data or help them in choice-making and issue fathoming. These knowledge-sharing exercises, both understood and expressed, can happen between staff, clients or staff and clients at the same time. In case anybody among them is having issues related to taking care of advances, they may not get the required data and information looking for for.

Lack of Uniform National and International Information Policy: The Need for participation among national and universal organisations and libraries included in library-related work debilitates the framework and makes superfluous duplication or, indeed, competition. If freely accessible assets are rare, cooperation and asset sharing become an arrangement to advance information. Participation is also fundamental among national data suppliers, including legislative and non-governmental organisations, the media, corporate companies, and the distribution division.

Lack of Needs Analysis: Numerous libraries are set up without a proficient needs investigation of the community, resulting in a data benefit based on presumptions, not actual needs. These libraries disconnect themselves from the common open and right supporters; their collection really serves as if it were a little parcel of clients, not an entire community, who benefit from the collection. Fair as a needs investigation is essential sometime recently building up a benefit, proceeding checking and assessment with the dynamic community for most significant utilisation of accessible assets for information spread.

Irrelevant Material: Irrelevant, obsolete and outdated collection greatly hinders knowledge promotion. Especially in libraries that lack funding, cannot afford continuous collection development, and depend on donations and similar help, which causes poor collection and attracts fewer readers; hence, the dissemination of knowledge and information is also low.

Conclusion

As an association, a physical and advanced area, and a well-recognized social institution, the library could be a standard setting for supporting, advancing and making unused information. Libraries may be interestingly situated as centres where all the disciplines come together, where understudies mingle, consider, and rest, and where the institution's mission and recognising characteristics meet with the broader world of information, past and display. Even though the library is still famously distinguished with books, it can also be a craftsmanship display, a space for voyaging shows, an execution middle, a lab, a producer space, and a press, which makes a difference in advancing information in society. It's a place where understudies can find who they are, where thoughts take birth, and where instructors can get back as they investigate inventive and open ways to share their discoveries. The library, as the common ground for all in any institution and a nearby point of research, can speak to and demonstrate values that interface and make the world a place where all are empowered to think openly, make, and share for the past display and future information. In conclusion, libraries are vital to educating advanced information, cultivating mental requests, and improving communities with different instructive and social encounters. Through their devotion to instruction, community engagement, and encouragement, libraries help people and communities thrive in an ever-changing world where each information searcher features a location to recover his/her information and data seeking.

References

1. MD. ASHIKUZZAMAN. Role of libraries in promoting information literacy and critical thinking skills in the digital age, *LIS Education Network.* from https://www.lisedunetwork.com/

role-of-libraries-in-promoting-information-literacy-and-critical-thinking-skills-in-the-digital-age/

2. Islam Nazmul, Islam Shariful and Rajk Abdur. (2020). Problems of knowledge management practices in libraries and information centres of Bangladesh. From https://journals.sagepub.com/doi/10.1177/0340035219894359
3. Krolak, Lisa. (2005). The Role of libraries in the creation of literate environments. from https://unesdoc.unesco.org/ark:/48223/pf0000146057.
4. Negi, Dheeraj. (2014). Soft skills for librarian.from https://www.slideshare.net/slideshow/soft-skills-for-librarian/37750342
5. Fister, Barbara. (n.d).Librarians supporting the new knowledge. From https://acrl.ala.org/newroles/?page_id=263
6. Gwyer, Roisin. (n.d). **A** list of must-have librarian skills for academic libraries. From https://librarianresources.taylorandfrancis.com/insights/librarian-skills-development/10-skills-librarians-need-future/

CHAPTER 16

Evolving University Library Services in the Light of COVID-19 Pandemic

S. Weerasinghe,
Senior Assistant Librarian
Science Library, University of Peradeniya, Sri Lanka
E-mail:-sureniw1@yahoo.com

Abstract

The sudden onset of the COVID-19 pandemic brought significant changes to almost every aspect of human lives, including university libraries. Despite the challenges, university libraries have transitioned to offering technology-driven online services in the post-pandemic era. This study investigates how university libraries are evolving and adapting to the changing landscape in the post-COVID-19 era. The study applied a qualitative approach using semi-structured interviews with six library professionals engaged in the university sector of Sri Lanka. By examining the perspectives of these library professionals, the study uncovers the strategies and innovations implemented by university libraries adapting to the new normal caused by the pandemic.

Keywords: Post covid era, University Library, Sri Lanka, qualitative

Introduction

The unforeseen outbreak of the novel COVID-19 pandemic tremendously transformed almost every aspect of human lives virtually overnight. Inevitably, universities and, in particular, university libraries were severely affected by this crisis. The COVID-19 situation caused libraries to undergo frequent closures and interruptions to regular functions and hindered almost all library services. In addition, one-on-one service interactions became impossible or less preferable. Library collections in printed format created barriers to information access, and thus, the value of printed collections declined (Cox, 2020). Nevertheless, the library staff had to overcome psychological distress and face new challenges with a positive mindset. The pandemic and its preventive social distancing norms led libraries to find pragmatic alternatives since online learning and hybrid information provisions became the 'New Normal' in the higher education system (Martzoukou, 2020). Inaccessibility of printed collections led libraries to seek other possible ways to make content promptly available. University libraries are rapidly transitioning to online services to satisfy their user needs. For survival of the pandemic, university libraries were compelled to create innovative information services and provide enhanced services to the scholarly community. Still in the post-pandemic era, university libraries continue providing technology-driven online services. As a consequence of the pandemic, university libraries are faced with the challenge of supporting their user base by continuously maintaining academic and research activities via remote and virtual platforms.

This study explores how university libraries are evolving and adapting to the changing landscape in the post-COVID-19 era. The study followed a qualitative approach using semi-structured interviews with ten library professionals engaged in the university sector of Sri Lanka. By examining the perspectives of these library professionals, the study attempts to uncover the strategies and innovations implemented by university libraries adapting to the new normal caused by the pandemic. Study findings will provide important insights into the evolving university library services amidst the challenges caused by the pandemic. The findings will contribute to the literature on library service delivery during crises and inform future strategies for enhancing library services in the digital age.

Method

This study employed a qualitative research design. Semi-structured interviews were conducted and audio-recorded. A pre-prepared semi-structured interview guide with open-ended questions was used to conduct the interviews. All interviews were transcribed non-verbatim and translated to English. For the interviews, 6 library professionals attached to the state university sector in Sri Lanka were selected, applying the snowball sampling method. Data were analysed using thematic analysis.

Results and Discussion

Table 1: Demographic Profile of the Subjects

Interview Number	Gender	Age Category
1	Male	31-40
2	Female	41-50
3	Female	41-50
4	Female	31-40
5	Female	50-60
6	Male	41-50

Through the thematic analysis of the interviews the following library services that have evolved due to the pandemic were revealed:

Enhancing the Library Web site

University libraries are improving their websites to provide library resources and services via the library webpage which is the main access point for the library user (Int.1). The interface of the library website is created in a user-friendly manner with simple navigation as well as in an eye-catching manner (Int. 1 and Int. 2 and Int.5). In addition, websites should be responsive and enable personalization for users (Int. 3). Parts of the websites are redesigned to direct user attention on to the online services being delivered (Int.3). In addition, information regarding the library such as seminars, programs hosted by the library and fine waivers, is also highlighted in the library website (Int. 4). Also, library website is being updated frequently to render timely information (Int.6).

Remote Access of Content

University libraries worked on rendering remote access to library electronic resources by applying strategies such as shibboleth access to subscribed databases (Int.1, Int. 2, Int. 4, Int. 6). Also, scanned copies of past papers, abstracts of Theses are made accessible via the library website (Int. 2, Int.3). Moreover, librarians are establishing negotiations with publishers and other content providers to gain free access to electronic resources (Int.3). Medawar and Tablet (2020) also pointed out that several prominent publishers including Sage, Elsevier and Springer have promptly responded to support librarians through creating hubs and launching pages to provide unlimited access to numerous resources.

Remote Interactive Services

Libraries have opened up services for users to consult information specialists virtually via modes such as chat, email queries and 'Ask a Librarian' (Int.5 and Int.6).

Online Library Orientations

Library orientation programs which were usually conducted physically in lecture halls were shifted to online platforms such as Zoom, Microsoft Teams, Google meet etc (Int.1; Int.2, Int. 5, Int. 6). Yet, the librarians are striving hard to create awareness and educate students in a fruitful way and to render them an experience similar to that in classroom sessions (Int.5).

Support Online Teaching and Online Research

University libraries play a vital role in improving the digital literacy of students, teachers and researchers so that they will possess adequate skills and competency to work in the new online context successfully (Int.3, Int. 4, Int. 6). Libraries assist the Faculty in producing instructional videos and rendering access to scholarly resources (Int. 1, Int. 4). Cox (2020) mentioned that, libraries could facilitate researches through developing virtual labs and using tools such as ORCHID to link various gateways with institutional repositories.

Enhancing Digital Content Services

Digital content processed by libraries is extended by including library guides, book chapters, free e-copy services etc. (Int. 1, Int.3). Also, Inter-Library Loan Services are enhanced to provide better services during the pandemic (Int.1; Int.4, Int.5). Libraries have lounged content page service for subscribed electronic journals and delivery of full text to academics through e-mail (Wijetunge, 2021)

Modified Reference Services

The pandemic made physical visits to the library almost impossible and thus, the library staff has taken measures to consistently attend to user inquiries which will help to fulfil their information needs via online mode (Int.1, Int2, Int.3, Int. 6). According to Cox (2020), to offer high-quality user services meeting with their expectations libraries need to seek for more "self-service" and "touch-less interactions" such as "self-checkout, curbside pickup, scan and deliver, and materials delivery" (Cox, 2020).

Advancement of Open Educational Resources (OER)

Due to the closure of libraries during the crisis, alternative pathways such as OER have come into light for the dissemination of information via institutional repositories (Int.4, Int. 5). OER permits free access, use, adaption as well as redistribution of content under no or limited restrictions. Libraries have taken initiatives to educate faculty members on the advantages of creating OER, free textbooks, and personalised pedagogical material, which help decrease student education costs (Int.1; Int.2 and Int.4).

Use of Social Media

Libraries have more massively embraced social media in order to connect with their users (Int. 1, Int.2; Int.5 and Int.6). Social media are used by libraries for promoting their resources, services and events (Int. 1, Int.2; Int.5 and Int.6). According to Medawar and Tablet (2020), Instagram, Twitter and Facebook are the heavily utilized social media platforms to serve these purposes.

Challenges Faced by University Libraries in Service Provision

COVID-19 has accelerated the digital transition of higher education institutions and libraries. The interviews revealed some challenges faced by university libraries in service provision. Even though technological advancements have created new roles and means of information delivery, lack of digital infrastructure has become a major barrier (Int. 4, Int.6). Some libraries may not have financial provisions as well as equipment to successfully complete the digitization of library material (Int.1 and Int.2; Int.5). Also, cultural as well as organizational barriers worsen this problem (Int.3). Another serious obstacle faced by librarians in providing information services to users is the Copyright laws (Int. 4, Int.5, Int. 6). It is mandatory to provide unrestricted access to various types of materials for students who are engaged in online education. Yet, copyright laws have built up many restrictions, and librarians must pay close attention to provide access to information without violating copyright laws. Librarians should create awareness about copyrights including fair use of materials for educational purposes among Faculty staff and recommend authors use open publishing initiatives such as creative commons licenses in publishing research(Int. 4, Int.5; Int.6).. Declination of library allocations is also a great hindrance to the purchasing and subscription of resources (Int.1 and Int.2). Nowadays electronic resources are heavily utilized by the scholarly community. Thus, it is imperative for university libraries to allocate a large proportion of funds for the development of electronic collections. In addition, library staff may not have sufficient skills to offer various online services (Int.3). On the other hand, university students may have the same problems of not having suitable devices and skills (language skills, use of e-resources, etc.) to receive library services (Int.4 and Int.6).

Conclusion

In conclusion, the COVID 19 crisis made a significant impact on university libraries, leading to the evolution of various innovative strategies. University libraries have adapted through improving their websites to offer better access to resources, providing remote access to content, rendering interactive online services, conducting online orientation programmes and reshaping reference services. Also, the advancement of OERs has played a vital role in assuring consistent access to information during the pandemic and in the post pandemic era. In addition, use of social media is important for libraries to engage with users and promote library services. It is clear that online library services have obtained prominence among information sources in the context of non-contact education. There is a need for university libraries to come up with strategies and programs for digital transformation. This is the time to reinforce open access, open research, open data and open publishing. It is also important that librarians educate and motivate faculty staff as well as researchers to publish their work under open access policies. University librarians should rethink about making printed content accessible for the scholarly community and increasing the visibility of available online resources. The COVID-19 pandemic has been a catalyst for change in university library services. The shift towards digital resources, virtual collaboration, and enhanced inclusivity has transformed the way libraries support students and researchers. In the post-COVID-19 era, university libraries will continue to evolve and adapt, using the lessons learnt during the pandemic to provide innovative services that meet the requirements of the academic community.

References

1. Cox, C. (2020). Changed, Changed Utterly. Inside Higher ED.:https://www.insidehighered.com/views/2020/06/05/academic-libraries-will-change-significant-ways-result-pandemic-opinion

2. Martzoukou, K. (2020). Academic libraries in COVID-19: a renewed mission for digital literacy. Library management.
3. Medawar, K. and Tabet, M.(2020). Library collections and services during Covid-19: Qatar National Library experience. Alexandria: The journal of National & International Library & Information Issues, 30(2-3), 178-190.
4. Wijetunge, P. (2021) Challenges imposed on Sri Lankan Libraries by COVID19 and new normal service paradigm.Available at :https://www.researchgate.net/publication/341671003_Challenges_of_Covid_19_on_Sri_Lankan_libraries
5. Zhou, J. (2021). The role of libraires in distance learning during COVID- 19, Information Development. 1-12, DOI:https://doi.org/10.1177/02666669211001502

CHAPTER 17

Role of Libraries in Promoting Knowledge

Ms. Padma Harsora
Research Scholar (Ph.D.)
Veer Narmad South Gujarat University Surat
E-mail: padma.harsora@gmail.com

Dr. Ajit Prajapati
Librarian
Government Arts and Commerce College,
Netrang, Bharuch, Gujarat
Email: ajit.prajapati2010@gmail

Abstract

Thanks to internet technology, many social media platforms like Facebook, Instagram, WhatsApp, YouTube, blogs, and so on have emerged. Every member of society, as well as several governmental, private, educational, and non-academic institutions, have grown reliant on these communication channels. Libraries, for example, use social media to promote and expand their services and information offerings. Modern inventions and technology, such as smartphones, mobile internet access, and social media, have presented librarians with new difficulties in meeting users' expectations and information needs in this digital age. Another significant difficulty is getting more people to the library and giving them access to resources and information. Because of this, academic libraries must offer cutting-edge services to draw in and pique users' interests if they are to thrive in the modern era of technology. Thus, this article has made an effort to offer information on which social media platforms can be used and what services academic libraries can offer to advertise their materials, data, and offerings.

Keywords: Academic Libraries, social media, Publicity, and Library and Information Services

Introduction:

We can classify the current era as ultra-modern. These days, communication methods have undergone significant change due to the ongoing advancements in science and technology. Internet technology has created numerous social media platforms today, including Facebook, Instagram, YouTube, blogs, and WhatsApp, which are now an integral part of a person's life and a crucial conduit for communication. All of these attachment tools have made every member of society, as well as numerous private and public academic and non-academic institutions, dependent. This also applies to libraries. Libraries also use social media for internal development, service and information marketing, and the spread of different library activities.

Any educational institution's library serves as its beating heart. Library materials were prized possessions in antiquity. It was also restricted to nobility only. As opposed to being knowledge repositories, libraries nowadays serve as information hubs. Conventional libraries are undergoing continuous transformations. In the digital age, librarians have new problems providing the information consumers require and demand. These innovations include social media, mobile internet access, smartphones, and other modern advancements. One significant difficulty is figuring out how to draw people into the library and deliver them services and information. To thrive in the modern era of technology, academic libraries must, therefore, offer cutting-edge services that pique users' interests and draw them in.

So, in this article, there are resources by academic libraries. What social media can be used to promote information and services? An attempt has been made to provide information on what services can be provided.

What is social media?

Two general terms make up social media. Initially, social media, then media. The term "social" in its original definition describes a state where people actively seek out social groups to join. for them to converse with each other about their ideas and experiences. Sociality is ingrained in human nature. They converse with individuals. To assist, to enable, to share, to collaborate. Like being involved in decisions. He thus makes distinct and varied entrances into society. And makes himself known. Put otherwise, a situation that an individual finds themselves in. Social interaction refers to the reciprocal relationship based on human interactions between people or groups, feeling actively linked to the group, and being conscious of the interests of the group.(Barevadiya, 2014)

Another word used in a collective meaning is "media," which is the word "media" in plural. Media is the aggregate term for all forms of media, including television, radio, newspapers, the internet, etc. Media so refers to a variety of media. It is a means of establishing communication with members of the community. This communication can take any form, including written, spoken, or electronic. (Swarn, 2014)

Therefore, social media is a combination of media and social, which is used to connect people in society. It is called social media. In the sense of technology, media that is used to share user-generated content and enhance collaboration through internet-based various technologies like computers, mobile, tablets etc., is called social media. Web, mobile and other device-based technologies through which people produce, consume and share content. In this one, the user can fulfill the roles of producer, distributor, editor and consumer. (Swarn, 2014)

Definitions of social media:

"Social media pertains to computer-based technologies that enable the exchange of thoughts, concepts, and data among extensive networks and communities. Social media is an online platform that lets people quickly share content—including documents, images, videos, and personal information. Individuals who utilize computers, tablets, or smartphones to access social media through web-based software or applications. (social-media.)

Social media is defined as forms of electronic communication, such as websites for local networking and micro-engaging. Through an online community, users can share information, ideas, personal opinions and other content." (Webster, 1976)

Use of social media in libraries: The main objective of social media use is to share and promote information and services. Apart from these, other objectives are as follows:

- Enhance reference services
- To share knowledge among users
- To promote various programs for libraries
- To modernise the image and e-reputation of the library
- Reach new audiences through potential users
- To promote library news and press releases
- To give users up-to-date information quickly
- To create discussion groups and collaborative work

Various social media and library services:

Social media is the independent variable, while the library services librarians provide to their users is the dependent variable. Dependent variables include library materials and functions such as books, journals, newspapers, maps, Internet-based resources, CD/DVD and lending services, reference services, indexing and instructing services, user education, etc. Are divided. The independent variables are social media like WhatsApp, Facebook, blog, Twitter, etc.

(Avhad, 2023), Librarians can use these social media platforms to advertise library services and initiatives. It also provides an innovative and effective way for libraries to stay in touch with their users. The following are popular social media platforms that librarians utilise to advertise library services and satisfy customers' information needs:

WhatsApp Messenger:

WhatsApp is a social media with popular instant free messaging and voice-over telephony services running on smartphones or Android-based cellphones. It was started in January 2009 by Jane Kumm and Brian Acton. Written messages between users. Allows the exchange of audio, video, images, thoughts, verbal messages, etc.(Acton, 2009)

The following services can be provided through WhatsApp in libraries:

- List of new books in the library. Periodicals and up-to-date information can be sent by grouping with readers.
- Cover photos of new books can be placed in reader groups.
- Librarians can send library notifications and instant messages to users instantly as well
- Can also get feedback.
- Up-to-date information that library users need can be sent instantly.
- Documents and materials can also be sent to the users at any time and even after the library's working hours.
- Users can post images and videos of library competitions, news, library orientation programs and competitions.
- It also allows librarians to interact with users through discussion groups, image tagging, receiving comments and feedback, and suggestions to improve library services.

YouTube:

YouTube is an important social media site for sharing videos, and it is widely used nowadays. It was founded on February 14, 2005, by Steve Chain, Chad Hurley, and Javed Karim. In which registered members can upload videos. Google bought it in November 2006 for $1.65 billion. In this way, non-registered members can watch different types of videos, such as TV shows, music videos, movie trailers, educational videos, etc., for free. However, paying a fee to watch some videos. (Steve Chain, Chad Hurley, 2005)

Libraries can offer the following services through YouTube:

- Readers can be encouraged to upload various library-related videos to YouTube.

- Most libraries use YouTube to create and share videos on library events, lectures, special talks, library visits, bibliography etc. to users.
- YouTube allows librarians to save videos related to favourite topics and also enables them to create playlists and share them among users.

Facebook:

Facebook is one of the widely used social media platforms, mainly for interaction and information sharing. Facebook is one of the most popular and library-friendly. It started in AD. Mark Zuckerberg, a student at Howard University, did it in 2004. Then, it was called Facebook. Then, in August 2005, its name was changed to Facebook. Facebook is a free social media service on the Internet. Through this, its members can interact with their friends, families and acquaintances. (Mark Zuckerberg, 2004)

By using Facebook, academic libraries provide the following services to their users:

- By using services like JSTOR Search and World Cat through Facebook, users can be in touch with their information needs, and information can be replicated. (Barevadia, 2014).
- Libraries can inform users by posting updated library information, programs and services.
- Facebook can connect and furnish details on novel and pre-existing print and digital materials…
- Enables users to access the contents of the library catalog without visiting the library or the library website. (Farkas, 2007).
- An online library helps users create study groups.
- The question paper facilitates access to the bank. This will allow users to access question papers without geographical limitations.
- Practical information about library hours, as well as website information, can be posted.

- Libraries' Facebook pages serve as a central point for user contact, and librarians can remind users about their services by posting images and up-to-date information about them.

Pinterest:

Paul Sciarra, Evan Sharp and Ben Silberman invented Pinterest. Its development began in December 2009, and the site was launched in March 2010 as a closed beta. The site was launched in an invite-only open beta. On Pinterest, users can upload, save, and categorize images on different boards. Pinterest's evolution depends on the interests of its users and its members to produce content. (Paul Sciarra, 2009)

Pinterest can be used in the library to:

- Photos of new books, magazines, etc., in the library can be uploaded to Pinterest.
- Academic libraries are experimenting with Pinterest as a new way to connect with students, faculty, and staff.
- As Pinterest is a collection of visual images, users collect images from the internet and help group them under the headings of their choice. Thus acting as a research portal.

Instagram:

Instagram was founded in 2010 by Kevin Sister Om and Mike Kreger. It was made available as a free IOS mobile application in October 2010. It was then launched for Android phones two years later. This app is available in 33 languages. Which can be used on smartphones and computers. You can send photos and videos from this to each other whenever you want. It can also be written and posted. This is similar to Facebook. However, live video chatting is not possible. Only images can be uploaded in this. (Kreger, 2010)

- Instagram can be used to post pictures related to collections in the library. For example, a US university posted a picture of an old phenology map related to their collection on the history of psychiatry

- Libraries use Instagram to ask users about their favourite authors. Library programs. Competitions may be announced. Photos of competition posters, staff preparing for the competition and other relevant photos can be used to inform the public and build excitement about the competition.
- Libraries are using Instagram to showcase their history. Instagram has proven to be a creative platform for reposting historical photos and films for libraries and other institutions.
- Library space can be shown. If the library space is user-friendly, they will be more attracted to the library and will use the library and information services more.

LinkedIn:

LinkedIn is a business social network service founded on December 28, 2002, by Rid Homan and launched in May 2003. (Homan, 2003)

You can search for a job by uploading a resume on this site. After uploading a resume, you can apply for a job in a company according to the company's requirements.

- This platform allows librarians to offer customised services like disseminating specific information.
- Using LinkedIn to connect with specialists in their industry, librarians can obtain professional information. (Chauhan, 2013)

Blogs:

Blogs are a type of personal web page, which can be written like a diary. It started in 1992. The person who writes blogs is a blogger, and this work is called blogging. Their topics can be general or specific. It provides news, information or ideas related to the topic. Most blogs are primarily in text form. However, some blogs are arts (art blogs). Photographs (photography blogs) are also in the form of videos and music. (Blog, 1992)

The following library services can be provided to the users using Bozza.

- Librarians in libraries can periodically send messages information on a particular topic or issue to users and get their opinions
- Users may be allowed to contribute content. They can write articles news on local issues and expect instant response from users
- Users may be allowed to contribute content. They can write articles news on local issues and expect instant response from users
- Provided by librarians as blogs enable user interaction
- Allows students to provide feedback on incoming services. News about library timings, events, competitions, and activities in the library can be flashed.
- Blogs allow librarians to create guides on various topics to meet student demand.
- A librarian can create a blog detailing the programs of projects undertaken on renovations taking place in the library.
- Librarians and users can find current information about various topics, usually through weblogs or blogs.
- Reference blogs can provide the correct information at the right time by providing advanced reference services.
- Blogs can be used for library outreach, dissemination of information, image building of the library, communication with internal and external users, and the arrival and promotion of new materials in the library collection

Twitter:

This is a free social networking and micro-blogging service. Twitter was founded on March 21,2006, by Jack Dorsey, Noah Glass, Biz Stone and Evan Williamson in San Francisco, California. Where users are free to express themselves without feeling ecstatic. Twitter has become very popular among the youth after its launch, Which provides up-to-date information to its users. It also provides a facility to send and read information to each other. Tweets are text-based posts of up to 140 characters and are displayed on the author's profile page and sent to other users. Tweets can be sent and received via an external application, the Twitter website, or the Short Messaging Service (SMS). This service is accessible on the internet, but the use of SMS requires a fee to be paid by the phone service provider. Till now, this service was available in English, but now many languages are also available, like Spanish, Japanese, German, French, etc...(Jack et al., 2006)

Twitter can be used to promote information services in the library as follows:

- The library's librarians can provide users with up-to-date information about new books, magazines, and daily events.
- Employees can inform the audience about daily operations, such as collecting frequently updated content through a microblogging app. Librarians can use this platform to send short messages or status updates.
- Users can use Twitter to communicate concerns or inquiries about a specific library-related issue, and they will receive prompt feedback.

Myspace

Myspace is a helpful resource that libraries may use to connect with a broader audience. So that a new generation can be reached and access the services provided by the library. For that, libraries should begin to understand Myspace's opportunities to reach users, especially the youth, and create their own Myspace page.

- Their communication can be increased with youth and college groups who spend much time on Myspace, and they can easily reach out to libraries.
- Mather Paksha gives more information about who the librarians are helping so that they can produce the information as per the users' desire.

- Through Myspace, library services can be reached and offered to users who have not previously taken advantage of library resources.

Flickr:

Flickr is a photo management service that allows users to upload and share high-quality photos, connect with friends, and stay in touch. It also provides easy ways to use social tagging to find great images and manage the search for supporters.

- Librarians use this tool to share and distribute images of new collections in the library. Pages of books and magazines and other reading materials via Flickr can be transmitted to users.
- Clicker allows librarians to upload and share images of library events, programs, and activities. Additionally, it enables tagging images with keywords. Related to this tag, Images will be more helpful in searching. (Flickr, 2008)
- Librarians can create discussion groups with users, and educational and subject-related photographs can be posted.
- It enables librarians to post videos for virtual library visits.

Library Thing:

Library Thing is a social cataloging web application for storing and sharing book catalog and various type of book meta data. It is used by authors, individuals, libraries and publishers. Tim Spalding developed Library Thing and went live on August 29, 2005. As of February 2021, it had 26,00,000 users and a catalogue of 155 million books.

- Librarians can use this to send lists of current publications to users.
- Users can access the catalogue from anywhere.
- Library Thing also serves to connect people with similar books.

Following are some examples of libraries using social media:

The ADA University Library of Azerbaijan's Facebook page was initially launched in October 2014, with about 3,300 likes. The use of the Facebook page increased the number of people coming to use the resources in the library and the circulation of new books.

The Glasgow University Library initially used Facebook in the United Kingdom (UK). The library now employs a hybrid strategy that uses the internet, blogs, Facebook, Twitter, and Instagram. The Otis Library uses Pinterest in a variety of ways, which has a library board where photos of libraries and their services are posted. Prince Library provides library stories and insights from around the world through Instagram.

In addition, other university librarians utilize Facebook. Some of these are as follows: Below is the link to the library's Facebook page.

https://www.facebook.com/OULibrary
https://www.facebook.com/BristolUniLib
https://www.facebook.com/nofglibrary
https://www.facebook.com/ADA University
Library httpswww.facebook.com Mahas library Services
https://www.facebook.com
pages
University-of-Nairobi library/265755873442721

Conclusion:

Thus, in today's 21st-century era, many social media have come into existence due to the internet. Which is widely used for communicating information. Librarians must constantly strive to adopt this new approach to providing information and services to library users through social media and constantly update themselves. Only then can one provide good, fast, up-to-date information and services to its users. Also, a new audience can be attracted. At the same time, information and services of the library can also be disseminated quickly, and the library will grow faster.

Reference

1. Acton, J. K. and B. (2009). *wikipedia.org*. https://en.wikipedia.org/wiki/WhatsApp
2. Avhad, S. (2023). Use of Social Media to Promote Library Services in the College Library. *International Journal of Science and Research (IJSR)*, *12*(11), 1353–1355. https://doi.org/10.21275/sr231118150311
3. Barevadiya. (2014). Use of Social Media for Library and Information Services, Libraries. *Towards Value Added Services.4th National Library Conference and 30th Library Conference of Gujarat Granthalaya Seva Sangh. Ahmedabad, Gujarat.*, pp. 158–162.
4. Blog. (1992). *wikipedia.org*. https://en.wikipedia.org/wiki/Blog
5. Chauhan, M. (2013). *Use of Social Media in Libraries at EDII, Gandhinagar on Redefining Libraries to Create Next Generation Libraries*. 1–46. http://alibnet.org/public/bookofpaper/ppts/85.pdf%0Ahttps://www.coursehero.com/file/56872623/85pdf/%0Ahttps://www.semanticscholar.org/paper/Use-of-Social-Media-in-Libraries-Chauhan/8761ec559db2e9189d0447eced2361246e23b687
6. Flickr, U. (2008). *Flickr*. 58–62.
7. Homan, R. (2003). *wikipedia.org*. https://en.wikipedia.org/wiki/Linkedin
8. Jack Dorsey, Noah Glass, B. S. and E. W. (2006). *wikipedia.org*. https://en.wikipedia.org/wiki/Twitter
9. Kreger, K. S. O. and M. (2010). *wikipedia.org*. https://en.wikipedia.org/wiki/Instagram
10. Mark Zuckerberg. (2004). *en.wikipedia.org*. https://en.wikipedia.org/wiki/Facebook
11. Paul Sciarra, E. S. and B. S. (2009). *wikipedia.org*. https://en.wikipedia.org/wiki/Pinterest

12. social-media. (n.d.). *investopedia.com*. Retrieved March 15, 2024, from https://www.investopedia.com/terms/s/social-media.asp
13. Steve Chain, Chad Hurley, J. K. (2005). *wikipedia.org*. https://en.wikipedia.org/wiki/YouTube
14. Swarn, S. (2014). *Social Media: Sampark Kranti ka Kal, Aaj or Kal.* Harper Collis Publishers India. https://www.scribd.com/book/427477597/Social-Media
15. Webster, M. (1976). *Webster's New Collegiate Dictionary*. G.&C. Merriam Company Springfield, Massachusetts, USA.

CHAPTER 18

Knowledge management in CBSC school libraries in Jodhpur

Nattha Ram
Assistant Librarian
Army Public School Jodhpur
E-mail: nattharam1894@gmail.com

Abstract

Knowledge is power, and it is a vital tool for information seekers. Today, knowledge has spread worldwide with the help of the internet. Further, it is vast and diverse in any field. The library is the heart of any institute, but when we talk about school libraries then, knowledge management must be done. In the internet era, the library plays a vital role in any field of knowledge management, especially school libraries. The school library is far behind in knowledge management.ICT and digital libraries are the right places for CBSE school libraries to achieve the goal of knowledge management.

Keywords: Knowledge seeker, Digital library

Introduction

Knowledge management is a scientific process that arranges knowledge in a proper, systematic, user-oriented, aim-based way, achieving goals with the help of this tool. It includes institutional mechanisms, information technologies and software for school libraries. In school libraries where the readers are minors, correct knowledge and information must be adequately provided so that they can make excellent use of knowledge management at the university and college levels.

Definition

Knowledge management (KM) identifies, organises, stores, and disseminates information. IBM

Knowledge management is the process of capturing, creating, sharing, using, optimising, and managing information, expertise, and insights in an organisation. E GYAN

Knowledge Management Generation, Circulation and Management

From the ancient time of human civilisation to today, information/knowledge has constantly improved lifestyle; in modern societies, information is interlocked with the growth of economic, political, social and cultural sectors. It can be divided into two types: explicit and implicit. Knowledge includes printed /non-printed material. It is invisible and often confined to the mind of a person. It is hard to codify and, therefore, difficult to communicate with others—explicit and implicit knowledge accomplishing the knowledge circulation systems.

Knowledge begins the process of classifying and cataloguing information. Knowledge management is an activity that manages information and expertise in an environment that supports knowledge creation, acquisition, organisation and storage. It is distributed, accessed, and how it is transferred.

Knowledge management is not an easy task for any librarian. Still, some tools help smoothly, such as Email, databases, spreadsheets, powerpoint, Voice-mail, data models, documents, drawings, references, and process plans.

The infrastructure of Knowledge Management

Information management enters libraries, and many libraries have ICT facilities for information access. The infrastructure required for effective KM is the school library, which has software, hardware, databases, networks, etc. Many technologies can be used for knowledge processing, production, and integration—an initiative from the management for incurring expenditure for the adoption and implementation of ICT.

The Role of Librarians in KM for The Digital Library:

The librarian acts as the lighthouse that disseminates information and knowledge in optimum quality and quantities to any information. Now, the time of AI and the internet, with the help of computers, taken librarians first row as knowledge managers. Computers are used in resource sharing, and digital content is more helpful for information seekers.

Digital content pulls societies together for global, local, and personal functions. The digital libraries of schools play a magical role in getting and sharing information resources among the students. NDLI and virtual libraries are the platforms for correct information. School libraries have more with the help of digital libraries.

Conclusion

KM is to be integrated with proper organisational management to build competitiveness. With the help of ICT, it has become ever-dynamic, which has to be managed effectively for storing and service. Knowledge management will be more accessible with the help of a digital library.

REFERENCE

1 Onehttps://www.egain.com/what-is-knowledge-management/

2 ESSENCE OF KNOWLEDGE MANAGEMENT IN LIBRARIES IN MODERN ERA Krishnamurti Singha

3 International Journal of Digital Libraries and Knowledge Management. Volume 3, Number 2 (2013), pp. 71-74 © Research India Publications

4 PSG Kumar, A Students Manual of Library and Information Science-2002,

CHAPTER 19

Transforming Libraries: The Convergence of Emerging Technologies in the 22nd Century after Pre and Post-Pandemic 2019

Dr. Pushpendra Singh
Librarian & Head Central Library G.L. Bajaj Group of Institutions, Mathura
om.mahaur@gmail.com

Vishal Saxena
Chief Librarian Central Library Babu Banarasi Das University, Lucknow
vishalsaxena7786@gmail.com

Abstract

With the proliferation of digital resources and the growing expectations of users, School/College/University libraries are finding it challenging to keep up with the changing landscape of information services. The emergence of technology has led to a paradigm shift in the functioning of libraries. Libraries have transformed from just book repositories to digital hubs of information. New technology has impacted various aspects of society, including library services. The study aims to explore the impact of emerging technologies on library services, focusing on artificial intelligence (AI), machine learning (ML), blockchains, and many more emerging technologies. In this article, the authors explore the future of libraries in the new era of technology. We will also analyse the impact of technology on libraries and look at how libraries are evolving to meet the changing needs of their patrons.

Keywords: Artificial Intelligence (AI), Digital Library, Virtual Library, QR technology, Mobile Library, etc.

Introduction:

The library is a critical component of society that provides access to information and knowledge. However, with the rapid technological advancements, libraries have been forced to adapt to remain relevant. It means that "Do people still use physical libraries?" or "Aren't you worried about becoming irrelevant?" or "Are you worried about libraries disappearing?" I never get asked what advances libraries are making or where I think libraries are headed. The questions always have a negative bent. The future of libraries is not something. They have been around longer than our modern memory likes to consider. Libraries have a long history, 5,000 years–long. However, people worry about them because of modern technological developments like the internet, computers, and smartphones. The internet is 40 years old, computers less than 80, and smartphones have been around for only 30 years. It is bold to think these advances would eliminate libraries rather than advance them. Now let us take a journey of libraries from their beginning in 400 BC to the 21st century.

Libraries from the past to present in the 21st century

- Early Libraries (4000 BCE - 1800 CE): Cuneiform tablets in ancient Mesopotamia, Papyrus scrolls in ancient Egypt, and Greece manuscripts in medieval Europe
- Printing Press (1440 CE): Johannes Gutenberg's invention revolutionised the production of books and led to the widespread dissemination of knowledge
- Public Libraries (19th century): Andrew Carnegie's philanthropy helped establish many public libraries in the United States and Europe
- Digital Libraries (20th century): The development of electronic storage and retrieval systems allowed for the creation of digital libraries

- Internet Libraries (21st century): The growth of the Internet and World Wide Web has led to the creation of vast digital libraries accessible to anyone with an Internet connection
- Mobile Libraries (21st century): The proliferation of smartphones and tablets has led to the development of mobile libraries, allowing people to access books, articles, and other resources on-the-go
- AI-Assisted Libraries (21st century): Advances in artificial intelligence have created intelligent libraries that can recommend books and resources based on a user's interests and reading history.

It is proven that with every transformation from century to century, libraries move towards advancement, not disappearing or becoming irrelevant. Now, we can say that technological advances will not eliminate libraries. Instead, libraries are becoming more powerful and advanced. Emerging technologies such as artificial intelligence (AI), machine learning (ML), and blockchain can potentially transform library services. This study aims to explore the impact of emerging technologies on libraries. The research methodologies adopt a literature review, and the data collected from relevant sources is analyzed using thematic analysis. The study found that emerging technologies have transformed library services by improving the efficiency of operations, enabling personalised services, enhancing user experience, and expanding access to information. However, some challenges in adopting these technologies include financial constraints, technical expertise, and privacy concerns. The study concludes that libraries must adapt to emerging technologies to remain relevant and enhance their services.

Literature Review:

Artificial Intelligence (AI) is a technology that enables machines to learn from experience, perform tasks that require human intelligence, and improve their performance over time. AI has transformed library services by improving efficiency, enabling personalised services, and enhancing user experience. For instance, libraries have used AI-powered chatbots to provide 24/7 assistance to users, answer reference questions, and provide personalized recommendations. The University of Utah Marriott Library implemented an AI chatbot that could accurately answer 69% of reference questions (Bennett, 2019).

With messaging apps on the rise, chatbots are increasing in popularity among businesses and consumers. Chatbots are artificial intelligence (AI) systems that enable customer engagement via messaging, text, or speech. Many are deployed on chatbot platforms such as Facebook Messenger, WhatsApp, WeChat, Slack, or text messages. Facebook's expansion with Facebook Messenger has allowed businesses to better reach their target audience through different APIs, and chatbots are becoming necessary in specific industries.

Despite the complexity of AI, machine learning (ML), and natural language processing (NLP), which are used to pick out content and context from conversations with users, many platforms and solutions are available to build a sophisticated chatbot. The increased use of messaging apps and the ease and accessibility of customizable apps prove that the chatbot industry will continue to grow and strengthen. As the industry matures, the underlying AI technology continues to evolve and become more sophisticated.

Machine learning (ML) is a subset of AI that involves using algorithms to learn from data and improve the performance of a task. ML has been used in libraries to improve information retrieval, automate cataloging, and provide personalized services. The National Library of Medicine (NLM) implemented an ML algorithm to improve information retrieval. The algorithm improved the relevance of search results by 40% (Chen, 2019).

Block chain is a distributed ledger technology that allows for secure and transparent record-keeping. Block chain has the potential to transform library services by enabling secure and transparent transactions, facilitating copyright management, and providing decentralized access to information. The British Library implemented a blockchain-based project to manage copyright. The project enabled authors to manage their copyrights and license their works to users (Hindawi, 2020).

Challenges in the Adoption of Emerging Technologies:

The adoption of emerging technologies in library services is not without challenges. Financial constraints, technical expertise, and privacy concerns are challenges in adopting emerging technologies. Libraries must invest in technology infrastructure and hire staff with high technical expertise to implement these technologies successfully. Privacy concerns are also a challenge, particularly with AI and ML technologies. Libraries must ensure that user privacy is protected and that data is used ethically.

Emerging technologies have transformed library services by improving efficiency, enabling personalised services, and enhancing user experience. Libraries must adapt to emerging technologies to remain relevant and enhance their services. However, there are challenges in adopting these technologies, including financial constraints, technical expertise, and privacy concerns. Libraries must address these challenges to successfully implement emerging technologies and provide better services to their users.

Libraries have traditionally been a physical space where people come to borrow books, access information, and study. However, with the advent of new technologies such as augmented reality, virtual reality, QR code technology, artificial intelligence, machine learning, the Internet of Things, blockchain, and the latest revolution in the digital world, i.e., Chat GPT, libraries are going to transform themselves into more interactive and engaging spaces. Especially how libraries adapt to these new technologies and the benefits they offer users.

Future Trends in Libraries in the 22nd Century

Libraries have been essential to human society for centuries, serving as repositories of knowledge and culture. However, the rapid pace of technological change and societal transformation raises questions about the future of libraries. This paper explores potential future library trends in the **22nd** century, considering emerging technologies, societal changes, and environmental factors. The study draws upon existing literature and expert opinions to identify potential future library trends. The paper concludes by offering recommendations for libraries to adapt and thrive in the future.

The role of libraries has evolved from collections of manuscripts and books to digital repositories of knowledge and culture. The **22nd** century is likely to witness significant changes in society, environment, and technology that will impact the future of libraries. This paper explores potential future library trends in the 23rd century.

Emerging Technologies:

The **22nd** century will likely see the emergence of advanced technologies that will transform how libraries function. For example, artificial intelligence and machine learning will play a significant role in library operations, such as cataloging, information retrieval, and user services. Virtual reality and augmented reality technologies will create immersive and interactive library experiences for users, enabling them to explore digital collections and cultural artifacts in new ways. 3D printing and other additive manufacturing technologies will allow libraries to create physical replicas of rare or fragile artifacts, expanding access to cultural heritage.

Societal Changes:

The **22nd** century is likely to see significant societal changes that will impact the role of libraries. For example, the continued growth of urbanization and globalization will increase demand for libraries as community gathering spaces, cultural centers, and local history and identity repositories. The growing diversity and complexity of society will require libraries to develop new services and programs that cater to the needs of different user groups, such as marginalized communities, immigrants, and refugees. The rise of a post-literate society, where visual and multimedia communication predominates, will require libraries to adapt to new information dissemination and literacy instruction modes.

Environmental Factors:

The **22nd** century is likely to see significant environmental challenges that will impact the future of libraries. For example, climate change and natural disasters will require libraries to develop disaster preparedness plans and sustainable practices that minimize their environmental impact. The growing awareness of environmental issues will require libraries to incorporate environmental education and sustainability initiatives into their services and programs. Developing off-world settlements and space colonization may require libraries to develop new information storage and retrieval models for extra-terrestrial environments' challenges.

Recommendations:

To adapt and thrive in the **22nd** century, libraries should consider the following recommendations. Firstly, libraries should invest in emerging technologies that enhance their operations and services, such as artificial intelligence, virtual reality, and 3D printing. Secondly, libraries should prioritize the needs of diverse user groups and develop programs and services that cater to their needs. Thirdly, libraries should incorporate environmental education and sustainability initiatives into their services and operations. Fourthly, libraries should engage in interdisciplinary collaborations with other institutions and organizations to address emerging challenges and opportunities.

Emerging technologies, societal changes, and environmental factors will likely shape the future of libraries in the 22nd century. Libraries must adapt and evolve to remain relevant and impactful in this changing landscape. The potential future trends identified in this paper offer insights into the challenges and opportunities that libraries may face. By embracing emerging technologies, prioritizing the needs of diverse user groups, incorporating environmental education and sustainability initiatives, and engaging in interdisciplinary collaborations, libraries can adapt and thrive in the **22nd** century.

"Here is a list of some popular and favourable online apps for e-books, magazines, anwebsitesre users spend their valuable time learning and getting knowledge worldwide":

S. No	Apps/Website	Details
1	Amazon Kindle	Amazon's Kindle app offers many eBooks and magazines for purchase and download.
2	Apple Books	Apple's Books app provides access to a wide range of eBooks and magazines for iOS and macOS users.
3	Aldiko	Aldiko is a popular e-book reading app that supports various file formats. While it does not offer its collection of free books, you can import and read free e-books downloaded from other sources.
4	Google Play Books	Google's Play Books app offers an extensive collection of eBooks and magazines that can be read on Android devices and web browsers.
5	Barnes & Noble Nook	The Nook app by Barnes & Noble provides access to a diverse library of e-books and magazines.
6	Kobo: Kobo's	The app offers a wide selection of e-books and magazines that can be read on various devices, including smartphones and e-readers.
7	Scribd	Scribd is a subscription-based service that provides unlimited access to many eBooks, audiobooks, and magazines.
8	Zinio	Zinio specializes in digital magazines and offers an app that allows users to browse and read various magazine titles.

S. No	Apps/Website	Details
9	Flipboard	Flipboard is a personalized news and magazine app that curates articles and stories based on your interests.
10	Readly	Readly is a subscription-based service that provides unlimited access to a large selection of magazines
.11	Texture(now Apple News+)	Texture, which has been acquired by Apple and integrated into Apple News+, offers a vast catalogue of digital magazines for a monthly subscription.
12	OverDrive	Over Drive is a platform that allows users to borrow eBooks and audiobooks from their local libraries.
13	Libby	Libby is an app by Over Drive that allows you to borrow e-books and audiobooks from your local library. You can sign in with your library card and access a wide selection of free e-books to borrow and download.
14	Project Gutenberg	Project Gutenberg offers over 60,000 free eBooks that can be downloaded and read on various devices.
15	Wattpad	Wattpad is a community-driven platform where users can read and share stories and eBooks for free.
16	Many Books	Many Books offers a free e-book app that accesses over 50,000 titles in different genres. The app allows you to download books for offline reading.

S. No	Apps/Website	Details
17	Book mate	Book Mate is a subscription-based service that provides access to a library of eBooks and audiobooks in multiple languages.
18	BookBub	BookBub is an app that notifies you about discounted and free e-books available on various platforms. It curates a selection of free e-books based on your interests and preferences.
19	Free Books	Free Books is an app that provides access to thousands of free e-books across various genres. The app allows you to download books for offline reading.
20	Open Library	Open Library is an open-source project that aims to create a web page for every published book, providing access to a vast collection of e-books.
21	Internet Archive	The Internet Archive hosts many digital materials, including e-books, texts, audio recordings, videos, and more.
22	HathiTrust Digital Library	HathiTrust is a partnership of major research institutions and libraries worldwide, offering a collection of millions of digitized books and other materials.
23	Europeana	Europeana provides access to millions of digitized cultural heritage items, including e-books, from European libraries, archives, and museums.

S. No	Apps/Website	Details
24	Digital Public Library of America (DPLA)	DPLA offers free access to a wide range of digitized materials, including e-books, from libraries, archives, and museums across the United States.
25	National Digital Library of India (NDLI)	(NDLI): NDLI is a digital library initiative that provides access to a vast collection of e-books and other digital resources from various sources in India.
26	Trove	Trove is an Australian digital library that provides access to a wide range of digitized resources, including e-books, newspapers, journals, maps, and more.
27	National Library of Australia	The National Library of Australia offers an extensive collection of digitized books, magazines, newspapers, and other resources.
28	Digital Library of the Caribbean (dLOC)	dLOC provides access to digital collections from libraries, archives, and museums in the Caribbean region, including e-books and other materials.
29	Digital NZ	DigitalNZ provides access to a wide range of digital content from New Zealand libraries, museums, and galleries, including e-books.

Global Artificial Intelligence Market Size 2021-2030

According to Next Move Strategy Consulting, the artificial intelligence (AI) market is expected to grow strongly in the coming decade. Its value of nearly 100 billion U.S. dollars is expected to grow twentyfold by 2030, up to nearly two trillion U.S. dollars. The AI market covers a vast amount of industries. Everything from supply chains, marketing, product making, research, analysis, and more are fields that will, in some aspect, adopt artificial intelligence within their business structures. Chatbots, image-generating AI, mobile

Artificial intelligence (AI) market size worldwide in 2021 with a forecast until 2030 (in million U.S. dollars)

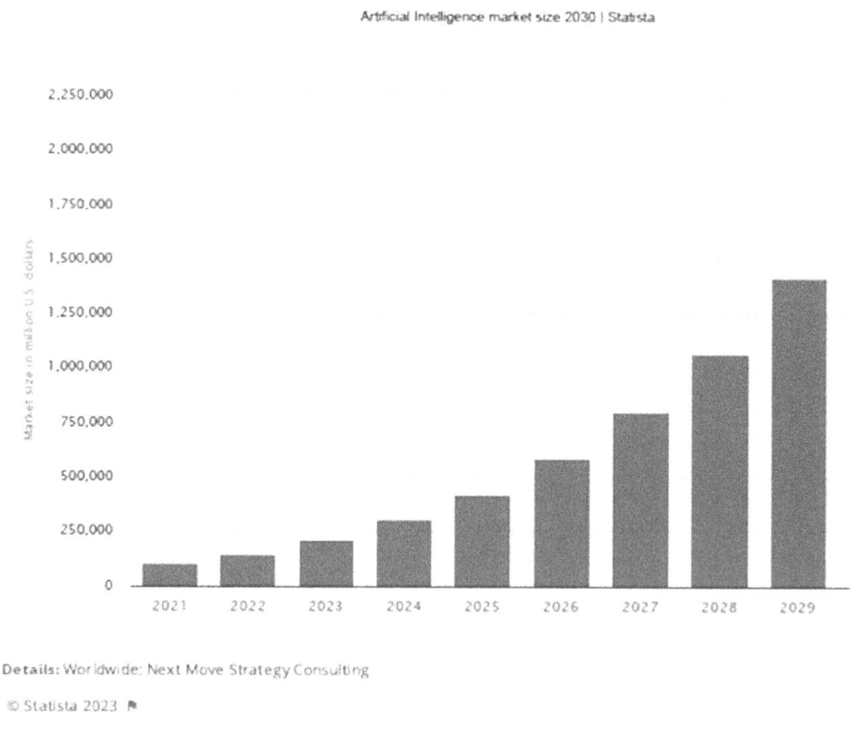

Challenges in the Adoption of Emerging Technologies:

The adoption of emerging technologies in library services is not without challenges. Financial constraints, technical expertise, and privacy concerns are challenges in adopting emerging technologies. Libraries must invest in technology infrastructure and hire staff with technical expertise to implement these technologies successfully. Privacy concerns are also a challenge, particularly with AI and ML technologies. Libraries must ensure that user privacy is protected and data is used ethically.

Libraries Using Technology in the Digital Age: A Review of the Literature

Libraries have long been known as a place to access information and learn. In the digital age, technology has transformed libraries into more than just a repository for books. Today, libraries use technology to give users access to digital resources, e-books, online databases, and virtual reality experiences. This literature review will examine how libraries use technology to enhance their services and meet the needs of their users in the digital age.

Digital Libraries:

Digital libraries have become a common feature in many libraries around the world. They offer users access to various digital resources, including e-books, audio and video recordings, and online databases. The development of digital libraries has made it possible for users to access information from anywhere, at any time, with an internet connection. Digital libraries have also made it possible for libraries to increase the reach of their services beyond their physical locations.

Online Catalogs:

Online catalogs have been an essential feature of libraries for many years. They have evolved to provide users with more than just a list of books. Today, online catalogs are integrated with library systems, allowing users to search for books, place holds, and even check out materials from their homes. Online catalogues have made it easier for users to find the resources they need and have helped libraries manage their collections more efficiently.

Virtual Reality:

Virtual reality (VR) has been gaining popularity in libraries worldwide. Libraries use VR to create interactive experiences that engage users in new and innovative ways. VR can be used to create simulations that allow users to explore historical sites, learn about science and technology, or experience fictional worlds. VR can potentially transform how libraries deliver information and engage users.

VR technology creates a simulated environment that users can interact with. Libraries can use VR to provide users with immersive experiences, such as exploring historical sites or visiting distant locations. VR can also be used to create interactive exhibits that allow users to explore complex concepts in a new way. For example, a library could use VR to create a virtual science lab, allowing users to conduct experiments in a safe and controlled environment.

Augmented Reality:

Augmented reality (AR) is a technology that overlays digital information onto the physical world. Libraries can use AR to provide users with an interactive experience, allowing them to explore books, maps, and other materials in a new way. For example, a library could use AR to create a virtual tour of the library, allowing users to navigate the space and find resources more efficiently. AR can also create interactive displays that provide users additional information about a topic.

Virtual Reality:

QR Code Technology:

QR code technology is a barcode that can be scanned using a smartphone. Libraries can use QR codes to provide users with additional information about books, displays, and exhibits. For example, a library could use QR codes to provide users with links to online resources related to a book or exhibit. QR codes can also create interactive scavenger hunts, allowing users to explore the library and discover new resources.

Mobile Libraries:

Mobile libraries have been around for many years, but the development of mobile technology has made them more accessible and convenient than ever before. Libraries are now using mobile technology to reach users where they are. Libraries use mobile applications to give users access to digital resources, online catalogs, and virtual reality experiences. Mobile libraries have the potential to make library services more accessible to people who might not otherwise be able to visit a physical library.

Technology has transformed libraries in the digital age. Libraries use technology to provide users access to digital resources, online catalogs, and virtual reality experiences. Libraries are also using mobile technology to reach users where they are. Technology has allowed libraries to increase the reach of their services beyond their physical locations and engage users in new and innovative ways. As technology continues to evolve, libraries will continue to adapt and use technology to meet the needs of their users.

Artificial Intelligence:

AI has revolutionised the way libraries function. Libraries use AI to improve their search engines, recommend materials to users, and automate various functions such as cataloging and indexing. AI can also be used to analyze user behavior and provide personalized services. In the future, libraries will increasingly use AI to optimize their operations and services.

The Impact of AI-Assisted Libraries in 2023:

A Look into the Future of Libraries: As artificial intelligence (AI) grows, libraries find new ways to integrate this technology into their services. AI-assisted libraries can potentially transform how we access and use library resources. In this article, we will explore the impact of AI-assisted libraries in 2023, looking into the future of libraries and how AI will shape their development.

Personalized Recommendations AI-assisted libraries can make personalized recommendations for users. AI algorithms can analyze a user's reading history, preferences, and interests to suggest books, articles, and other resources that match their interests. This can save users time and help them discover new resources they might not have found otherwise. In 2023, AI-assisted libraries will continue to refine their recommendation algorithms to provide even more accurate and personalized suggestions.

Improved Accessibility: AI-assisted libraries can also improve user accessibility. AI algorithms can make library resources more accessible for people with visual impairments or other disabilities. For example, AI can convert text to speech or provide audio descriptions of images. In 2023, we can expect more libraries to use AI to make their resources more accessible to everyone.

Enhanced Search Capabilities AI-assisted libraries can also enhance search capabilities. AI algorithms can help users find the information they need faster and more accurately. For example, AI can identify keywords, synonyms, and related concepts to help users find resources relevant to their search. In 2023, we can expect AI-assisted libraries to improve their search capabilities even further, making it easier for users to find the needed resources.

Virtual Assistance AI-assisted libraries can also provide virtual assistance to users. AI chatbots can be used to answer common questions, provide assistance with library resources, and even recommend books or other materials. This can provide users with quick and efficient access to information outside of library hours. In 2023, we can expect to see more libraries using AI chatbots to provide virtual assistance to users.

Challenges and Considerations While AI-assisted libraries have the potential to revolutionize the way we access and use library resources, there are also some challenges and considerations to keep in mind. For example, there is a risk that AI algorithms may perpetuate biases or reinforce existing inequalities. Additionally, there is a need to ensure that users' data and privacy are protected. Libraries must carefully consider these challenges and work to address them as they integrate AI into their services.

AI-assisted libraries can potentially transform how we access and use library resources. In 2023, we expect to see continued development and refinement of AI-assisted libraries, with improvements in personalized recommendations, accessibility, search capabilities, and virtual assistance. As libraries continue to integrate AI into their services, it will be essential to address the challenges and considerations associated with this technology to ensure that AI is used in a way that benefits all users.

Write a full-text research paper on 1. The impact of emerging technologies on library services: With the rapid advancements in technology, it is crucial to study how new technologies such as artificial intelligence, machine learning, and blockchain will affect library services

Machine Learning: Machine learning algorithms are used to analyze large volumes of data, such as user behavior patterns, to provide insights that can be used to improve library services. Machine learning can be used to automate processes, such as data classification, and optimize search algorithms. Machine learning can also help libraries identify trends in user behavior, which can be used to improve the services offered.

Internet of Things:

The Internet of Things (IoT) is a network of communication devices and sensors. Libraries can use IoT to automate various functions, such as monitoring temperature, humidity, and lighting levels. IoT can also be used to track library materials and prevent theft. Libraries can use IoT to provide personalized services, such as recommending materials based on the user's location.

Artificial Intelligence (AI) and Machine Learning (ML) are emerging technologies that have the potential to revolutionize how libraries organize and provide access to information. Libraries have always been a vital resource for the dissemination of knowledge and the preservation of cultural heritage. With the advent of AI and ML, libraries can now leverage these technologies to enhance their services and provide more efficient and effective access to information. This research paper explores AI and ML applications in libraries, their impact on library services, and ethical considerations around their use.

Applications of AI and ML in Libraries

AI and ML have many library applications, from automating routine tasks to improving information discovery and retrieval. One example of AI and ML in libraries is the use of chatbots. Chatbots can assist users with routine tasks such as renewing books, locating resources, and answering basic reference questions. Chatbots can also provide personalized recommendations to users based on their search history, borrowing behavior, and preferences.

Another example of AI and ML in libraries is predictive analytics. Predictive analytics can anticipate user needs, identify potential areas of interest, and tailor services accordingly. For example, predictive analytics can recommend resources to users based on their search history, demographics, and preferences. Predictive analytics can also identify potential areas of research interest and tailor outreach efforts.

AI and ML can also be used to enhance information discovery and retrieval. One example is using natural language processing (NLP) to improve search results. NLP can be used to understand the context of user queries and provide more relevant search results. NLP can also extract key concepts from documents and provide more precise search results.

Impact of AI and ML on Library Services

The impact of AI and ML on library services is significant. These technologies can help libraries provide their users with more efficient and effective services. By automating routine tasks, libraries can free up staff time for more complex tasks such as research support and outreach. Libraries can enhance user engagement and satisfaction by providing personalized recommendations and tailored services.

AI and ML can also help libraries adapt to changing user needs and preferences. As users increasingly rely on digital resources and expect more personalized services, libraries can leverage these technologies to meet those expectations. By providing more relevant search results, personalized recommendations, and tailored services, libraries can better serve their users and remain relevant in an increasingly digital world.

Ethical Considerations around the Use of AI and ML in Libraries:

While using AI and ML in libraries offers many benefits, it raises ethical considerations. One concern is the potential for bias in algorithms. AI and ML systems rely on data to make decisions; if that data is biased, the system's outputs will also be biased. This can have implications for access to information and equity.

Another concern is privacy. AI and ML systems rely on large amounts of data to make decisions, and if that data includes personal information, there is a risk of privacy violations. Libraries must ensure that they are collecting and using data in a way that respects user privacy and confidentiality.

Data analysis and interpretation

Survey responses:

The survey questionnaire was sent to all 500 Faculties, students, and Library professionals, out of which 180 valid responses were received, giving a response rate of 36%. A response rate of 36% is generally considered quite good, especially for surveys involving a more significant population like faculties, students, and library professionals.

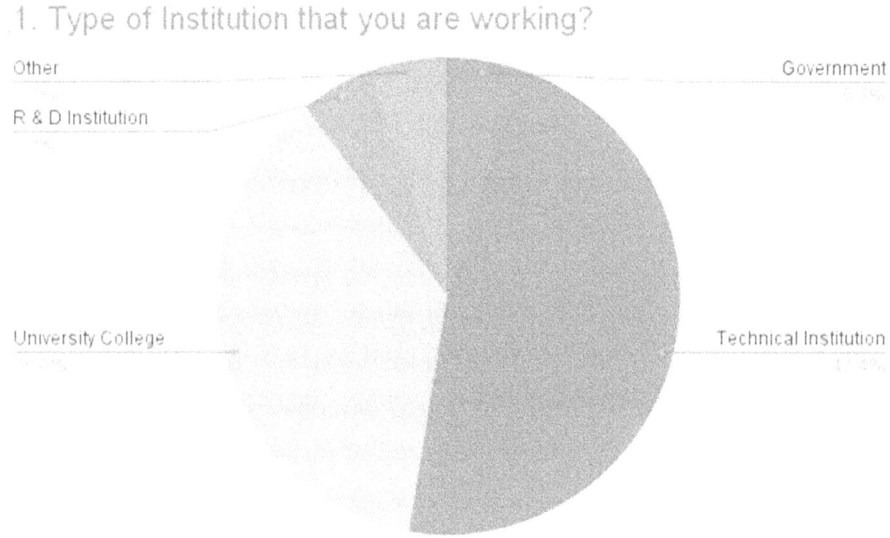

Fig.:1. Type of Institutions

Figure 1 shows the type of institutions in which the respondents work; 5.3% of Government Institutions of the respondents work in government institutions. These could include libraries and educational institutions funded and operated by the government. 47.4% Technical Institutions, the largest group of respondents, comprising 47.4%, work in technical institutions. These institutions may include technical universities, engineering colleges, vocational schools, or other technical education-focused establishments. 5.3% R&D Institutions of the respondents are affiliated with Research and Development (R&D) institutions. These institutions typically focus on scientific research and technological advancements. 36.8% Universities and Colleges of the respondents are from universities and colleges. These are higher education institutions offering a range of academic programs and degrees, and 5.3% Other Institutions, the remaining 5.3% of the respondents are from institutions that do not fit into the abovementioned categories. These could include private educational institutions, non-profit organizations, or other specialized institutions.

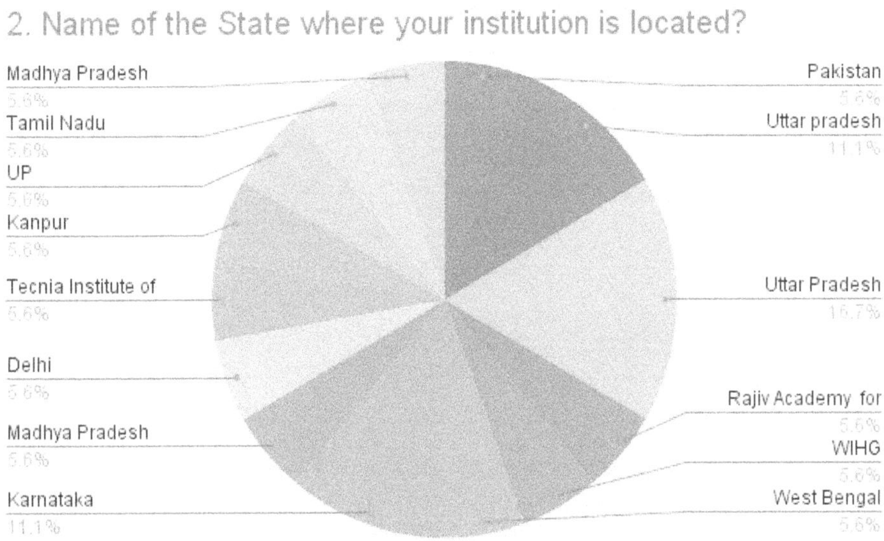

Fig. : 2. State where institution located

Figure 2 shows that for geographical location, Pakistan Division (5.6%): 5.6% of the respondents are from the Pakistan division, which may refer to a specific administrative division or region within Pakistan. Madhya Pradesh (11.2%): The largest group of respondents, 11.2%, are from Madhya Pradesh in India. Tamil Nadu (5.6%): In India, 5.6% of the respondents are from Tamil Nadu. Uttar Pradesh (33.4%): 33.4% of the respondents are from Uttar Pradesh in India. Kanpur (5.6%): 5.6% of the respondents are specifically from the city of Kanpur, located in Uttar Pradesh, India. Tecnia Institute of Advanced Studies (5.6%): 5.6% of the respondents are affiliated with Tecnia Institute of Advanced Studies, an educational institution in Delhi, India. Delhi (5.6%): 5.6% of the respondents are from Delhi, India. Karnataka (11.1%): 11.1% of the respondents are from Karnataka in India. Rajiv Academy for Technology & Management (5.6%): 5.6% of the respondents are affiliated with Rajiv Academy for Technology & Management, an educational institution in India. WIHG (5.6%): 5.6% of the respondents are affiliated with WIHG, which may refer to the Wadia Institute of Himalayan Geology in India. West Bengal (5.6%): 5.6% of the respondents are from the state of West Bengal in India.

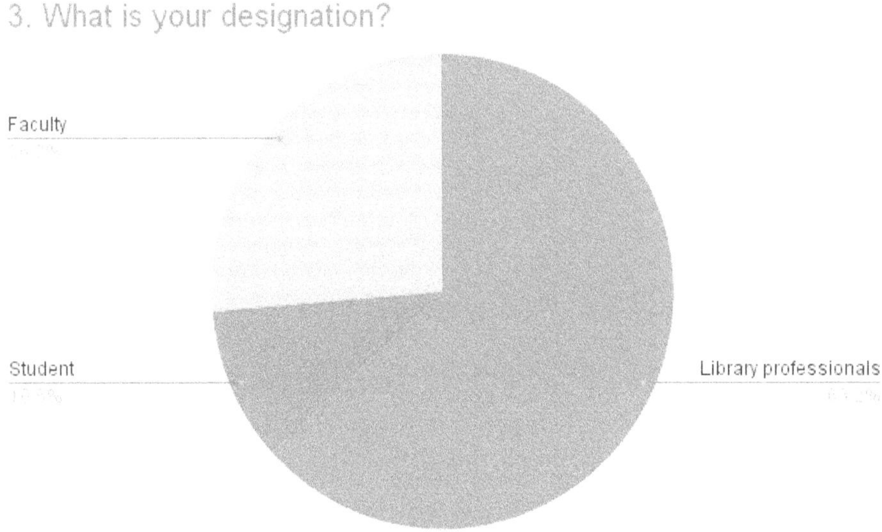

Fig.: 3. Designation of the respondents

Figure 3 shows the percentage of the respondent's designation, in which 26.3% of the respondents are faculty members from the teaching field. These individuals are likely professors, lecturers, or instructors working in educational institutions. 10.5% of the respondents are students from the field of study. These individuals are currently enrolled in educational programs, such as undergraduate or postgraduate courses, researchers, etc. 63.2% Library Professionals, the largest group of respondents, comprised of 63.2%, are library professionals who belong to the library sector. These individuals work in various capacities within libraries, such as librarians, assistants, administrators, etc.

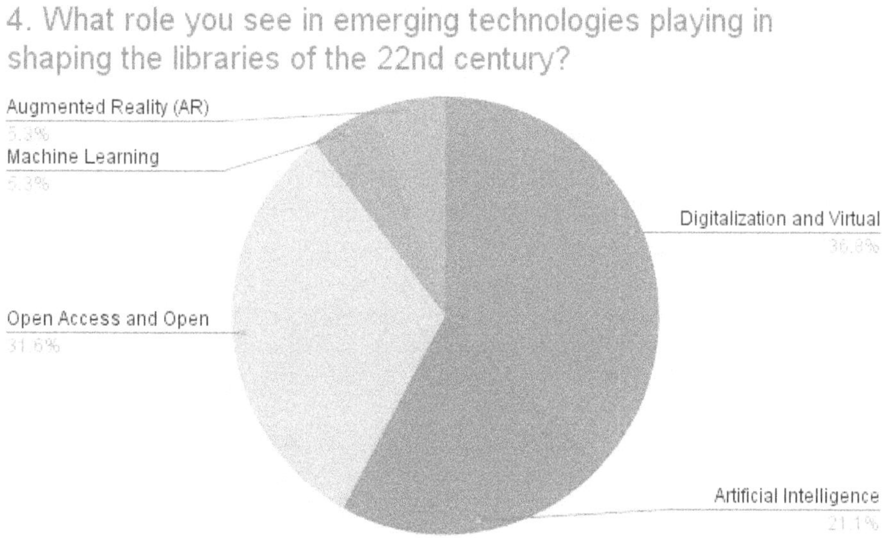

Fig.: 4. Emerging technologies playing in shaping the libraries of the 22nd century

Physical book collections will likely coexist with vast digital repositories accessible through virtual reality (VR) and augmented reality (AR) technologies. Figure 4 shows that 5.3% of augmented reality (AR) and virtual reality (VR) represent these technologies that enable users to experience virtual book collections, immersive storytelling, and interactive learning experiences, enriching the library experience beyond physical book collections.5.3 % Machine Learning can enhance library services by providing personalized recommendations, improving search algorithms, and automating various tasks, leading to more efficient and tailored user experiences.31.6% of Open Access and Open Educational Resources (OER) represent the Libraries that are likely to embrace open access initiatives, providing users with free access to a vast array of digital resources and educational materials, promoting knowledge sharing and accessibility.

36.8% Digitalization and Virtual Libraries represent that the digitalization of resources will expand, enabling libraries to build extensive virtual collections accessible through online platforms, making information available to users anytime and anywhere. 21.1% Artificial Intelligence (AI) technologies can optimize library operations, from chatbots providing instant assistance to intelligent content curation, making libraries more efficient and user-friendly.

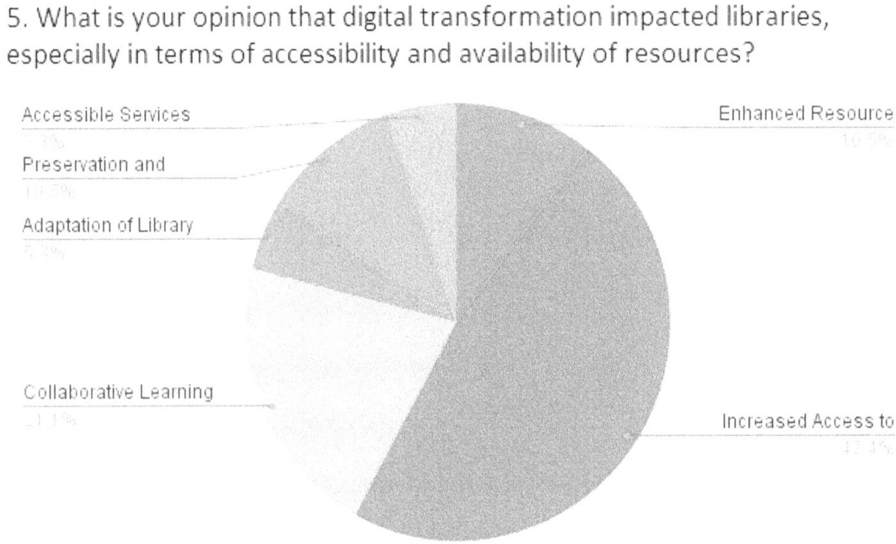

Fig. 5. Digital transformation impacted libraries, especially in terms of accessibility and availability of resources

Digital transformation has significantly impacted libraries, particularly in terms of accessibility and availability of resources. Digital technologies and the internet have revolutionized how libraries operate and provide services to their patrons. Figure 5 shows that 5.3% of digital resources services can be designed to be more accessible to individuals with disabilities. Features like text-to-speech, screen readers, and adjustable font sizes cater to a broader range of users, promoting inclusivity. 10.5% Preservation and Conservation represent the Digital transformation that has facilitated the preservation and conservation of fragile and rare materials. High-resolution digitization and digital backups help protect valuable resources from physical deterioration.5.3% Adaptation of Library Spaces represents the transformation brought about by digital technologies that have changed library spaces' concepts, values, and functions. Libraries have evolved into dynamic, user-focused hubs that combine the benefits of physical and digital resources to cater to the diverse needs of their communities and adapt to the ever-changing landscape of information and communication. 21.1% Collaborative Learning and Sharing represent the Digital technologies that have enabled libraries to engage in resource-sharing and collaborative projects more efficiently. Interlibrary loan systems and digital repositories promote knowledge sharing among institutions. 10.5% Enhanced Resource Discovery represents the Digital transformation that has made vast information and knowledge accessible to library users. Online databases, e-books, e-journals, and digital archives have expanded the range of resources users can access remotely, regardless of location or time zone.47.4% Increased Access to Information represents the digital resources and online databases available 24/7, allowing users to access information conveniently. This has significantly increased the availability and accessibility of resources beyond traditional library hours.

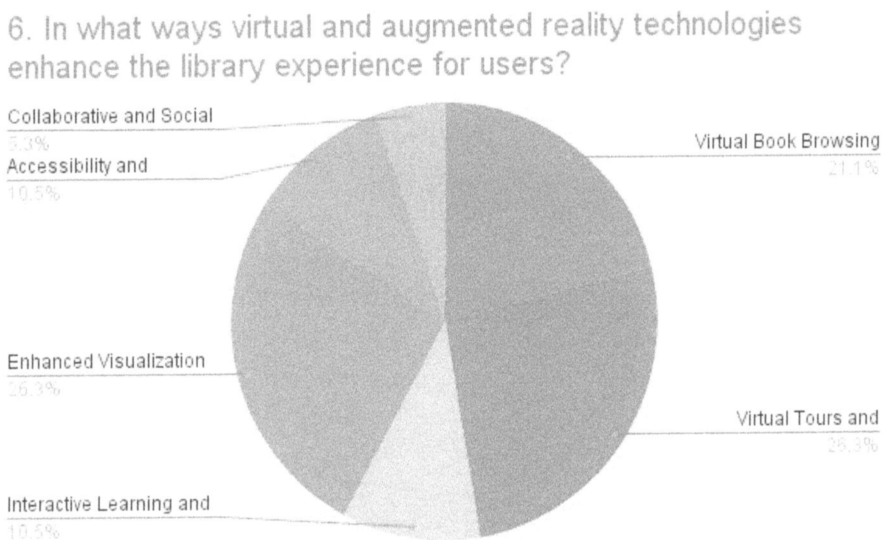

Fig.: 6. Virtual and augmented reality technologies enhance the library experience for users

Figure 5 shows that 5.3% of Collaborative and Social Experiences represent these technologies and turn libraries into interactive hubs where users can collaborate, share knowledge, and engage in collaborative learning experiences. 10.5% Accessibility and Inclusivity represent that Virtual and augmented reality can make libraries more accessible and inclusive for all users, regardless of their abilities or backgrounds. 26.3% Enhanced Visualization and Data Exploration represent that these technologies offer innovative ways to present complex information, making it easier for users to understand and explore data. 10.5% of Interactive Learning and Storytelling represent the Virtual and augmented reality technologies that provide hands-on, immersive educational experiences, transforming passive information consumption into engaging learning opportunities. 21.1% Virtual Book Browsing represents this application allows library patrons to browse through digital book collections in an immersive and interactive manner, enhancing the discovery and exploration of books, and 26.3% Virtual Tours and Exploration represent these technologies enable users to embark on immersive journeys, exploring diverse places, historical sites, cultural landmarks, and even fictional worlds without leaving the library.

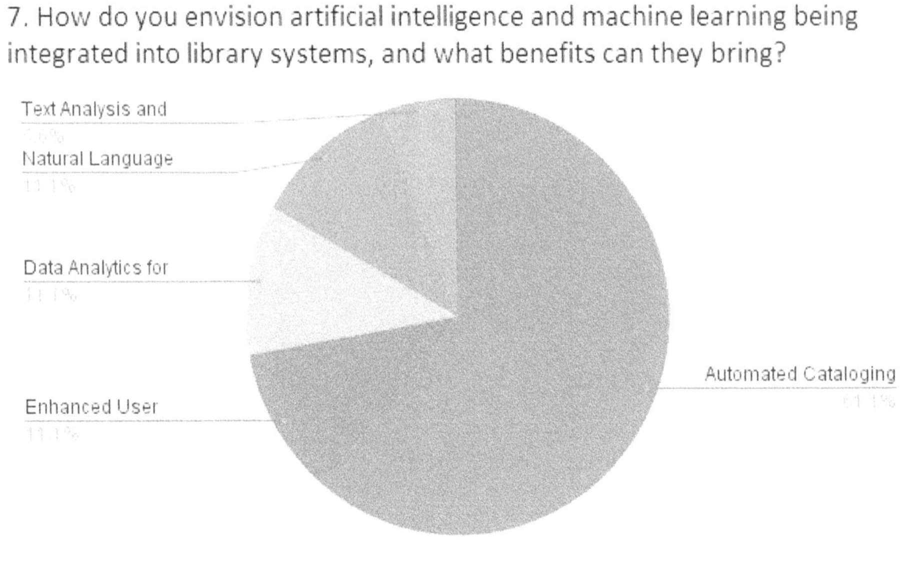

Fig.: 7. Artificial intelligence and machine learning being integrated into library systems, and what benefits can they bring

Integrating artificial intelligence (AI) and machine learning (ML) into library systems can revolutionize how libraries operate, offer services, and engage with users. Figure 7 shows that 5.6% of Text Analysis and Content Extraction can assist in extracting valuable information from texts and documents, aiding researchers in data analysis and knowledge discovery. 11.1% Natural Language Processing (NLP) and AI can aid in real-time language translation, making library resources more accessible to users worldwide, including those with language barriers. 11.1% Data Analytics for Collection Development can analyze user behavior and library usage data, providing valuable insights into user preferences, resource popularity, and overall library performance. AI can assist librarians in analyzing user trends and demand patterns to make informed decisions about collection development and management, ensuring the library's offerings align with user interests and needs. 11.1% Enhanced User Experience can analyze user interactions and preferences to create interactive and engaging experiences, such as virtual book clubs, personalized reading challenges, and gamified learning activities. 61.1% Automated Cataloguing and Metadata Management can automate the cataloging and metadata management process, reducing manual labour and ensuring consistent and accurate data organization.

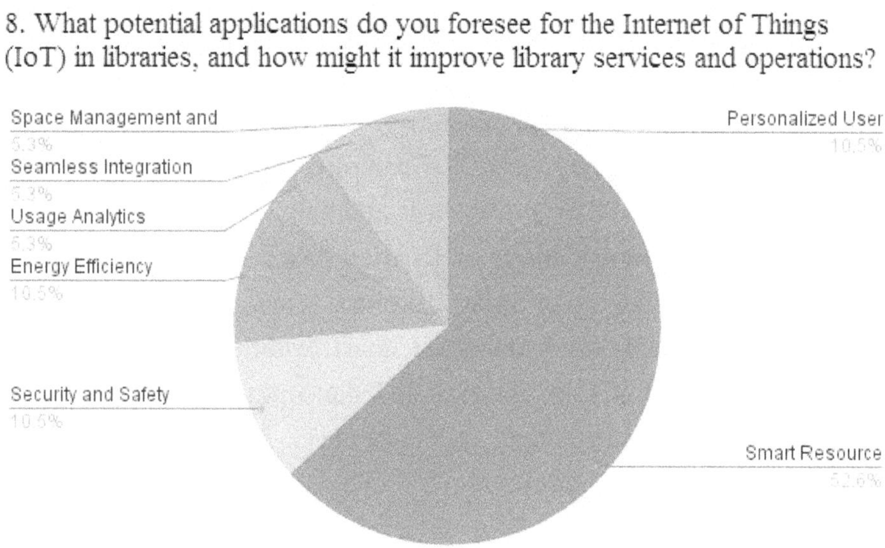

Fig.: 8. Potential applications do you foresee for the Internet of Things (IoT) in libraries, and how might it improve library services and operations

Figure 8 represents the potential applications of the Internet of Things (IoT) in libraries and how each application can improve library services and operations. It shows that 5.3% of Space Management and Optimization represent that the IoT can help optimize library spaces by using sensors to monitor occupancy and usage patterns. This data can assist in rearranging furniture, allocating study areas, and optimizing the use of available space for the convenience of library users. 5.3 % Seamless Integration with Digital Services represents that the IoT can enable seamless integration between physical and digital library resources. For example, smart devices can facilitate instant access to digital collections or interactive displays, bridging the gap between physical and virtual library experiences. 5.3% Usage Analytics represent IoT sensors that can gather library space and resource use data. Analyzing this data can provide valuable insights into user behavior and preferences, enabling informed decision-making for enhancing library services. 10.5% Energy Efficiency represents that the IoT can contribute to energy-efficient operations by automatically controlling lighting, heating, and cooling systems based on occupancy and environmental conditions, leading to cost savings and reduced carbon footprint. 10.5% Security and Safety represent the IoT-powered security systems that can enhance library safety by monitoring entrances, exits, and restricted areas. Real-time alerts can be sent to staff in case of security breaches or emergencies. 10.5% Personalized User Experience represents the IoT can offer personalized experiences to library users based on their preferences and behaviors. For instance, personalized book recommendations or location-based services can enhance user satisfaction, and 52.6% of Smart Resource Management represents the majority of respondents who identified smart resource management as a crucial application of IoT in libraries. IoT can optimize resource allocation, track inventory, and automate tasks like check-in/check-out, leading to more efficient library operations.

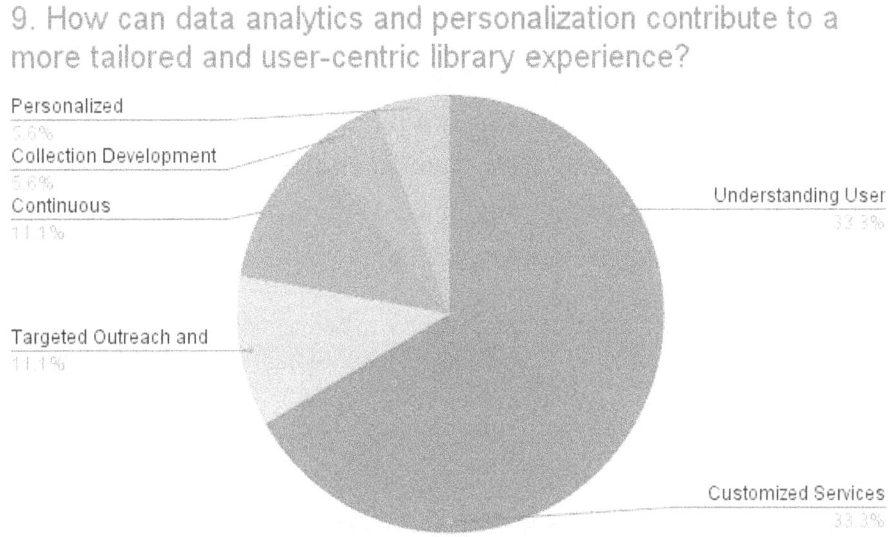

Fig.: 9. Data analytics and personalization contribute to a more tailored and user-centric library experience

Figure 9 represents the 5.6% personalized recommendations data analytics that can analyze user behavior, reading history, and interests to offer personalized book recommendations. This tailored approach helps users discover relevant resources, increasing user satisfaction and engagement. 5.6% Collection Development and Resource Allocation By analyzing user data, libraries can make informed decisions about collection development and resource allocation. This ensures that the library's offerings align with user preferences and needs, optimizing the relevance of available resources. 11.1% Continuous Improvement and Evaluation data analytics can be used to evaluate and improve library services and operations continuously. By monitoring user feedback and engagement metrics, libraries can identify areas for enhancement and make data-driven decisions to improve user experiences. 11.1% Targeted Outreach and Communication personalization allows libraries to send targeted communications to users. Based on their interests and past interactions, users can receive relevant event invitations, updates on new resources, and personalized newsletters, fostering greater engagement. 33.3% Understanding User Needs and Preferences Data analytics is crucial for understanding user behavior, needs, and preferences. It enables libraries to gain insights into how users interact with library resources and services, helping them adapt and cater to diverse user requirements. 33.3% Customized Services and Interfaces personalization enables libraries to offer customized services and interfaces. This may include personalized research assistance, individualized digital platforms, and curated reading lists, enhancing the user experience.

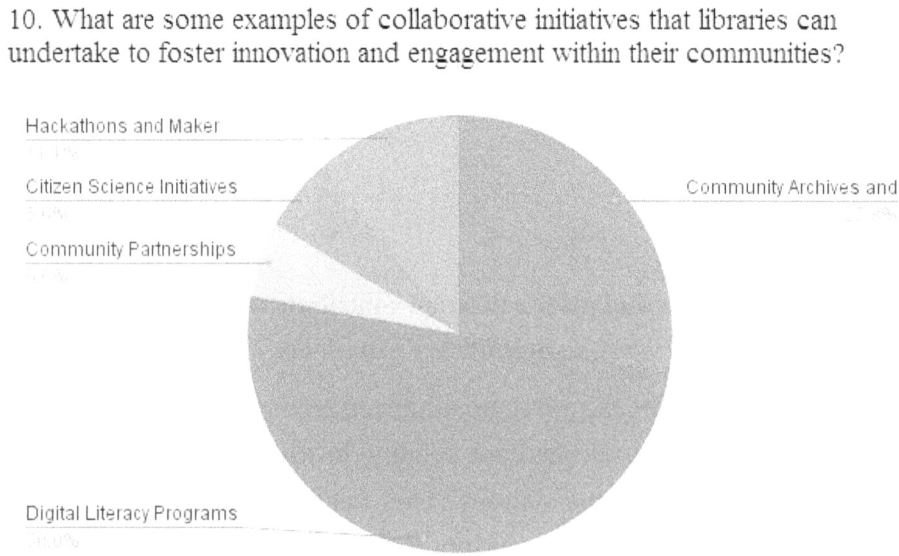

Fig.: 10. Examples of collaborative initiatives that libraries can undertake to foster innovation and engagement within their communities

Figure 10 shows that 11.1% of Hackathons and Maker Spaces libraries can organize hackathons and establish maker spaces in collaboration with technology companies, universities, or community organizations. These initiatives provide a platform for community members to collaborate on innovative projects, such as app development, robotics, or creative arts, fostering a culture of hands-on learning and exploration. 5.6% Citizen Science Initiatives collaborating with scientific institutions or environmental organizations, libraries can launch citizen science programs. These initiatives involve community members in data collection and research projects, contributing to scientific discovery and raising awareness about local environmental issues. 5.6% Community Partnerships collaborating with various community organizations, businesses, educational institutions, and libraries can form partnerships to address community needs. These partnerships may lead to joint events, workshops, or shared resources, enhancing the library's impact and relevance within the community. 50.0% Digital Literacy Programs libraries can lead digital literacy programs in collaboration with tech companies, schools, or local government. These programs aim to improve digital skills and access to technology for community members, empowering them to navigate the digital world effectively. 27.8% of community archives and oral history projects collaborating with local historical societies, museums, universities, and libraries can curate community archives and conduct oral history projects. These initiatives preserve local history, culture, and heritage, encouraging community members to actively participate in preserving their collective memory.

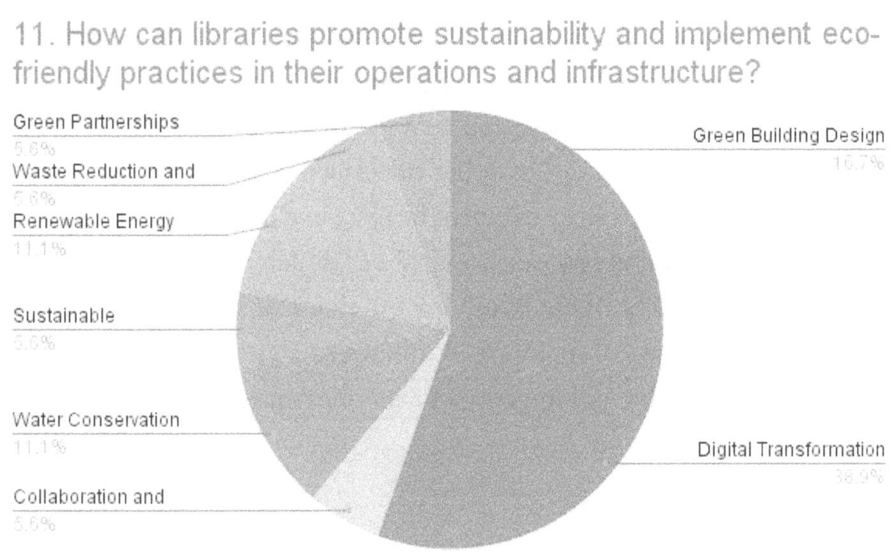

Fig.: 11. Libraries promote sustainability and implement eco-friendly practices in their operations and infrastructure

Figure 11 shows that 5.6% of Green Partnerships libraries can partner with local environmental organizations, community groups, or businesses prioritizing sustainability. Collaborating with these partners can lead to joint initiatives and events that promote eco-friendly practices and raise awareness about environmental issues within the community. 5.6% Waste Reduction and Recycling libraries can implement waste reduction measures, such as encouraging patrons to use reusable bags or promoting digital materials. Additionally, establishing recycling programs for paper, plastic, and other recyclables can significantly reduce waste generation. 11.1% Renewable Energy Sources libraries can transition to renewable energy sources, such as solar, wind, or geothermal power, to reduce their reliance on fossil fuels and decrease their carbon footprint. 5.6% Sustainable Procurement libraries can prioritize purchasing eco-friendly and sustainable products. This includes using recycled paper, energy-efficient appliances, and environmentally friendly office supplies. 11.1% of Water Conservation libraries can implement water-saving measures, such as installing low-flow faucets and toilets and using drought-resistant landscaping to reduce water consumption. 5.6% Collaboration and sharing libraries can collaborate and share resources with other organizations to optimize efficiency and minimize waste. This could involve sharing equipment, materials, or expertise with community partners. 16.7% Green Building Design libraries can incorporate sustainable design principles when constructing new buildings or renovating existing spaces. Utilizing eco-friendly building materials, optimizing natural lighting, and implementing energy-efficient heating and cooling systems are examples of green building practices. 38.9% of Digital Transformation libraries can promote digital resources, e-books, and online services to reduce the use of paper and physical materials. Embracing digital transformation not only reduces environmental impact but also offers greater accessibility and convenience to patrons.

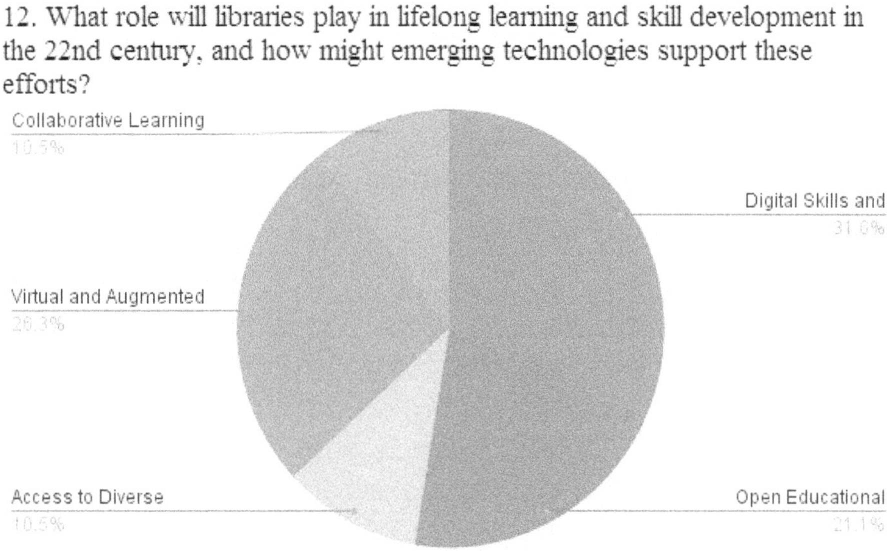

Fig.: 12. Role will libraries play in lifelong learning and skill development in the 22nd century, and how might emerging technologies support these efforts

Figure 12 shows that 10.5% of Collaborative Learning Spaces libraries will provide collaborative learning spaces encouraging knowledge exchange and group work. These spaces will be equipped with advanced technologies, interactive displays, and multimedia resources to facilitate group projects and foster a sense of community-based learning. 26.3% Virtual and Augmented Reality learning emerging virtual and augmented reality technologies will revolutionize library learning experiences. Patrons can explore historical events, visit distant places, or engage in simulated practical training, making learning more immersive and engaging. 10.5% Access to Diverse Learning Resources Libraries will continue to expand their collections to include diverse learning resources, from traditional books and e-books to online databases, e-journals, and multimedia content. Emerging technologies will enable libraries to curate vast digital repositories accessible to learners worldwide. 31.6% Digital Skills and Technology Training libraries will actively provide their patrons digital skills and technology training. Workshops and courses will be offered to help individuals navigate digital tools, online platforms, and emerging technologies, empowering them to be digitally literate and adaptable in a tech-driven world. 21.1% of Open Educational Resources (OER) libraries will embrace open educational resources as a valuable addition to their collections. OER, including open textbooks, lecture notes, and educational videos, will enable learners to access quality educational materials freely, making learning more accessible and affordable.

13. What challenges do you anticipate libraries facing in adopting and implementing these new technologies, and how can they be overcome?

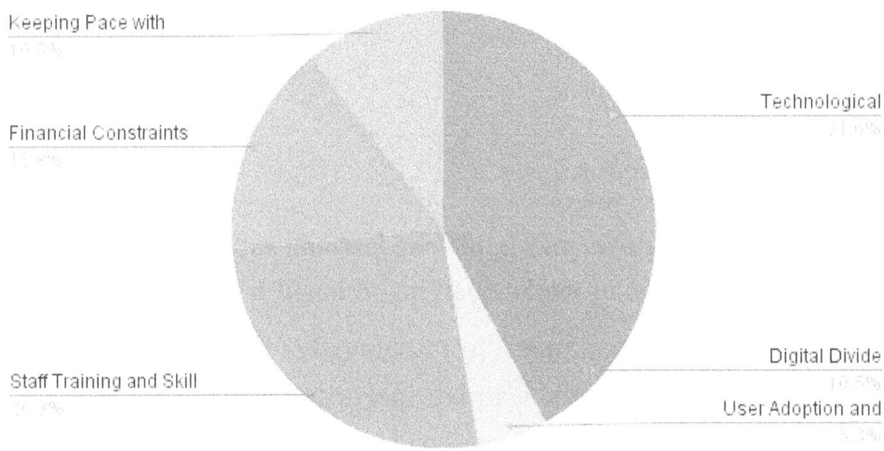

Fig.: 13. Challenges do you anticipate libraries facing in adopting and implementing these new technologies, and how can they be overcome

Figure 13 shows that 10.5% Keeping Pace with Technological Advancements the rapid pace of technological advancements can be overwhelming for libraries, making it challenging to stay up-to-date with the latest innovations. To address this challenge, libraries can monitor continuously, attend technology conferences and workshops, and collaborate with technology experts or consortia to stay informed about emerging trends. 15.8% Financial Constraints: Implementing new technologies can be financially demanding for libraries, particularly those with limited budgets. Libraries can explore grant opportunities, seek financial support from local governments or community sponsors, and prioritize technology investments based on their potential impact on patron services. 26.3% Staff Training and

Skill Development Training library staff to effectively use and support new technologies is essential for successful implementation. Libraries can invest in staff development programs, offer online training courses, and partner with technology companies to provide hands-on training sessions for staff. 31.6% of Technological Infrastructure libraries must have a robust technological infrastructure to support integrating new technologies. This includes reliable internet connectivity, up-to-date hardware and software, and secure data storage systems. Libraries can conduct technology assessments to identify infrastructure gaps and develop plans for upgrades or improvements. 10.5% Digital Divide Ensuring equitable access to technology can be challenging, as not all patrons may have the necessary devices or internet connectivity. Libraries can address this by providing public computers and Wi-Fi hotspots and partnering with community organizations to offer digital literacy programs to bridge the digital divide. 5.3% User Adoption and Digital Literacy Some library patrons may hesitate to adopt new technologies due to a lack of familiarity or digital literacy skills. Libraries can address this by offering user-friendly interfaces, conducting digital literacy workshops, and providing personalized assistance to patrons needing support.

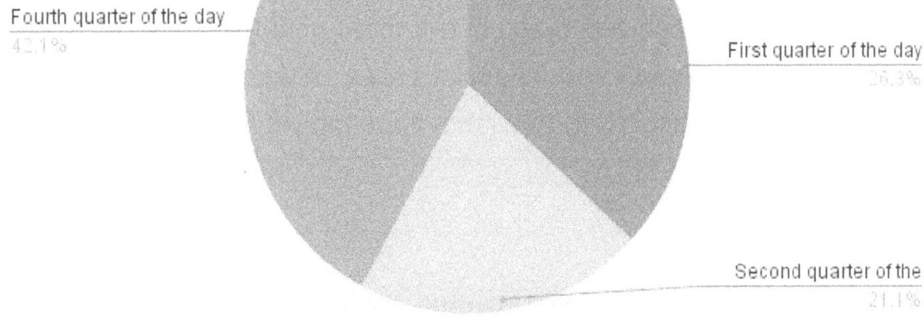

Fig.: 14. Frankly speaking, how much time do you spend on social media platforms every day

Figure 14 shows that 42.1% of users spend their fourth-quarter time of the day on the social media platform, 10.5% of users spend their third-quarter time of day, 26.3% of users spend their first quarter of the day, and 21.1% of users are spending his second-quarter time of the day on the social media platform.

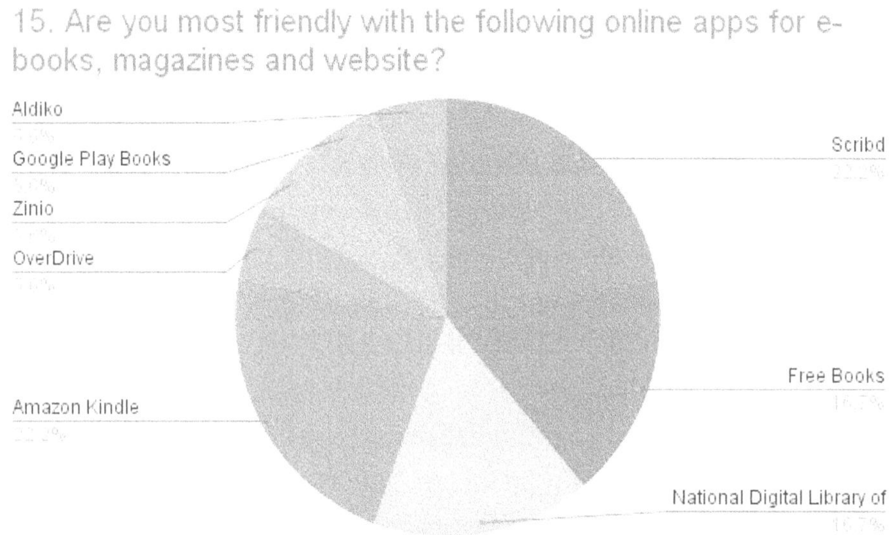

Fig.:15. Most friendly with the following online apps for e-books, magazines, and website

Figure 15 shows that the users used 5.6% Aldiko, 5.6% Google Play Books, 5.6% Zinio, 5.6% OverDrive, 22.2% Amazon Kindle, 22.2% Scribd, 16.7% Free Books, and 16.7% National Digital Library of India (NDLI). Based on response, the users may choose these platforms based on factors like the selection of books and magazines, ease of use, pricing, availability in their region, and specific features they find appealing.

Conclusion:

AI and ML have the potential to revolutionize how libraries organize and provide access to information. These technologies offer many benefits, including automating routine tasks, enhancing information discovery and retrieval, and tailoring services to user needs and preferences. However, their use also raises ethical considerations around bias and privacy. Libraries must carefully consider these issues as they integrate AI and ML into their services to ensure that they are providing equitable and ethical access to information.

Blockchain:

Blockchain is a decentralized, secure, transparent ledger that stores and manages data. Libraries can use a blockchain to store user data securely, such as by borrowing history and personal information. Blockchain can also create a decentralized lending system where users can lend and borrow materials directly from each other.

ChatGPT:

ChatGPT is a language model that can understand and respond to natural language. Libraries can use ChatGPT to provide personalized services to users, such as answering questions and recommending materials. ChatGPT can also automate various functions, such as responding to user inquiries and providing feedback.

The emergence of AI, machine learning, IoT, blockchain, and ChatGPT has transformed how libraries function. Libraries are increasingly becoming digital information hubs, providing personalized services to users. In the future, libraries will continue to use these technologies to optimize their operations and improve the services offered. However, ensuring that these technologies are used ethically and with user privacy in mind is important.

The advent of large language models such as ChatGPT can transform how users interact with library resources and services. ChatGPT is a deep learning model that uses natural language processing to generate human-like responses to user queries. This paper explores the impact of ChatGPT on institutions' library and information services.

Advantages of ChatGPT in Library and Information Services: The integration of ChatGPT into library and information services offers several benefits. Firstly, ChatGPT can provide an instant response to user queries, reducing the wait time for users. Secondly, ChatGPT can handle multiple queries simultaneously, enhancing library services' efficiency. Thirdly, ChatGPT can personalize responses to user queries based on their search history, improving the quality of search results. Fourthly, ChatGPT can assist users in navigating complex databases, reducing the time required to find relevant information.

Challenges of ChatGPT in Library and Information Services: The integration of ChatGPT into library and information services also presents some challenges. Firstly, the accuracy of ChatGPT responses can be affected by the data quality used to train the model. Secondly, ChatGPT may not understand the context of user queries, leading to irrelevant responses. Thirdly, the lack of transparency in ChatGPT's decision-making process can raise concerns about bias and discrimination. Fourthly, using ChatGPT may reduce the interaction between library staff and users, affecting the quality of services.

Case Studies:

Several institutions have integrated ChatGPT into their library and information services. For example, the University of California, Berkeley, has implemented a chatbot that uses ChatGPT to answer user queries. The chatbot can answer questions about library resources, opening hours, and study spaces. The University of Arizona has also implemented a chatbot that uses ChatGPT to provide personalized responses to user queries. The chatbot can assist users in finding relevant information and navigating complex databases.

Recommendations: To integrate ChatGPT effectively into library and information services, institutions should consider the following recommendations. Firstly, institutions should ensure that the data used to train the model is diverse and representative. Secondly, institutions should allow users to speak with a human librarian if they require further assistance. Thirdly, institutions should ensure that ChatGPT's decision-making process is transparent and explainable. Fourthly, institutions should regularly evaluate the effectiveness of ChatGPT in improving library services.

Integrating ChatGPT into library and information services can transform how users interact with library resources and services. The advantages of ChatGPT include providing instant responses to user queries, handling multiple queries simultaneously, personalizing responses, and assisting users in navigating complex databases. However, the integration of ChatGPT also presents challenges such as accuracy, context, transparency, and reduced interaction between library staff and users. Institutions should consider the recommendations provided in this paper to integrate ChatGPT effectively into their library services.

Benefits of Technology for Libraries:

Adopting new technologies can provide many benefits to libraries and their users. Technology can help libraries increase user engagement, improve resource access, and create new revenue streams. Technology can provide users a more interactive and engaging experience, making finding and accessing resources easier. Libraries are adapting to the new era of technology by embracing augmented reality, virtual reality, and QR code technology. These technologies offer many benefits to libraries and their users, including increased engagement, improved access to resources, and a more interactive experience. As technology evolves, libraries must stay ahead of the curve and explore new ways to enhance their services.

The emergence of AI, machine learning, IoT, blockchain, and ChatGPT has transformed how libraries function. Libraries are increasingly becoming digital information hubs, providing personalized services to users. In the future, libraries will continue to use these technologies to optimize their operations and improve the services offered. However, ensuring that these technologies are used ethically and with user privacy in mind is essential.

References:

1. Bennett, L. (2019). Marriott library uses artificial intelligence to answer student questions. University of Utah News. *https://unews.utah.edu/marriott-library-uses-artificial-intelligence-to-answer-student-questions/*
2. Chen, S. (2019). How machine learning is changing the face of libraries. OCLC Next. *https://www.oclc.org/en/next/blog/*
3. Aharony, N., & Fox, R. (2017). Libraries and artificial intelligence: Opportunities and challenges. Library Hi Tech, 35(1), 144-155.
4. Kucirkova, N. (2019). Libraries and emerging technologies: The future of innovation and impact. Journal of Librarianship and Information Science, 51(3), 721-730.
5. Singh, M., & Sharma, A. (2018). Blockchain technology: Opportunities and challenges for libraries. International Journal of Information Science and Management, 16(2), 47-52.
6. Verma, R. (2020). Emerging technologies and their impact on libraries: A review. International Journal of Information Dissemination and Technology, 10(3), 137-144.
7. Wei, J., & Li, J. (2019). The impact of artificial intelligence on libraries. The Electronic Library, 37(2), 204-215
8. https://www.statista.com/statistics/1365145/artificial-intelligence-market-size/
9. https://www.worldometers.info/geography/7-continents/